Apocalyptic Dread

THE SUNY SERIES

HORIZONS OF CINEMA

MURRAY POMERANCE | EDITOR

Also in the series

William Rothman, editor, *Cavell on Film*

J. David Slocum, editor, *Rebel Without a Cause*

Joe McElhaney, *The Death of Classical Cinema*

Apocalyptic Dread

American Film at the
Turn of the Millennium

Kirsten Moana Thompson

STATE UNIVERSITY OF NEW YORK PRESS

Published by
State University of New York Press, Albany

© 2007 State University of New York

Printed in the United States of America

For information, address State University of New York Press,
194 Washington Avenue, Suite 305, Albany, NY 12210-2384

Production by Marilyn P. Semerad
Marketing by Anne M. Valentine

Library of Congress Cataloging-in-Publication Data

Thompson, Kirsten Moana.
    Apocalyptic dread : American film at the turn of the millenium / Kirsten
Moana Thompson.
        p. cm. — (SUNY series, horizons of cinema)
    Includes bibiographical references and index.
    ISBN-13: 978-0-7914-7043-5 (hardcover : alk. paper)
    ISBN-13: 978-0-7914-7044-2 (pbk. : alk. paper)
    1. Horror films—United States—History and criticism.   2. Disaster
films—United States—History and criticism.   3. Science fiction films—
United States—History and criticism.   4. Apocalypse in motion pictures.
I. Title. II. Series.

PN1995.9.H6T47 2006
791.43'6160973—dc22   2006013425

10 9 8 7 6 5 4 3 2 1

To Noelle Couvreur,
With love.

Contents

Illustrations

Acknowledgments

This book had its origins in my doctoral dissertation, which I completed at the Cinema Studies Department at New York University in 1998. Instrumental to writing this dissertation were the members of the NYU dissertation seminar, whose suggestions, questions, and interventions helped shape my work. My warmest thanks to Antje Ascheid, Alex Keller, Marcos Becquer, Bruce Brasell, Cynthia Lucia, Roy Grundmann, David Lugowski, Paula Massood, and Jill O'Brien, and especially to Dr. Chris Straayer, whose generosity of time and patience in leading this group was vital in helping us all through the dissertation-writing process.

A special thanks to Roy Grundmann who has been a crucial editor, interlocutor, guide, and friend through the numerous drafts of this project, and who helped me with the difficult task of reshaping the dissertation into a book. I am eternally grateful for his help at an early point when I felt stymied. I also wish to thank my friend Paula Massood for reading drafts, making suggestions, and providing her ever-valuable copyediting for this and other writing projects. I also wish to thank my doctoral advisor, Robert Stam, and the other members of my dissertation committee—Toby Miller, Chris Straayer, and Judith Halberstam—for their suggestions and responses to various drafts of the dissertation and to its defense. I also thank the staff members of the Cinema Studies Department Isabelle Freda, Ann Harris, and Ken Sweeney, who in numerous ways, both personal and professional, helped me navigate my way through my PhD at NYU. Thanks also to Professor William Simon, Chair of the Cinema Studies Department, and Professors Robert Sklar and Richard Allen, who contributed to my intellectual growth at NYU.

My warmest thanks to Peter Sacks, Valery Manenti, David Kalal, Gita Reddy, and Catherine Sears, who as my friends and moral support spent many hours with me watching movies, smoking cigarettes, and talking through things throughout the arduous yet fun years of graduate

school. Thanks also to my family—to my sisters Andrea and Nicola
Thompson, and to my mother, Sigrid Thompson, for their support in my
adventures in academia. My love also to my numerous family members—
uncles, aunties, and cousins scattered around the world from Samoa to
New Zealand and Germany.

My thanks also to Wayne State University, which provided financial
support in the form of a release from teaching duties in my sabbatical in
2003. My thanks to Dr. Richard Grusin and all the members of the
English Department, and especially to my friends and colleagues Kathryne
Lindberg, Sheila Lloyd, Ted Pearson, Donna Landry, and Gerald Maclean,
and to my film colleagues Robert Burgoyne, Cynthia Erb, and Les Brill
for their support and advice in my years in the Motor City.

My thanks to SUNY Press for bringing this project into print, to
anonymous reviewers A and B, and to my series editor, Murray Pomerance,
Interim Director James Peltz, freelance copyeditor, Wyatt Benner, and
Director of Production, Marilyn Semerad, for their guidance and suggestions for revisions at various stages of this project. Special thanks also to
Ronit Bezalel and Mark D. Phillips for permission to reproduce their
personal photographs.

An earlier version of chapter 2 was published as "Cape Fear and
Trembling: Familial Dread," *Literature and Film: A Guide to the Theory
and Practice of Film Adaptation*, ed. Robert Stam and Alessandra Raengo
(New York: Blackwell, 2004) 126–47.

The photo in figure 3.3, Cabrini-Green "White" Towers, appears
courtesy of Ms. Ronit Bezalel.

The photo in figure 6.2, "The Face of the Devil?" appears courtesy
of Mr. Mark D. Phillips.

Figures 2.1, 2.3, and 3.2 are promotional publicity stills, which appear
courtesy of PhotoFest.

1

Apocalyptic Dread, Kierkegaard, and the Cultural Landscape of the Millennium

A HUGE METEOR IS ON A COLLISION course with earth. A giant radioactive creature threatens Manhattan as Godzilla goes on a rampage. Volcanoes spew lava and huge tidal waves threaten cities. Outbreaks of the Ebola virus spread through the United States. The devil has come to town and it is the end of days. In the last decade of the twentieth century, a new cycle of Hollywood disaster movies from *Independence Day* to *Godzilla*, and from *Deep Impact* to *Volcano*, depicted crisis on a global scale. Survivalist groups began stockpiling supplies, businesses anxiously evaluated their computer systems in light of the Millennium (or Y2K) bug,[1] and unknown to the public, the Clinton administration arrested a series of individuals who had been plotting to blow up Los Angeles and New York in the "Millennium plot." As the marker of a new year, decade, and millennium drew closer, long-standing apocalyptic anxieties about the overdetermined year 2000 became evident in American popular culture, public policy, and journalism. This anxiety about the future and about the end of the world drew upon long-standing eschatological prophecies about Armageddon drawn from Revelations, Daniel, and other Christian and Jewish apocalyptic texts.

I will argue that these social anxieties, fears, and ambivalence about global catastrophe, which I call *apocalyptic dread*, took explicit narrative form in American cinema of the late nineties and continued into the first

1

years of the twenty-first century. Furthermore, this dread was a new manifestation of a long-standing American apocalyptic tradition. A blend of providential and messianic elements in Puritan Calvinism, this tradition first became apparent in the science-fiction cinema of the cold war, reemerged in the seventies with separate cycles of science-fiction and demonic films, gained further prominence under a turn to social conservatism under Reagan in the eighties, and reached a hysterical peak in the nineties in a cycle of horror, disaster, and science-fiction films explicitly focused on the approaching millennium. After 9/11, this dread took new forms with anxieties about the rise of Islamic fundamentalism and terrorism from within.

From the demonic dread in the family emblematized by the seventies' horror films *Carrie*, *The Omen*, and *The Exorcist*, to more recent science fiction like *Strange Days* and *End of Days*, in which the turn of the millennium became an explicit narrative focus, Hollywood repeatedly creates fantasies about the end of the world. Fredric Jameson suggests that science-fiction's affinity for the dystopian is symptomatic of the genre's "deepest vocation . . . to demonstrate and dramatize our incapacity to imagine the future," *and* that this failure of imagination is not individual but rather collective and ideological (246–7). Constance Penley suggests "we *can* imagine the future, but we *cannot* conceive the kind of collective political strategies necessary to change or ensure that future," and that, as a result, science-fiction films repeatedly replay resistance to alien invasions in the form of romanticized messiahs or small guerilla groups, rather than through systemic political change (64). Geoff King and Tanya Krzywinska suggest that this failure of imagination leads to representations of "the present or future [that] are sometimes shaped in the mould of supernatural terrors from the past" and that bring "the millenial fear of Judgement Day into the hi-tech present." (53)

Although apocalyptic dread is most explicitly evident in the science-fiction and disaster films of the last decade (1995–2005), this dread permeates well beyond these traditional genres. An unexamined component of dread that my book seizes on can be found in nineties' cinema within the horror/crime hybrid. Unlike science fiction or the disaster film, the horror hybrid turns to the family under threat—not (merely) from asteroids, aliens, or replicants, but rather from the internal conflicts and traumas that my case studies explore. *Apocalyptic Dread* examines a particular and historically situated set of horror relations within the family, in both its past and present formations, and between the family and workplace, and family and society. In particular, I suggest that in the nineties, hybrid crime/horror films are consumed with apocalyptic dread, or a free-floating anxiety and ambivalence about the future that is displaced onto the specific dread embodied by each film's monster, and that dramatizes a compulsive eschatological need to perceive and decode signs. This wider mood of dread pervades many genres, and the case studies that follow this chapter will include a melodrama-thriller (*Cape Fear*), a psychological horror film (*Candyman*), a melodrama (*Dolores Claiborne*), a serial-killer film (*Se7en*), a science-fiction thriller (*Signs*), and a science-fiction disaster film (*War of the Worlds*). In these case studies, a monstrous figure, the uncanny double of what the family has repressed, emerges and threatens apocalyptic vengeance because of the specific crimes for which the family are responsible. Produced by the repression of specific traumas, yet disavowed, these narrative monsters continue to repeat themselves as pathological symptoms, figured through the uncanny. These traumas are of rape (*Cape Fear*), lynching and miscegenation (*Candyman*), domestic violence and incest (*Dolores Claiborne*), serial murder (*Se7en*), a husband's loss of his wife and faith (*Signs*), and paternal failure (*War of the Worlds*). But apocalyptic dread's guiding tropes of cataclysmic violence, prophetic revelation, and radical transformation do not exhaust themselves in the familial narratives evident in my case studies; they also link the familial to the public sphere by pointing to broader historical fragmentation and change.

Through my readings of *Cape Fear* (Martin Scorsese, 1991), *Candyman* (Bernard Rose, 1992), *Dolores Claiborne* (Taylor Hackford, 1995), *Se7en* (David Fincher, 1995), *Signs* (M. Night Shyamalan, 2002), and *War of the Worlds* (Steven Spielberg, 2005), I will consider the ways in which apocalyptic dread maps the demonic, the eschatological, and the uncanny across the family. I also use these films as indicators of how popular culture negotiates anxieties about the subject, family, and future at this point of historical transition. But before doing so, I want to take a closer look at apocalypticism as a religious, historical, and sociocultural fear formation, as well as at a particular subgenre or fear formation of apocalyptic dread that I call *millennial dread*, and that appeared in the last decade of the old millennium.

Apocalypse Now

Apocalyptic dread can be defined as that fear and anxiety about the future and about the anticipated end of the world. A transliteration of the Greek word *apokalypsis*, apocalypse broadly means to "uncover or disclose." As Mick Broderick has observed, the apocalypse is commonly confused with doomsday, disaster, catastrophe, and terminus. These popular misconceptions overlook what Lois Parkinson Zamora calls the apocalypse's other dialectical meanings—those of revelation, triumph, order, and the millennium (qtd. in Broderick 252)—and it is these other connotations of apocalypse that emerge as prominent components of apocalyptic dread's 1990s twin, *millennial dread*. They ultimately converge in the belief, visualized in many doomsday scenarios, that the average apocalypse isn't all bad—at the very least, it can teach us a lesson, so long as we're able to read the signs . . . In this sense, the millennial and the apocalyptic shall be discussed in close conjunction with one another.

Apocalyptic literature consists of those parts of the Bible and other Jewish and Christian books that embody an apocalypse, or revelation, given through a prophetic vision of the future.[2] Apocalyptic literature such as Ezekiel and Daniel in the Old Testament and the last book in the New Testament, Revelations, concerns itself with the end of world and the final confrontation between God and the powers of evil. In these narratives, the conflict frequently culminates in a world catastrophe, and with a messianic figure triumphing over evil.[3] Nineteenth-century American fundamentalism understood history as marked by discrete stages, between which there were abrupt transitions marked by violence, such as the expulsion from the Garden, the Flood, and so on (Strozier 9). Similarly the *eschatos*, or end of the world prophesized in Revelations also has discrete stages, with the Rapture (the time at which saved souls are suddenly lifted up to heaven), followed by the Time of Tribulation (the seven years when the Antichrist will rule over the world through an international body) and the battle of Armageddon (the Antichrist fights Christ on the Plains of Jezreel near modern-day Megiddo in Israel). All of them culminate in the Final Day of Judgment and the end of the world, when God triumphs over the Antichrist and rules for a thousand years. In this framework the apocalyptic encompasses the following meanings: the revelatory (prophecy), the destructive (cataclysm/disaster), the grandiose (wild predictions), and the climactic (decisive).

Millennialism refers to a specific form of eschatological belief that draws from Judeo-Christian apocalyptic literature and that understands that the end of the world has been both preordained by God and prophesied in the Bible. Its followers believe one must spiritually and psychologically prepare for it. As a specifically Protestant fundamentalist philosophy, premillennialism (also called dispensationialism) understands history in terms of the past (original sin, the first coming of Christ) *and* the future end-time (the Second Coming, the battle of Armageddon) before the day of Final Judgment. It understands time as measured from the birth of Christ and believes that the year 2000 (or 2001) is the beginning of the third millennium. American millennialism has deep roots in the belief systems of the Puritans who, through the sermons of Increase Mather and John Cotton, understood themselves as God's chosen people, establishing their New World settlements in anticipation of the Second

Coming. In Christopher Sharrett's terms, they understood the nation's future as "a divinely ordained historical destiny which, when violated or ignored, will cause a cataclysmic retribution" (221). Emerging from the Judeo-Christian apocalyptic tradition and Puritan Providentialism, millennialism was a more specific manifestation of a broader cultural context of dread, and as millennial dread awaited the overdetermined year 2000 in the last decade of the twentieth century.

What shall be the sign of your coming and the end of the world?

—Matthew 24.3

As a consciousness of the end of the world, apocalyptic or millennial thinking reflects and depends upon *hermeneutics*, or the interpretation of signs to predict and prepare for the future. Repeatedly when disaster struck, eschatological thought understood political, social or physical disruption as portents of the beginning of the end of the world; the enormous devastation wrought by the bubonic plague in the fourteenth and fifteenth centuries and the threat of Islamic invasion in the sixteenth century prompted the return of these anxieties. Similarly, at the end of the second millennium, many fundamentalist, evangelical, or Pentecostal[4] groups interpreted geopolitical events (particularly war and unrest in the Middle East) as signs of the coming of the end of the world. Natural disasters (storms, floods, volcanic eruptions, global warming) and man-made crises (monetary collapses, scandals, coups, and revolutions) were the second staple source for eschatological interpretation.[5] As Charles Strozier's research into the psychology of American fundamentalism has demonstrated, its social appeal is closely linked to anxieties about global threats; he says, "I would argue that our historical moment is fraught with a new kind of dread, for we live with the real scientific possibility that either through nuclear warfare, or choking pollution, or vastly increased rates of disease, especially cancer, we could actually end human existence" (158). Biblical prophecy thus offers an overdetermined narrative in which political and cultural change, together with violence, crime, and natural disasters, is retrospectively understood within the comforting terms of God's plan.

In this way then, history is understood as a series of signs (or portents) of the end-time, which those who have been given the gifts of prophecy by God can decode. According to Hal Lindsay, author of *The*

Late, Great Planet Earth (1970), there will be seven signs signaling the end-time: war, revolution, plague, famine, earthquake, religious deception, and "strange occurrences in space." The twentieth century has certainly seen no shortage of occurrences that, from a millenarian perspective, fit into these seven sign groups. Political events from the formation of the United Nations and the state of Israel (1948) to more recent battles in the Middle East with the two Gulf Wars (1991, 2003) have been read as signs of the coming of the Antichrist, who it is believed will appear in a time of geopolitical chaos before the second coming of Christ. Religious authors such as Lindsay, Pat Robertson (*The New World Order*), Salem Kirban (*666 and 1000*), and Larry Burkett (*The Illuminati*) have offered themselves as hermeneutic prophets, connecting cryptic passages of apocalyptic literature to contemporary events, and warning believers that the end-time is at hand (Melling 88). Robertson's *New World Order* (1992), which sold 500,000 copies on its release and spent weeks on the *New York Times* best-seller list, was but a part of a commercial spike in sales of prophecy literature, which together with popular sermons and calls to religious hotlines reflected a belief that the first Gulf War was a fulfillment of prophetic literature and a sign that the end-time approached.[6] This fascination with overdetermined narratives, paranoid conspiracies, and hermeneutic decoding continues with the enormous financial success of a more recent novel, Dan Brown's *The Da Vinci Code* (2003), which is now a Hollywood movie (Ron Howard, 2006). After all, as Peter and Paul Lalonde suggest in *The Mark of the Beast*, "If you're not paranoid, it's because you're not paying close enough attention to the imminence of evil in the last days" (qtd. in Melling 91). For fundamentalist Christians, September 11, 2001, seemed to augur the end of days, and sales of prophecy literature increased by 71% in the weeks immediately following the disaster, including huge sales for the apocalyptic Left Behind series, whose authors, Tim LaHaye and Jerry B. Jenkins, had already displaced John Grisham as the top adult-fiction writers of the nineties.[7] But again, the reason these apocalyptic fantasies emerged was not that they filled a vacuum left by world history. They have supplemented—and consistently alluded to or explicitly drawn on—the real-life history of the world, peppered as it is with all kinds of disasters and apocalyptic moments.

Historical Context of Apocalyptic Dread

Rupturing the first half of the twentieth century, the two World Wars and the Holocaust were cataclysmic events; indeed as Nancy Ammerman has noted, World War I prompted an increase in interest in all things apocalyptic, giving rise to three international prophecy conferences between

1914 and 1918 (77). The Second World War and especially the Holocaust have also been described as "the revelatory, traumatic, apocalyptic fulcrum of the twentieth century" (Berger 391). After 1945, decolonization in Africa, Asia, and the Pacific began, as the world divided into two poles during the cold war, and in the United States rising paranoia about Communism and fears about atomic power and the H-bomb took displaced form in the invasion narratives of science-fiction cinema. In the second half of the century, the battle for civil rights in the United States intensified, and American cities began to burn after the murder of Martin Luther King, Jr. in 1968. In the seventies the trauma of Watergate and the Vietnam War, together with the energy crisis and recession, split the country and gave rise to a culture of paranoia that was acted out on television, in tabloids, and on movie screens.[8]

In response to rapid sociocultural changes over the last forty years, an increased cultural conservatism and (re)turn to fundamentalist religions (which could be termed another "New Awakening" in American history) has become increasingly prominent, and is a key dimension of what I call apocalyptic dread. In 1976, which *Time* declared to be "The Year of the Evangelical," Jimmy Carter became the first Southern Baptist to be elected president, and three years later Jerry Falwell formed the Moral Majority. Although membership in mainline churches has fallen in the last thirty years, membership in fundamentalist and evangelical churches (Jehovah's Witnesses, Church of God in Christ, and Assemblies of God, among others) continued to grow exponentially through the eighties and nineties. Anxieties about the changing role of women in the wake of the feminist movement of the seventies, and about the gay-rights movement after Stonewall, led to conservative political campaigns that decried sexual promiscuity, pornography, any form of birth control, premarital sex, and public "immorality." By the eighties, Christian conservatism was now flexing its political muscle as a voting bloc. Under Reagan it became an increasingly important part of the Republican base, with the political wing of the conservative movement led by organizations like Jerry Falwell's Moral Majority, James Dobson's Focus on the Family, Ralph Reed's Christian Coalition, and Gary Bauer's American Values. A "religion gap" or political difference in voting patterns between the secular and the faithful first became evident with Nixon's election in 1972. This gap widened under Reagan and both Bushes and largely favored the Republican Party, which has attracted the fundamentalist religious voter (with certain exceptions) (Page 2004). Today it is estimated that there are more than 60 million born-again Christians (Hendershot 177).

In 1992 at the Republican National Convention, Pat Buchanan's keynote address decried social changes relating to sexuality, the family, and society, declaring that America was now in a "culture war" over social values. Divorce rates of 50%, the rise of single-parent families, extended family parenting, and gay civil partnerships and adoptions are all examples of challenges to traditional notions of the nuclear family. In fact, the conventional understanding of the nuclear family as consisting of a male breadwinner, female homemaker, and several children is based on a historical model of relatively brief duration, beginning in the 1920s and reaching its highpoint in the 1950s (Mintz 352–62). In the 1980s, the reassertion of "family values" as a political slogan by the Republican Party was a marker of conservative anxiety about these social changes. The principal targets of this conservative reaction were feminists, liberals, and homosexuals. In 1989, Jerry Falwell claimed that American society was corrupted from within by an unholy trinity of Communists, feminists, and homosexuals. From Pat Robertson's prediction in 1998 that a meteor and tornadoes would destroy Orlando and Disneyland for holding an unofficial "Gay Day," to Stan Craig, a pastor at the Choice Hills Baptist Church in Greenville, South Carolina, who described gays "as a stench in the nostrils of God," incremental victories in gay civil rights have mobilized increased right-wing political and social activism. Much of the language of opposition of the religious Right was expressed in apocalyptic terms, as when Robertson made a series of prophecies on May 27, 1998, on *The 700 Club*, the Christian Broadcasting Network talk show, in which he urged, "I would warn Orlando that you're right in the way of some serious hurricanes, and I don't think I'd be waving those flags in God's face if I were you." Robertson also warned that the widespread practice of homosexuality "will bring about terrorist bombs, it'll bring earthquakes, tornadoes and possibly a meteor" and that his warning "is not a message of hate. This is a message of redemption" (Robertson, *700 Club*). Indeed, after the fall of Communism in 1991 and the rise of "postfeminism," it became the third leg of Falwell's unholy triad—homosexuals—who increasingly bore the burden of millennial meaning. More recently, Stephen Bennett, an evangelical writer for the American Family Association, described May 17, 2004, when gay same-sex marriage licenses began to be issued in Massachusetts, in telling terms as "the day the earth stood still." Speaking in characteristically apocalyptic terms, he said America was "a nation awaiting the Almighty's response. We know the days are short and evil, so let us redeem the time doing what we were called to do—winning the lost to Christ."

With the election of George W. Bush, whose political father is the culturally conservative Ronald Reagan rather than the former president George H. W. Bush (1988–92), the relationship between Christian conservatives and the Republican Party became ever closer. Continuing

Reagan's focus on social values, and taking up a phrase by the equally conservative pope John Paul II (1978–2005), the Christian wing of the Republican Party argued that their policies were part of a "culture of life." Policy struggles between the Republican administration, the judiciary, and local and state governments were central in debates about abortion, stem cell technology, gay marriage (in 2004), and euthanasia and medical technology in end-of-life issues, the latter foregrounded in 2005 by the Terri Schiavo case.[9] Echoing the Scopes trial of 1925, battles over the teaching of evolution in schools returned through the late nineties in local school-board elections in Ohio, Oklahoma, and Kansas, as conservative Christian groups were increasingly successful in arguing that so-called intelligent design (a fictive cover for creationism) should be given equal time with evolution in science classrooms.[10] Most recently, Christian conservative activism has even led to a dozen IMAX theaters in the South (a number of which were in science museums) refusing to show the film *Volcanoes* in 2005, because of its brief references to evolution.[11] The defeat of John Kerry in the 2004 presidential election and the public debate over exit polls, in which self-identified "morals" voters referred to social issues as a compelling factor in their election of George W. Bush continue to foreground the social significance of the close alliance between the religious Right and the Republican Party.

In this sense, those who were puzzled by Bush's victory, and in their minds kept going over the previous six months in search of early signs of their own doomsday, may want to consider that the writing was, in fact, on the wall by April 2004. However, the proverbial wall that is of interest here is not the primaries or any state or national poll, but the American movie box-office. Mel Gibson's *The Passion of the Christ*, an eschatological tale of the first order, had by then become the box-office sensation of the year. But the film's gargantuan success was hardly due to any crossover appeal—quite the opposite. The movie, whose dark sectarian revisionism fueled its violent spectacle to brutalizing effect, would surely have withered on the vine, had it not been for the droves of religious fundamentalists who worshipped at this movie's altar. Meanwhile, evangelical Christian–produced media broke out of its market niche and began to influence popular culture and mainstream thinking. In the seventies, evangelical cinema like Donald W. Thompson's prophecy series *A Thief in the Night* (1972), *Distant Thunder* (1978), *Image of the Beast* (1981), and *The Prodigal Planet* (1983) were produced and distributed on 16 mm to a specialty market of church audiences. By the turn of the new millennium, evangelical cinema adopted a new approach, using stars and high production values in *The Omega Code* (Robert Marcarelli, 1999) and its sequel *Megiddo: The Omega Code 2* (Brian Trenchard-Smith, 2001). Funded by the Trinity Broadcasting Network, these films became the first evangelically produced films to receive a wide theatrical release to general audiences. As part of their strategy of mainstream appeal, they appropriated the generic conventions of the horror, science-fiction, and Hollywood action blockbuster, blending them with an apocalyptic narrative.[12] *The Omega Code* and its sequel integrated conservative and isolationist anxieties about the United Nations into narratives by showing the Antichrist character, Stone Alexander (Michael York), becoming a political leader of a UN-like body. Just as Damien Thorn's global corporation provided political cover for his secret identity as the Antichrist in *Omen 3: The Final Conflict* (Graham Baker, 1981), so *The Omega Code*'s narrative fictionalized contemporary geopolitical events in the Middle East and reflected conservative hostility to the United Nations, by depicting it as instrumental to the rule of the Antichrist. In fact, *The Omega Code* suggests that the Antichrist *is* the United Nations, and not only threatens American sovereignty, but—literally—signifies the end of the world.

Heather Hendershot's important recent study *Shaking the World for Jesus* traces the enormous productivity of the evangelical media industry, which in recent decades has expanded its market, selling everything from Christian rock music to rapture videos and feature films (179–80). Religious broadcasting on television and radio have also increased, as have sales of religious paraphernalia (from $1 billion in 1980 to $4 billion in 1996). From book publishing to direct-to-video productions, religious media is a multimillion-dollar industry (Shorto 60–61). Shrewdly adopting mainstream genres and aesthetic conventions, whether in publishing, cinema, videos, or rock music, Christian media's representational strategies made Jesus the new action hero. Timothy Weber, president of the Memphis Theological Seminary, explained the enormous commercial popularity of the Left Behind apocalyptic fiction series (which has since been adapted to film) in these terms: "The culture war fits into the premillennialists' expectation of the end of history—the decline of civilization, the breakdown of morality, a general breakdown of order. The warrior Jesus returns to set everything right again" (qtd. in Kirkpatrick, "Return" A6). The commercial success of apocalyptic literature and films were echoed in the enormous grosses of *The Passion of the Christ*, which led ABC to broadcast a previously shelved film, *Judas*, in March 2004, and it has already led Hollywood to reevaluate theological themes as an important untapped market (Waxman, "Hollywood" B5). The release of C. S. Lewis's *The Chronicles of Narnia: The Lion, The Witch, and the Wardrobe* (Andrew Adamson, 2005), together with accompanying Christian and secular soundtracks, continues this trend. Unsurprisingly, Mel Gibson's new film *Apocalypto* (2006) frames its story of Mayan decline in eschatological terms. More recently, Hollywood has hired "faith and family" consultants to examine scripts for objectionable content and to assist in promoting their films to Christian markets; and Sony studios has now partnered with the Christian production company Cloud Ten to make the third installment of the Left Behind series (Waxman, "Passion of the Marketers" C3). In the same way that Gibson's *The Passion of the Christ* blended horror conventions with Christian eschatology, LaHaye and Jenkin's novel *Glorious Appearing* described Jesus's triumphant and violent second coming as if it were a version of *Dawn of the Dead*: "Men and women soldiers and horses seemed to explode where they stood. It was as if the very words of the Lord had superheated their blood, causing it to burst through their veins and skin. Even as they struggled, their own flesh dissolved, their eyes melted and their tongues disintegrated" (Kirkpatrick, "Return" A1).

Just as Christian media has appropriated the generic conventions of horror, the action film, and science fiction, so Hollywood has found itself turning to theological subject matter, and this reorientation also underscores the generic hybridity of apocalyptic dread. Beginning in the eighties, the increased political power of Christian conservatism in the Republican Party, together with the increasingly high-profile debate over the "culture wars," "family values," and the "culture of life" began to infiltrate commercial American cinema. It is worth taking a closer look at some of the ways in which Christian millennialism and apocalyptic eschatology have become prominent themes in Hollywood films.

Apocalypticism and Cinema

Apocalypticism has long had a close connection to the science-fiction genre, for both are concerned with a fantasy about the future and a dread that the world will end. Early films taking such theories ranged from *The Comet* (1916) and *End of the World* (1916) to *Metropolis* (1926) and *Things to Come* (1936). Scholars from Kim Newman to Sean Cubitt have suggested that in science-fiction films of the fifties, fears of the cold war and Communism became displaced into narratives about public invasion and private contamination. Classic invasion narratives such as *The Day the Earth Stood Still* (1951), *The War of the Worlds* (1953), and *It Came from Outer Space* (1953) constructed visions about malevolent invaders from outer space descending on American cities, while *I Married a Communist* (1950), *Invasion of the Bodysnatchers* (1956), and *I Married a Monster from Outer Space* (1958) singled out the family as the main target. The cycle took a realist turn with the apocalyptic fear of nuclear annihilation in *On the Beach* (1959), *Fail-Safe* (1964), *Dr. Strangelove* (1964), and *Crack in the World* (1965). In the seventies, low-budget exploitation films like *No Blade of Grass* (1970), *Ultimate Warrior* (1975), and *Death Race 2000* (1975), and higher-budget films like Franklin J. Schaffner's *Planet of the Apes* (1968–73) and George Miller's *Mad Max* (1980–85) series continued the dystopian postapocalyptic cycle, even influencing the western (the protagonist of *High Plains Drifter* [1973], turns out literally to be the devil). (Broderick 269). In the eighties under the Reagan administration, which itself merged public policy and science fiction in its Strategic Defense Initiative (Star Wars), the science-fiction genre returned with commercial profligacy. Increasingly sophisticated computer-generated imagery (CGI) enabled new spectacles in the extraterrestrial or supernatural subgenres, from *Star Wars* (1977) to *Close Encounters of the Third Kind* (1977), *Poltergeist* (1982), *E.T.* (1982), and the sequel-fertile ur-narratives, Ridley Scott's *Alien* (1979) and James Cameron's *The Terminator* (1984). Not a few of them had millennial components or undertones.

The nineties saw an explosion of apocalyptic dread as Hollywood used fears about the year 2000 as fodder for its story lines, commodifying contemporary anxieties about global warming and climate change into quasi-plausible doomsday plots, with a cycle of disaster movies that continues into the more recent era with *The Core* (2003) and *The Day After Tomorrow* (2004). Whereas the disaster cycle of the seventies had a rather localized focus on individual ships, buildings, or cities—consider *Poseidon Adventure* (1972), *Earthquake* (1974), and *The Towering Inferno* (1974)—disaster movies of the nineties were global in scope. Developments in special effects enabled new visual spectacles and obviated expensive location shooting and casts of thousands in *Twister* (1996), *Independence Day* (1996), *Volcano* (1997), *Deep Impact* (1998), and *Armageddon* (1998).

Further, this cycle included films that blended action, disaster, and horror genres with an explicit or implicit dystopian narrative focus on the end of the world and/or the approach of the year 2000, bringing what Geoff King calls "the millennial fear of Judgment Day into the high-tech present." They were typified by *Terminator 2: Judgment Day* (1991), *Nostradamus* (1994), *Strange Days* (1995), *12 Monkeys* (1995), *The Prophecy* (1995), *End of Days* (1999), and *The Matrix* (1999) (King and Krzywinska 53). In fact, the disaster movie had never entirely gone away; twenty-five disaster movies appeared throughout the eighties. But in the nineties fifty-six disaster movies were released, with fourteen films released in the peak year 1997 (Keane 73). In the post–cold war era, nuclear weaponry had renewed purpose, and in disaster films like *Armageddon* protected us against giant comets or asteroids plummeting to earth, or was a shield against terrorist states or individuals on earth.

Beginning in the late sixties and accelerating in the eighties, Hollywood studios, network stations, and cable television became divisions of global media conglomerates like General Electric, Viacom, Matsushita, News Corp, and AOL TimeWarner. In the mid-nineties, the magazine divisions of conglomerates like TimeWarner began to target a perceived rise in readers' socially conservative values and religious interests, and it devoted cover issues to themes relating to religion, God, heaven, and spirituality.[13] In part reflecting the increasing cultural conservatism of the recent era and the conservative commercial imperatives of their conglomerate parent companies, Hollywood's second major cinematic cycle took an explicitly theological turn, with stories about messianic figures, angels, ghosts, or devils.[14] From *Stigmata* (1999), with its high production values and the presence of stars, to the low-budget *Eye of God* (Tim Blake Nelson, 1997) and *The Eighteenth Angel* (William Bindley, 1997), Manichaean oppositions of good and evil had renewed character functions in hybrid genres that blended the supernatural, theological, and quasi-scientific (Fowkes; Martin and Ostwalt; Lyden). Geoff King has shown how films like *Demon Seed* and TV shows such as *The X-Files* and *Buffy the Vampire Slayer* recycled medieval notions of the demonic or supernatural, using technology to explain the resurrection of vampires and demons, as they came to haunt contemporary settings.[15] Hollywood's turn to the Bible for inspiration fetishized the theological as narratively exotic, using the devil and the diabolical as a compelling and seductive spectacle in *The Devil's Advocate* (1997), *Fallen* (1998), *End of Days* (1999), and *The Exorcism of Emily Rose* (2005). Television shows also capitalized on stories with supernatural and, more specifically, theological narrative components.[16] The NBC miniseries *Revelations* (2005) featured Natasha McElhone as a nun investigating signs of the end of days, and debating faith with the scientist Bill Pullman. *Revelations* is one of the most explicit ways in which apocalyptic dread continues to pervade American culture, five years after the turn of the millennium. As Kevin Rafferty, the president for entertainment of NBC who gave the green light to *Revelations* and *Medium*, observed recently, "In the tumultuous times we live in, apocalyptic theory and big existential questions tend to be on the rise" (qtd. in Poniewozik 56).

Fusing apocalyptic themes with the disaster and science-fiction genres, the demonic cycle of the late nineties epitomized by *End of Days* was closely connected to the theological cycle, if not a subgenre of it, but also drew from a similar cycle in the seventies, in which key films like *The Exorcist* (William Friedkin, 1973), *Carrie* (Brian DePalma, 1976), *The Shining* (Stanley Kubrick, 1980), and the *Omen* (sequels 1976–91, remake 2006), brought together evil and horror in the family in the form of a child possessed by the devil.[17] Whether possessing the firstborn or only child (*The Omen, The Exorcist, The Good Son, The Exorcism of Emily Rose*), or the home itself (*Amityville Horror, Poltergeist*), the devil was the new dramatis persona.[18] Initiating this cycle, *Rosemary's Baby* (Roman Polanski, 1968) suggested that the principal site of threat was the family and the home. These demonic figures represented threats to social and institutional normality figured through the state, church, and family, and these films' narratives of struggle with the devil offered clarity and meaning in social contexts of chaos and uncertainty. As Paul Wells has noted, "The horror film in the post-*Psycho* era has also seen the symptomatic collapse of assurance in, and promotion of, the family and conservative family values. Children, once the epitome of innocence, become configured as the monster, partly to illustrate the proliferation of evil as a natural phenomenon" (85).

Related to the demonic cycle were those films which featured children or young adolescents with strange psychic or telekinetic powers, such as *Carrie* (Brian DePalma, 1976), *The Shining* (Stanley Kubrick, 1980), and *The Fury* (Brian DePalma, 1978), or children who have a special relationship with the extraterrestrial or supernatural, as we will see in *Signs*, as well as *The Sixth Sense* (M. Night Shyamalan, 1999) and *The Children of the Corn* cycle (1984–2004). Because these supernaturally gifted adolescents were often abused, usually by a monstrous parent, as in *The Shining* (1980) and *Carrie* (1976), this cycle also suggested that horror's threat was no longer just external but could be *internally* located in the family. For example, in *Carrie* the eponymous heroine is provoked into acts of homicidal rage after the repeated abuses of her repressive mother and sadistic classmates. Carrie's mother is a fanatical Christian who has repressed her own sexuality since the "sin" of her daughter's conception. In this way, demonic vengeance transformed tales of teenage angst about sexuality, desire, and the transition to adulthood into domestic melodramas, and suggested that violent horror was the consequence of psychosexual repression. As Paul Wells suggests, "domestic space had become the locality for the worst of horror" (17) and as Robin Wood has shown, horror became specifically American and familial ("Hollywood" 87). Whether in the form of the psychotic father of *The Shining* or the diabolical children of *The Exorcist* and *The Good Son*, the relationship between normality and monstrosity was profoundly unsettled. These tales of demonic children dramatized a personalized and familial evil, and they did so through parables with a theological trajectory and an eschatological outcome; that is, horror not only threatened the family from within, but also was preordained to triumph over it.

The demonic horror cycle also adopted an eschatological trajectory, linking the diabolical to prophecies about the end of the world. As the prologue to *The Omen* ominously suggests, "Here is wisdom. Let him that hath understanding count the number of the beast, for it is the number of a man, and his number is 666" (Rev. RSV 13, 16). The child Damian Thorn is the Antichrist foretold in Revelations. In a sequel, *The Final Conflict* (1981), a now adult Damian muses in exasperation, "[O]ne thing these pedantic Christians believe in is sticking to the letter of their prophecies." As I have suggested, eschatological prophecy is a central component of apocalyptic dread, in which the interpretation of signs becomes a central narrative issue. The nineties' cycle of diabolical horror fuses the emphasis of seventies' horror on the interpretation of signs with the apocalyptic dread of the fin-de-siècle. In *End of Days* (Peter Hyams, 1999), the devil (Gabriel Byrne) has just a few days before the turn of the new millennium to find a young woman, Christine, who is destined to be his bride. Based on a celestial alignment calculated by Gregorian monks, the last hour of the old millennium has been prophesied as the time "when a thousand years have ended, [and] Satan shall be loosed from his prison," and if the consummation occurs, Satan will triumph and the end of days begin. Alluding to *The Omen*, a priest (Rod Steiger) rejects the common understanding that 666 is the mark of the beast, claiming that it is really its mirror image, or 999, and thus refers to 1999, or the eve of the millennium. Merging the action conventions of *Terminator 2: Judgment Day* and other key films in Arnold Schwarzenegger's career, the final conflict between the devil and Jericho (Schwarzenegger) requires extensive shoot-outs and an arsenal of heavy weaponry. As with *Terminator 2*, Arnold must rescue a young woman from her murderous attacker in order to prevent the end of the world. However, as the pope intones at the beginning of the story, "the prophecy calls for faith," and it is ultimately the restoration of Jericho's faith (which he had lost because his wife and daughter had been murdered) rather than his heavy weaponry that enables him to sacrifice his life and triumph over the devil.

This issue of sacrifice and the importance of faith as a weapon is shared by an earlier film: *The Seventh Sign* (Carl Schultz, 1988), a thriller-horror about the Second Coming and the fulfillment of Revelations. In it many natural disasters—from hailstorms to solar eclipses and seas full of dead fish—are signs of the *eschatos*. Demi Moore plays Abby, a pregnant woman who becomes convinced that a strange man named David who boards with her is determined to kill her unborn baby. A biblical prophecy found in the book of Joel describes seven signs that prefigure the end of the world. A mixture of Jewish and Christian apocalypticism, the story is centrally concerned with the interpretation of seven seals, which reveal the imminence of the world's end. The narrative also alludes to the notion of the Guf, described in the Talmud as the place where unborn souls first stay in heaven, and which when empty becomes the seventh and final sign that the world will end. Ultimately, in order to save her unborn child, Abby sacrifices her own life, and breaks the cycle of signs that is leading to the apocalypse. Here Abby becomes a Christological savior figure whose sacrifice saves the world again, but unlike the original Christian story, Abby's identity as a mother is central to her messianic function. Like *The Forgotten* (Joseph Cohen, 2004), in which a mother's primal bond with her son triumphs over a strange alien experiment, *The Seventh Sign* reveals many of the key tropes of apocalyptic dread in the last decade: the importance of prophecy and the decoding of signs; the role of political and natural disasters as signs of the *eschatos*; the fearful anticipation of the future and the turn to faith as a defense; and finally, the narrative centrality of the family in the ultimate conflict between good and evil.

These dimensions are further echoed in *Stigmata* (Rupert Wainwright, 1999), which like *End of Days* stars Gabriel Byrne, this time playing Andrew Kiernan, a scientist-priest who "has not prayed for a very long time" and whose job is to investigate apparent miracles on behalf of a division of the Vatican called the Congregation of the Causes of the Saints. Kiernan becomes involved in the case of a young atheist named Frankie Page (Patricia Arquette), who has developed inexplicable stigmatic bleeding and who suffers from supernatural scourging. Puzzled by Frankie's atheism, because, in his words, stigmatics are deeply religious people "with no exceptions," Frankie's supernatural powers and visions ultimately restore Kiernan's faith. The film borrows liberally from *The Exorcist* in its scenes of physical possession and levitation, and replays the crisis of faith faced by Father Damien Karras in *The Exorcist*. Not unlike the *DaVinci Code*, *Stigmata* is also a conspiracy thriller with the Vatican deeply invested in preventing the publication of a long lost Gospel scroll, the Gospel of Thomas, which purports to reveal Christ's own words. Like a similar Vatican group in *End of Days* who try to kill Christine, the Congregation is determined to kill Frankie in order to keep the Gospel from the public. Thus, in *End of Days*, *Stigmata*, and *The Seventh Sign*, we see the return of the demonic cycle from 1988–99, foregrounding female characters whose bodies are central to theological prophecy. Whether through pregnancy, motherhood, or masochistic suffering, these women restore the faith of male characters, in order to save the world for Christianity.

These films suggest that the nineties only intensified a trend which began over the preceding thirty years, in which the family became front and center in the horror genre, and in which social anxieties about change become figured through narratives in which the family was under attack, whether from monsters, aliens, or diabolical children. As the century clicked over from 1999 to 2000 (or 2001), the new millennium was greeted variously, with theological fervor, social apprehension, or bored indifference. Although the transition into the new century passed uneventfully, since 9/11 dread and fear have regained prominence in the public sphere and become politically instrumental tools for a messianic Bush administration.[19] With American wars in Afghanistan and Iraq, the creation of the Department of Homeland Security, aggressive public surveillance, and the open-ended nature of the administration's war on terror, public dread about future occurrences of terror became so pronounced that the government had to construct a color coding alert system in order to quantify and manage dread; that is to say, dread was both politically instrumental and potentially chaotic. In the next section, I suggest that the anxieties and ambivalences attached to the family and the tensions and social conflicts that transform it from without and within manifest themselves in a form of dread that emerged in the nineteenth century as a product of particular sociocultural and philosophical factors. In order to understand these formations and the dread that they produced, I now turn to the work of the man who first conceptualized and explained them, taking up the concept of dread from philosopher often overlooked in film studies: Søren Kierkegaard.[20]

Kierkegaard and Dread

The indefiniteness of what we dread is not just lack of definition: it represents the essential impossibility of defining the "what." This withdrawal of what-is-in-totality, which then crowds around us in dread, this is what oppresses us.

—Martin Heidegger, "What is Metaphysics?" Lecture (1929)

Therefore I must point out that it is altogether different from fear and similar concepts that refer to something definite, whereas anxiety [dread] is freedom's actuality as the possibility of possibility.

—Søren Kierkegaard, *The Concept of Dread*

Kierkegaard's philosophy emerged from the Enlightenment turn to parliamentary democracy and (since the Renaissance) the de-privileging of theology in an increasingly secular world. Often described as the first existentialist, Kierkegaard understood individual existence as the primary ground for knowledge and, following Descartes, understood truth as subjectivity. His assault on traditional Western philosophy (and specifically that of Plato and Hegel) and on the religious complacency that arose from centuries of established Christianity led to a new form of philosophy that understood that reality was subjective and that only through radical, self-conscious choice could an authentic, ethical (and ultimately Christian) existence be reached. My turn to Kierkegaard is partly prompted by the contradictions presented by a secular, modern, knowledge-based society in which millennial and apocalyptic beliefs not only have a continuing presence in American culture, but indeed have proliferated in recent decades. Anxiety about the future and about the radical implications of free will in contemporary society lead us to Kierkegaard, because his theorizations about the paradoxical and ambivalent dimensions of anxiety (dread) suggest that the implications of knowledge and freedom of choice are not just liberating, but also deeply terrifying.

Colloquial meanings of dread refer usually to (a) a great fear, especially in the face of impending evil, or (b) extreme uneasiness in the face of a disagreeable prospect; a third, more archaic meaning suggests something causing awe or fear. By contrast, rather than being a straightforward fear *of* something, Kierkegaardian dread differs from fear in that its object is indeterminate. It has three principal components, which we shall look at in turn: first, radical freedom (or the moral dread occasioned by absolute choice), which gives rise to a fear of the future and which is mediated by past actions; second, a paradoxical ambivalence that is connected to the uncanny; and third, a connection to the cataclysmic qualities of trauma.

> When we consider the dialectical determinations of anxiety, it appears that exactly these have psychological ambivalence. Anxiety (dread) is a sympathetic antipathy and an antipathetic sympathy.
>
> —Søren Kierkegaard, *The Concept of Dread*

In *Fear and Trembling* (1843) and *The Concept of Dread* (1844), Kierkegaard understood dread (or more accurately translated, "anxiety/anguish") as the epistemological condition of existence, defining it as a "sympathetic antipathy or antipathetic sympathy" or the state in which "we desire what we fear, but fear what we desire" (*Concept of Dread* 38); that is, it is a paradoxical form of desire *and* fear. We love our desire, and our desire prompts dread, so in a sense we also desire our dread. Because Kierkegaard's understanding of dread was paradoxical, I see important linkages to the ambivalent dimensions of horror spectatorship. I use "dread" firstly to suggest the ways in which my case studies foreground the paradoxical qualities of attraction and repulsion—to a monster, to a fear, to an urban legend. These qualities are a significant, yet undertheorized, experiential and intellectual dimension of horror spectatorship. Consequently, I suggest that cinematic dread is profoundly ambivalent and is about the conflicting desire to know and yet not know, to see and yet want to look away.

Dread, Radical Freedom, and the Future

> When it is assumed that the prohibition awakens the desire, one acquires knowledge instead of ignorance, and in that case Adam must have had a knowledge of freedom, because the desire was to use it. The prohibition induces in him anxiety, for the prohibition awakens in him freedom's possibility.
>
> —Søren Kierkegaard, *The Concept of Dread*

Because the subject lives between possibility and the next possibility, subjectivity is essentially temporal. For Augustine, "we fear to fear" but cannot do otherwise, because in Kierkegaard's words "anxiety is always anxiety about one's self" (qtd. in Anz 47). As part of this notion of radical freedom, Kierkegaard also understood dread to be an expression of the *consciousness of the future*; as Sartre would say, "I await myself in the future. Anguish is the fear of not finding myself there." In *The Concept of Dread*, Kierkegaard writes that "anxiety [dread] is about tomorrow," because the future is fraught with possibility (80). For Kierkegaard, human beings face a future that is a tabula rasa of unknown choices, and yet at the same time always already mediated by Adam's original sin. In this sense, and like trauma, dread is open-ended, yet historically mediated by what has *already happened*.

Kierkegaard argues that dread resides in absolute "freedom," that is, in an invocation of existential choice that is *not* related to fear, but rather to the radical embrace of *possibility* as a necessary and intimate part of one's own existence, and therefore as terrifying and tempting as a yawning abyss. Consequently, dread is rooted in the *voluntary* nature of one's freedom—whether to sin, to kill oneself, or to kill others—and to the intense and ambivalent feelings that are aroused by that radical freedom. Kierkegaard tells us the story of Adam, whom God warns not to eat the apple hanging on the Tree of Knowledge. Adam dreads this freedom, which is not the eating of the apple per se, but rather the *possibility* to do so that is produced by the taboo. For as soon as God announces his prohibition, he awakens in Adam the possibility of the prohibition's transgression, and so prohibition prompts desire (cf. Romans 7:7 RSV "I should not have known what it is to covet if the law had not said 'You shall not covet.' "). When Adam then takes an apple from the tree and eats it, he breaks God's prohibition and commits the first (original) sin. For Kierkegaard, Adam's dread (absolute freedom) and Adam's sin (eating of the Tree of Knowledge) were identical, and therefore dread is *the ground of all knowledge*, because Adam's voluntary act implies an understanding of the epistemological nature of his choice.

Before Adam's sin, man is in what Kierkegaard calls "a dreaming state" (38). In this state of innocence, dread was a dread of "nothing," of mere possibility. Then after original sin's transgression, the nothing of dread becomes a fear of something (objective dread). After the Fall, there are two kinds of sinners: those who dread the good and those who dread sin. Yet hidden in each is a desire for the other; that is to say, hidden in the dread of sin, is a desire to sin, and hidden in the dread of good is a desire for the good. Further, the form in which dread is encountered is determined by culture, and for Kierkegaard sensuousness or sexuality becomes associated with sin as the object of dread.[21] We are always condemned to choose (like Adam before the tree) and the burden of that radical freedom is the production and magnification of dread. As a result, dread plays a key role in producing a consciousness of sin, and by extension makes possible the role of faith. Without absolute freedom, there is no dread, and without sin, there can be no faith. Despair or "the sickness unto death" is the flight from radical freedom, or the resistance or unwillingness to exercise this choice. At the same time, radical freedom fills one with horror and makes one tremble, because the future stretches before one, completely unwritten and absolutely dependant on one's own choices, which is what I will later call *moral dread*. Dread's ambivalent admixture of desire and fear—whether to see, to know, or to choose—produces a vertiginous effect, which Kierkegaard likens to the dizziness we feel when we approach a precipice and are consumed with the irrational impulse to jump off it: "One may liken dread to dizziness. He whose eye chances to look down into the yawning abyss becomes dizzy" (*Concept of Dread* 55). This vertiginous impulse bears remarkable similarities to some of the things that Edgar Allan Poe explores. He writes in his short story "The Imp of the Perverse,"

> But out of this our cloud on the precipice's edge, there grows into palpability a shape far more terrible than any Genius or any Demon of a tale. And yet it is but a Thought, although one which chills the very marrow of our bones with the fierceness of the delight of its horror. It is merely the idea of what would be our sensations during the sweeping precipitancy of a fall from such a height. And this fall—this rushing annihilation—for the very reason that it involves that one most ghastly and loathsome to all the most ghastly and loathsome images of death and suffering which have ever presented themselves to our imagination—for this very cause do we now the most impetuously desire it. And because our reason most strenuously deters us from the brink, therefore do we the more unhesitatingly approach it.

In the story the narrator speaks of having committed the perfect crime. Triumphantly delighted in getting away with his crime, suddenly the very fact of his unsuspected guilt gives rise to an irresistible urge for the narrator to confess. Poe likens this to peering over a precipice. Tormented by the impulse to confess, and by the knowledge that only he has the absolute freedom to do so, Poe's narrator eventually does confess. If he had not confessed he would never have been punished, but the thought of confessing produces such a powerful urge to reveal his secret guilt that the narrator is impelled to do so and ultimately does condemn himself by his own words. Radical freedom (to confess, to jump) always produces a concomitant dread, which is a compelling mixture of attraction *and* repulsion, of desire *and* revulsion, for in Kierkegaard's words "it alarms and fascinates us with its sweet anxiety" (*Concept of Dread* 55).

Dread is also connected to a presentiment about the future, or an inchoate feeling that the future is in some way foreordained; it is "a certain presentiment [*anelse*][that] seems to precede everything that is to happen, but just as it can have a strong determining effect, it can also bring a person to think that he is as it were predestined" (Kierkegaard, *Journals*, 1, 38). Kierkegaard insisted that even though we have a predisposition to sin, we nonetheless always have a (terrifying) choice. In other words, the anxiety produced by radical freedom in which our future depends only on our own choices and actions can also produce a compensatory response of predetermination, a feeling that the future is not frighteningly open after all, but reassuringly preordained by God. In a similar way, I will use apocalyptic dread to refer to that fear of the future that past events always already mediate, and that defends against existential dread (or the fear of freedom) with a compulsive desire for prophetic signs. Thus far we have discussed two key elements in Kierkegaardian dread: (1) the radical freedom of choosing or not choosing, and (2) the fear of the future. These elements are also operative in another theoretical paradigm of anxiety to whose connections with dread I will now turn.

Dread's Link with the Uncanny

> Anxiety is when, in this frame, something appears that was already there, much closer to the house, the *heim*: the host.
>
> —Anthony Vidler, *The Architectural Uncanny:*
> *Essays in The Modern Unhomely*

Freud understood the uncanny as "that which arouses dread and horror," or "that class of the frightening which leads back to what is known of old and long familiar" (340). Freud's famous reading of the uncanny in E. T. A. Hoffmann's "The Sandman" considered the paradoxical etymological relationships between *heimlich* and *unheimlich*; on the one hand, *heimlich* signifies that which is familiar, homely, or agreeable, and on the other hand, it signifies that which is concealed, hidden or secret, this latter meaning coinciding with its ostensible etymological opposite, *unheimlich*. The familiar and the unfamiliar thus form a complex interrelationship that evokes the uncanny in those strange, yet familiar, things that arouse dread and horror. The uncanny signals the emergence of what Schelling described as "that which ought to have remained hidden but has come to light" (qtd. in Freud 364). The uncanny makes visible the repressed, and is characterized by certain elements like burial alive, dismembered limbs, animism, magic and sorcery, omnipotence of thoughts, the fear of death, involuntary repetition, and castration. The figure of the double or doppelgänger is a privileged form of the uncanny and one that foregrounds the thematic relationship between self and monster with which horror is concerned. Freud notes that the uncanny figure of the double (which Otto Rank suggested was a psychic defense against death) was the process by which "the subject identifies himself with someone else, so that he is in doubt as to which his self is, or substitutes the extraneous self for his own" (qtd. in Freud 356). Psychologically, the doppelgänger is experienced *otherwise*, as an uncanny replica of the self, and is therefore twice as frightening because of that very similitude. The alien invasion narratives of the fifties like *Invasion of the Body Snatchers* (Don Siegel, 1956) and *I Married a Monster from Outer Space* (Gene Fowler, Jr., 1958) foregrounded the threat to the domestic space of the family by making the familiar uncanny through aliens "taking over" the bodies of humans (King and Krzywinska 51). In popular culture, and particularly in science-fiction narratives, Freud's uncanny double characteristically appears through the figure of the robot or automaton, suggesting anxieties about human identity and the body. Some films illustrating this are *Westworld* (Michael Crichton, 1973), *Blade Runner* (Ridley Scott, 1982), and the more recent *A. I.: Artificial Intelligence* (Steven Spielberg, 2001) and *I, Robot* (Alex Proyas, 2004).

In the case studies that follow we will see a concern with the double figured most prominently in *Candyman*, *Se7en*, and *Cape Fear*. In these three films, repressed national or familial secrets erupt and challenge the family, in the displaced and doubled form of the monster that comes to haunt them. Thus, as we shall see through Max Cady and Samuel Bowden in *Cape Fear*, or Helen Lyle and Candyman, or John Doe and Detective Somerset in *Se7en*, and also with the humans and aliens in *Signs* and *War of the Worlds*, the monster disrupts the boundaries between self and other, and calls into question notions of normality with which self, family, or nation are invested. The monster as double then is a figure for the return of the repressed. The effect of this emergence of repressed urges, desires, or secrets and its distinctive paradoxical combination of the familiar and the strange arouse dread or horror in the subject. Thus, both the uncanny and dread involve an uneasy oscillation between wanting to know and not knowing, wanting to see and yet not seeing. Whereas Kierkegaard considered that dread signals absolute freedom (and therefore cannot end), Freud was interested in how sin, guilt, or anxiety begins (in order that they may be cured). *Apocalyptic Dread* thus considers the temporal connection in the historical dimensions of dread (past/future), and trauma (past/present). The past and present are not only articulated in terms of cultural anxiety but have also retained a certain cataclysmic or catastrophic quality, which as we recall is one of the four aspects of the apocalyptic (along with the revelatory, the grandiose, and the climactic), and which is shared by another key theoretical paradigm of public as well as private anxiety: that of trauma.

Dread and Trauma

From the Greek word *traumat*, "trauma" means wound. But ever since psychoanalysis has illuminated the psyche in topographical terms that liken it to a body part, trauma has also become the privileged term to describe the injuries a subject incurs in her/his psychic evolution and history. The difference between psychic trauma and bodily traumas such as wounds, fractures, and concussions resides in the fact that psychic trauma is far less easily detectable, not only because its locus is the mental realm, but also because the psyche has its own ways of protecting itself against injuries, or of fighting for its survival. Many of these protective devices have a time coefficient that further displaces any past psychic injury. Post-traumatic stress disorder, according to the American Psychiatric Association, is a collection of symptoms such as nightmares, flashbacks, dread, and depression that suggest that the experience or reception of an overwhelming event is not fully assimilated, and that consequently repeatedly possess an individual (209). Freud argued that the way the psyche masters a trauma is through its reiterative repetition, and claimed that psychoanalysis offered a therapeutic resolution through the uncovering of repressed memories.[22]

Not only is trauma the product of its repetition, but also of the ways in which the subject repeats or represents an event to themselves, and is therefore symptomatic of this memorial violation of the ego. Cathy Caruth suggests that trauma is the expulsion from the psyche of the memory of

an overwhelming event, because it was an event unregistered at the time
(it was "too soon"). Consequently, because of its horrific experiential
dimensions, trauma poses a conundrum as a historical event that registers
symptomatically *because* the subject never fully incorporated it in a *temporal* sense (Caruth, "Unclaimed Experience" 3–7). Given this paradoxical
atemporality, trauma does not engender mere repression or defense (as
with hysterical or neurotic symptoms), but produces a *temporal delay* or
ellipsis that enables the individual to survive. The impact of trauma follows in this very belatedness, for outside the temporal confines of the
initiating traumatic event, memories repeatedly recur through flashbacks,
nightmares, and intrusive thoughts. As a literal symptom, trauma is constituted by its lack of integration into consciousness as history. In other
words, trauma is a historical symptom in which personal narratives of self,
identity, and history are disrupted by a symptomatic dissociation. Time
doesn't diminish memories that lie in the unconscious because, as Mary
Ann Doane suggests in her recent study of modernity and time, the
unconscious is a "space, a storehouse, a place outside of time, infinitely
accommodating, where nothing is ever lost or destroyed" (42). Thus,
memory as flashback is a visual representation that has no integrated
place in the past *or* the present. Horror spectatorship also plays on this
"too soon" of trauma, this sudden quality of a violent act that frightens
us with unexpected violence or its red herring (the false alarm). Trauma,
as Caruth understands it, is an interruption of history, and a failure of
integration, but I would suggest that trauma's failure to integrate into
narrative history collapses Kierkegaard's existential dread (indeterminate
anxiety) and object dread (the fear of the monster) into each other. It
replaces the inchoate fear of the future and of radical freedom with another narrative, and one that is apocalyptic.

The Relationship between the Apocalypse and Dread

Thus far, we understand that recent apocalypticism emerges out of the
increased political and cultural influence of Christian fundamentalism in
the last thirty years. As a form of premillennial dispensationalism, this form
of Christianity is intrinsically concerned with the end-time, and thus with
the future, and it is hermeneutically hungry for signs and prophecies that
might signal the beginning of the end. Anxiety about the future unites the
world of dread with the apocalyptic focus on the *eschatos*. If existential
freedom prompts an intense dread or ambivalence and anxiety about the
future, apocalyptic Christianity understands the future in the eschatological
framework of an ending, preordained by God. Apocalyptic dread, then,

refers to that tendency that adopts an overdetermined Manichaean and eschatological understanding of the world, and that transforms the random, the aleatory, and the meaningless into the preordained, overdetermined, and meaningful, and by so doing obviates the dread that existential choice and the open-ended future prompt.

If historical trauma engenders symptomatic repetition and return, dread is a field that subtends or complements the uncanny and erupts in the topographical and mythological circulation of horror. In the following chapters *memorial dread* is a marker of the ambivalence, anxiety, and apprehension involved in *remembering*—that is, it refers to the resistance to remembering and acknowledging the past traumas, betrayals, and secrets *that one already (albeit sometimes unconsciously) knows*. Memorial dread, or the paradoxical desire to both know and not know, is thus closely connected to *scopic dread*, which presents the act of seeing what one already knows (but has repressed), as dread-infused and closely tied to trauma and the horror of the visible. This dread is reflected in our spectatorial ambivalence, in the tension between wanting to see and dreading what we do in fact see. Bound up with Kierkegaard's "sympathetic antipathy and antipathetic sympathy," scopic dread involves the attraction and repulsion that the horror genre's monster traditionally prompts. Scopic dread takes a specific form in the psychological or physical horror that confronts each family. The theme of scopic dread is further underscored by *specular dread*—that is to say, a dread that attaches to a figure that in its doubled or mirrored form provides an uncomfortable challenge to the characters in each film, and that embodies the repressions that the characters themselves disavow. This theme of doubling or specularity is a further link to the uncanny, and each of my case studies will show a disavowed relationship between the protagonist and the monster as uncanny mirror images of each other.

In the late nineties, anticipating the turn of the century and millennium became a self-conscious form of apocalyptic dread, or what I have called millennial dread. After the transition, and more particularly after 9/11, apocalyptic dread continued in displaced form and has become conflated with a pervasive anxiety about terrorism. While Hollywood's disaster spectacles of the nineties suggest truly apocalyptic dread in their anxious imaginings of the end of the world, the case studies of hybrid horror that follow this introduction suggest more coded anxieties about family, patriarchy, religion and "family values." This dread is apocalyptic because it is informed by characters like Max Cady in *Cape Fear* and John Doe in *Se7en* who claim that their violent and cataclysmic acts of retribution have been preordained by God. In *Dolores Claiborne* this apocalyptic narrative is displaced onto more natural forces of transformation in the form of a lunar eclipse, and in *Signs*, and *War of the Worlds* this eschatological dread becomes explicitly aligned with an alien invasion that threatens the end of the world. Whether through monsters, aliens, or natural forces, the agents of my case studies carry with them the dual function of the apocalypse: of prophetic revelation and violent transformation.

Chapter Outlines

Focusing on J. Lee Thompson's 1962 classic *Cape Fear* and Martin Scorsese's 1991 remake, chapter 2, "*Cape Fear* and Trembling: Familial Dread," considers the ways in which these films were a dialogue with their different cultural and historical production contexts. It understands the second film as the monstrous return of the repressed desires, fears, and violence in the family, whose threat was contained in the original. Both films deal with historical memory and sexual dread that, in displaced form, become mediated and embodied in the figure of Max Cady, a predator who vows revenge against the Bowden family. The historical traumas of racism, slavery, and lynching remain inchoate in the haunted mise-en-scène of *Cape Fear*, but they become narratively explicit in chapter 3, "Strange Fruit: *Candyman* and Supernatural Dread." This chapter examines the uncanny function of Candyman as national allegory, foregrounding the ways in which memorial dread erupts in the topographical and mythological circulation of an urban legend. It suggests that *Candyman* is a metanarrative about the spectatorial pleasures of watching and hearing tales of horror, in which both dread and doubt are always at stake. In chapter 4: "*Dolores Claiborne*: Memorial Dread" we move away from the broad historical intersection of national and familial trauma in the preceding two chapters to melodrama's more constrained domestic focus on familial secrets of incest and domestic violence, and we examine how the family home becomes a traumatic site of spatial and memorial dread. Although *Dolores Claiborne*'s conclusion is one in which a family transcends the trauma that has initially divided it, in chapter 5, "*Se7en* in the Morgue: Dystopian Dread," we then turn to a narrative in which a serial killer effects the complete destruction of the family, and in which trauma can neither be repressed nor overcome. This chapter argues that *Se7en*'s portrait of a serial killer who models his crimes on the seven deadly sins is a self-reflexive meditation on both dread and the apocalypse, yet it also suggests that the film's unexpected and horrific conclusion brings about the reemergence of existential dread—a dread that even after the execution of the film's serial killer cannot be completely contained. Chapter 6, "*Signs* of the End of the World: Apocalyptic Dread" examines M. Night

Shyamalan's postmillennial *Signs* (2002) and suggests that dread continues and intensifies after 9/11. Although the film's mysterious crop circles turn out to be the initial signs of an alien invasion, the film's "signs" provide a conservative framework for addressing a crisis of faith and that ultimately unify and restore the family and its patriarch at a moment of global crisis. Finally, chapter 7 looks at another alien invasion film, Steven Spielberg's *War of the Worlds* (2005), which like *Signs* mediates national and global crisis through patriarchal redemption and the survival of the nuclear family. As another postmillennial film its uncanny exploration of man and machine also suggests that the trauma of 9/11 and the war on terrorism have produced new forms of dread.

2

Cape Fear and Trembling

Familial Dread

You're scared, that's OK. I want you to savor that fear. You know the South evolved in fear—fear of the Indian, fear of the slave, fear of the damned Union. The South has a fine tradition of savoring fear.

—Private eye Kersek, in *Cape Fear* (1991)

P RIVATE EYE KERSEK'S OMINOUS description of fear in Martin Scorsese's *Cape Fear* (1991) invokes a dread rooted in the history of slavery, colonialism, and the faded Confederacy. Here fear is everywhere: in New Essex, the small town in the deep South where our narrative family, the Bowdens, live; in their lavish house with its elaborate facade and Spanish moss, reminiscent of the plantation houses of the antebellum South; and in the swamps and mists that surround the Cape Fear River, to which they flee. Kersek expresses a pleasure in the savoring of fear, a fear that attaches to particular national historical repressions, and whose specific objects are Native American, Black, and Northerner. From William Faulkner to Carson McCullers, the Southern Gothic mobilized tropes of stolen land and bartered bodies, hidden burials and family secrets. Embedded in the past, Confederate and Union crimes repeatedly haunt the narratives of the American Gothic, and in the disavowal of these traumas, historical memory becomes dread itself.

The two cinematic adaptations of *Cape Fear* (1962, 1991) are a dialogue with their different cultural and historical production contexts, with the second film showing the return of the repressed desires, fears, and violence, whose threat was contained in the original.[1] John McDonald's novel *The Executioners* (1957) was the source material for both films, and all three versions tell the story of the Bowden family, who become threatened by Max Cady, a white ex-convict who has just been released from prison after serving a lengthy term for rape (see table 2.1). Cady has a prior relationship with the father and lawyer, Samuel Bowden, who either as witness or negligent defense attorney in the respective film adaptations is responsible for Cady's imprisonment. Upon his release from jail Cady is determined to take his revenge on Bowden's family. Cady stalks, harasses, and threatens the family, and in both screen versions presents a particular sexual threat to the Bowden daughter. The story climaxes with a final battle between Cady and the family, which in two of the versions ends in Cady's death.

In Martin Scorsese's *Cape Fear* (1991), Detective Kersek's musings on historical dread ("the South has a fine tradition of savoring fear") are addressed to Samuel Bowden (Nick Nolte), as they lie in wait to trap and kill Max Cady (Robert De Niro), who is stalking Bowden's family. Kersek suggests that fear is the necessary catalyst and justification for the illicit violence required in the defense of the family. Similarly, in J. Lee Thompson's *Cape Fear* (1962), Bowden (Gregory Peck) does not hesitate to use his wife and daughter as bait to catch Cady (Robert Mitchum), because, as he proudly notes, they come from "pioneer stock." Both films suggest that the defense of the (white, nuclear) family is parallel to historical actions of violent appropriation and displacement of the "Other" in American history, whether of Indians, African Americans, Unionists, or Northerners. Bowden's use of his wife and daughter as bait also recalls the paranoid racist fantasies of white women in peril from rape, whether by Indians in the captivity narrative in *The Searchers* (John Ford, 1956), or by Unionist ex-slaves in *The Birth of a Nation* (D. W. Griffith, 1915). Through the apocalyptic figure of the monster Max Cady who embodies the Bowden's sexual dread, Cady foregrounds what Louis Gross calls "the singularity and monstrosity of the Other; what the dominant culture cannot incorporate within itself, [it] must project outward onto this hated/desired figure" (90). Both films relive earlier historical traumas of American violence, but mediate and displace historical memory through sexual dread, as embodied in the figure of Max Cady, and both films implicate the family as morally hypocritical and therefore doomed to failure in the mastery of these traumas.[2]

Table 2.1. Principal Differences between Book and Films

The Executioners (1957)	Cape Fear (1962)	Cape Fear (1991)
Author: John D. MacDonald	Director: J. Lee Thompson Screenplay: James R. Webb	Director: Martin Scorsese Adapted screenplay: Wesley Strick
Cady rapes Australian woman during W. W. II. Spends thirteen years in jail.	Cady rapes American woman. Imprisoned for eight years.	Cady rapes sixteen-year-old, in Atlanta in 1977. Imprisoned for fourteen years.
Bowden is witness to rape.	Bowden (a prosecutor) is witness to rape and testifies against Cady.	Bowden is Cady's defense attorney. He buries a report of the rape victim's "sexual promiscuity."
Bowden family: Sam and Carol Bowden, Nancy (15) & two sons: Bucky & Jamie. Marilyn, family dog.	Bowden family: Samuel and Peggy Bowden, Nancy (15). No sons. Marilyn, family dog.	Bowden family: Sam and Leigh Bowden, daughter Danny (15). No sons. Benjamin, family dog.
Bowden is not adulterous.	Bowden is not adulterous.	Troubled Bowden marriage. Sam is having an affair with coworker Lori Davis.
Cady's "combat fatigue" suggests a reason for his violent behavior. Cady rapes and abducts his ex-wife, who has remarried.	Cady is raped in prison. On release, Cady rapes, abducts, and beats wife for three days. Wife won't press charges. Cady rapes Diane Taylor, a "fallen" beauty queen. She refuses to testify.	Cady is betrayed by his attorney's malfeasance. Cady is raped in prison. Cady rapes and mutilates Lori Davis, Bowden's lover. Cady murders Detective Kersek and Graciela, the family maid. Cady rapes Leigh and intends to rape Sam and Danny.
Mother witnesses death of dog.	Family witnesses death of dog.	Mother witnesses death of dog.
No houseboat.	Mother and daughter alone on houseboat as bait.	Family all on houseboat.
Bowden wounds Cady with a bullet and Cady later bleeds to death.	Bowden wounds Cady with a bullet but does not kill him.	Bowden strikes Cady with a rock, but he dies by drowning.

Figure 2.1. Max Cady (Robert Mitchum) and Peggy Bowden (Polly Bergen) in *Cape Fear* (1962). © Universal Pictures/Photofest

In 1962, the first cinematic *Cape Fear* was released amid the desegregation struggles in the South, and only six months later, its star Gregory Peck would play the defense attorney Atticus Finch in *To Kill A Mockingbird* (Robert Mulligan, 1962),[3] an important film that directly addressed the question of race in the South. As with his earlier role in *Gentleman's Agreement* (Elia Kazan, 1947), Peck's casting as a lawyer in *Cape Fear* aligned his liberal and idealistic star persona with the heroic role of the activist lawyer then prominent in the legislative battles of the civil rights movement in the fifties and early sixties. Peck plays Bowden, a prosecutor whose eyewitness testimony about Cady's rape of a woman led to his eight-year imprisonment, for which Cady intends to take revenge by raping Bowden's daughter. The violence and murder that met freedom riders in the early civil rights era forms the displaced historical context for the all-consuming dread that the Bowdens feel at Cady's hands. At the same time, the illegal violence with which Bowden increasingly responds to Cady's threats suggests the corruption of the law in a period of widely publicized institutional violence in the South epitomized by the fire hoses of Chief Bull Connor.[4] As J. Hoberman has observed, the centrality of this historical context for Thompson's portrait of Max Cady "conjures up the bogie of a terrifying rapist—albeit white—who proved inconveniently conversant with his 'civil rights.' In its nightmarish way *Cape Fear* managed to suggest both what terrified the white South and the terror the white South itself inspired" (Hoberman 8).

The first *Cape Fear* displaces the paranoid myth of the black rapist onto the white hipster figure of Robert Mitchum's Cady, who through his class and regional identity as a poor white Southerner shares with African Americans a certain marginalized position in relation to the privileged middle-class family, the Bowdens.[5] Cady's outsider status, together with the film's mise-en-scène, invokes the history of racial violence in the South, in which sexual threats to white women were a common pretext for lynchings from the Scottsboro boys to Emmett Till. Robert Mitchum's Cady, more bohemian hipster than lumpen pro-letarian, greets everyone as "daddy" and "man" and seduces his first victim in a jazz bar. As a bohemian, Mitchum's Cady is another figure of cultural anxiety for conservative authority in the late fifties and early sixties. He exemplifies Mailer's "White Negro," for which he is cursed as a "shocking degenerate" by establishment man Sam Bowden. Nearly thirty years later, Scorsese's Cady will recall this characterization, espe-cially when he pretends to be Danny's pot-smoking, Miller-reading drama teacher. Like the first *Cape Fear*, Scorsese's remake also articulates white anxieties about minorities who demand civil rights and due process, anxieties displaced onto a vigilante response to a poor Southern *white* monster, who in turn, is fully aware of his civil rights and skilled in his knowledge of the law.

At the same time, Scorsese's remake is a far different tale from the anxious yet utopian original, with its Eisenhower family threatened by the sleepy leers of a predatory Robert Mitchum. Instead, Scorsese presents the Bowden family in a violent Darwinian struggle for survival, which leaves it tenuous and traumatized, in a startling undermining of hege-monic Hollywood representations of the family. Through his uncanny recasting of Robert Mitchum, Gregory Peck, and Martin Balsam in cameo appearances, Scorsese's remake is a dialogical subversion of the first *Cape Fear* in which they all originally starred.[6] Upstanding Sam Bowden in the original, Peck now plays Cady's ingratiating and pompous Southern law-yer, Lee Heller; Mitchum, the original Max Cady, is now a genial yet dodgy detective, only just this side of the law,[7] and Martin Balsam moves from being a police chief to being a sanctimonious Southern judge who quotes Booker T. Washington. The sexual violence hinted at in the purr-ing physicality of Robert Mitchum becomes baroque in the sexual sadism of Robert De Niro's Max Cady, whose intense performance style and violent psychotic roles in *Mean Streets* (1973) and *Taxi Driver* (1976) offered additional menace to his star persona. With his prison cell filled with photos of Joseph Stalin, Robert E. Lee, and Christian martyrs that hint at his political sympathies and psychological identifications, Cady is an ironic signifier of Pentecostal evangelism ("granddaddy used to handle snakes") and the poor white working class.[8] Here is another form of folklore, this time rural, Southern, and Gothic. Indeed, screenwriter Wesley Strick's transformation of Cady's character for the remake self-consciously drew upon the very violence toward and murder of Jewish and African American activists that formed the bloody backdrop to the civil rights movement at the time of the first *Cape Fear*'s release. Emphasizing the historical, Christian, and Southern dimensions of Cady's monstrosity, Strick observed, "I wanted to make Max Cady a kind of monster of the South, a kind of creature who had crawled out of the muck of the South—the aspects of the South that were the most kind of primitive (sic) and to me as a New York Jew, the most terrifying."[9] As J. Hoberman suggested above, Strick's purposeful rewriting of Cady's character suggests the ambivalence of historical dread, embodying both violent racist Southern resistance to the civil rights movement, and also, in a displaced form, white fear about minorities who were demanding equal rights under the law (8). As monster and doppelgänger of Samuel Bowden, Cady becomes the external figure of dread for a family already fractured by the conflicts engendered by the father's ethical lapses. Combining class resentment with apocalyptic urgency, Scorsese's Max Cady is horrifying in his hubristic grandiosity. Bearer of the punishments of Judgement Day, Cady embodies the law of dreadful revenge.

If the horror of rape, mutilation, and violent death is the obvious threat that Cady bears, the parallels that connect him to his alter ego, the self-righteous lawyer Samuel Bowden, link horror to theology in an ethical interrogation of justice and law, crime and punishment. Not unlike an Ibsen play for the nineties, this portrait of a flawed white middle-class nuclear family critiques the ideological complacency proffered by J. Lee Thompson's original. Scorsese's version exposes the chasms and ideological struggles over the constitution of the contemporary nuclear American family and the repressions that its hegemonic representation as white, suburban, and middle-class necessitates. In *Family Fictions*, Sarah Harwood's study of popular films of the eighties under Reagan (1997), the family is a central trope, that, in its heterosexual, nuclear, and white hegemonic form is ideologically privileged in the form of "family values" by the Republican Party and the Christian Coalition, among others, and yet radically altered in its material formations and cinematic representations.

At the same time, white liberal conservatism also was evident by the Clinton era. The term "political correctness," initially coined by the Right, came to mark centrist discomfort with the social change attendant to multiculturalism, affirmative action, and the assertion of civil rights by minorities. The earlier emergence of gay rights in the late sixties and early seventies and the increasing queer activism in response to the AIDS epidemic under Reagan in the eighties constituted social challenges to hegemonic understandings of family, sexuality, and marriage; moreover, they drew upon the equal rights legacy of the civil rights movement. As chapter 1 argued, *apocalyptic dread* marks a particular and historically situated set of horror relations both within the family and between the family and society, which first emerged in the last three decades and intensified in the nineties. In his transformation of Max Cady into an apocalyptic figure of crime and punishment who becomes the Bowden family's dreaded and uncanny other, Scorsese's remake of *Cape Fear* critiques the nostalgic myth of the American family presented in the first film by representing the transformations of the family in the nineties, suggesting both conservative and liberal anxieties about social change to the white middle-class family. Not unlike the original *Cape Fear*, the remake reflects the fact that society has not come to terms with its own violent social conflicts and hypocrisy, and ultimately suggests the illusion of social progress.

One example of this debunking of apparent social progress reflects both the impact of feminism in the thirty years between the two films and the continuing limitations of that social transformation. In Thompson's *Cape Fear*, Cady's second rape victim is Diane Taylor (Barrie Chase), a "fallen" pageant queen who refuses to testify against him, not because of any uncertainty as to Cady's conviction (which the narrative implies would be inevitable with her testimony), but *because* of the social and familial disgrace as a rape victim. Initially in a catatonic stupor after her rape, Diane refuses to communicate with the police and abruptly leaves town. Similarly, the Bowdens would not let their daughter Nancy testify against Cady for sexual stalking, out of the same fear of social stigma. This is an important difference from Wesley Strick's screenplay for Scorsese's *Cape Fear*, in which Cady's victim Lori Davis (Illeana Douglas) refuses to testify *because* she is a legal officer and therefore understands the ways in which power functions in the legal system against rape victims ("This time I'm on the other side"). She knows that she was drunk and flirting with Cady in a public space, and foresees what defense attorneys do to rape victims like her in cross-examination: "They crucify them and just laugh about it later." Even with contemporary rape shield laws that today protect rape victims from interrogations about their sexual history, the prosecution and conviction of rape falls far below estimated offenses. Lori's decision not to file a complaint indicates her professional understanding of the ideological biases of the legal system, notwithstanding the changed social context of two decades of second-wave feminism. Not unlike the first *Cape Fear*, apparent societal progress, in this case toward gender equality in the wake of the feminist movement, is called into question, as trauma again breaks through the veneer of liberalism's social victories of the last three decades. In light of this drastically altered social landscape, Scorsese's remake instituted key character changes in the Bowden family, far from the ethical idealizations of the original—creating a portrait of a fractured, embittered family unit. Shifting from the unruffled righteousness of Gregory Peck's Bowden to the hysterical self-righteousness of Nick Nolte's Bowden, and from the feline stalking of Robert Mitchum's Cady to the monstrous grievance of Robert De Niro's Cady, the remake is a radical change.[10]

Cape Fear and Trembling

1 **dread** vb. {ME dreden, Fr. OE draedan} vt. (bef. 12C) 1a: to fear greatly, (archaic): to regard with awe, **2:** to feel extreme reluctance to meet or face ~ vi: to be apprehensive

2 **dread** n. (13c) **1a:** a great fear esp. In the face of impending evil 1 b: extreme uneasiness in the face of a disagreeable prospect<~ of a social blunder:

archaic : awe 2: one causing awe or fear

3 **dread** adj. (15c) **1:** causing great fear or anxiety **2:** inspiring awe

—Websters (1988 1st edition)

Cape Fear (1991) constructs an atmosphere of spectatorial dread and fear that threatens the limited boundaries of what Isabel C. Pinedo has described as *recreational terror*, or that which offers the spectator the illusion of mastery (5). Both diegetic and nondiegetic sound form part of the texture of the mise-en-scène's evocation of all-encompassing dread, and signal the Bowden family's increasing loss of control. Imitating the agitated string motifs and distinctive edginess that were so familiar from Bernard Herrmann's scores for Hitchcock, Elmer Bernstein's reorchestration of Herrmann's original score, together with the film's skillful use of anxiety-inducing sound effects, creates an agitated aural landscape. Red-herring trick shots frighten the viewer with fake threats that are natural or technological, as we see with abrupt jump cuts to extreme close-ups of a telephone, ringing with a strident loudness. Jarring montages, repeated zooms, canted angles, and Herrmann's use of fortissimo horn passages in a belligerent score all offer a heightened spectatorial experience of anticipatory dread.

Scorsese unveils the multiple repressions and disavowals of the past that have a continuing presence in the Bowden family, and that constitute the historical and familial dread that envelop the narrative. Here everyone has a secret to hide: the parents, Sam and Leigh Bowden (Jessica Lange), have a marriage that is evidently in trouble, due to Sam's repeated adulterous affairs. Sam has also committed legal and professional malfeasance in his original defense of Max Cady, by uncannily "burying" a report of the sexual history of the rape victim; a report that Cady will claim later would have mitigated his sentence. This difference complexifies Max Cady's character as both monster and victim in the remake. Leigh has had a nervous breakdown and "lost time." She is embittered with her husband and disappointed in her teenage daughter Danny (in a breakout role for Juliette Lewis), who also has secrets and strange memories of her childhood holidays, of "those days in the boat." The dread that haunts the Bowdens is based on guilt, ambivalence, and conflict, and as such, is an internal form of shameful and disavowed knowledge, which leads us to Kierkegaard. Failing to acknowledge unconscious desires and past traumas produces a *historical* dread (the fear of the return of the repressed) that displaces *existential* dread (the fear of absolute freedom). The Bowden's secrets and unconscious desires become displaced onto the object dread of horror's compellingly fearful monster—as it rises from the swamps of the Cape Fear River in the form of Max Cady.

With its location in the Deep South, the menacingly named Cape Fear River in North Carolina constructs a visual and spatial metaphor for the ways in which traumatic memory of the past (of historical and personal crimes) produces a dread-infused present. Designed by Saul and Elaine Bass, *Cape Fear*'s (1991) opening credit-sequence is a series of lap dissolves of the eponymous river, and Elmer Bernstein's adapted score establishes the tone of an ominous mise-en-scène. Reflections of double-exposed inchoate images appear beneath the waters. Barely discernible are a chain of images: a swooping hawk (at the introduction of De Niro's credit), several murky faces, a rolling eyeball, a mouth, teeth, a human figure with long hands, and finally, a drop of water that moves vertically downward as the image fills with a bloodred saturation.[11] This then dissolves into a saturated red close-up of Danielle Bowden's eyes, followed by a gray-and-white negative photographic image of her, which then shifts into color and zooms out (see figure 2.2). From the mise-en-scène of the Gothic South to Danielle's psyche, the sequence already foreshadows the metastatic spread of Cady's presence.

Figure 2.2. Negative Image of Danielle Bowden's Eyes in *Cape Fear* (1991). Digital frame enlargement © MCA/Universal Pictures

At this moment, the narrative's opening voice-over begins, foregrounding the thematic centrality of Danielle's memory: "My reminiscence. I always thought that for such a lovely river, the name was mystifying—Cape Fear. When the only thing to fear on those enchanted summer nights was that the magic would end and real life would come crashing in." Danielle's opening and closing voice-overs bracket *Cape Fear*'s narrative as her own—whether as nightmare, Gothic story, or unconscious fantasy, we are never sure. This narrative bracket is unique to Scorsese's version and is literally embodied in the close-ups of her eyes, dissolving from saturated red to negative grey and white, and then to color, and in reverse order at the film's end. After we zoom out from her eyes, we see Danny standing in front of what appears to be a classroom blackboard, over which running water is reflected, perhaps from outside rain. Her dress is formal, as if she were dressed for school, and so the entire narrative could be her homework assignment that we hear about later: to write a story modeled on the reminiscence formula of Thomas Wolfe's *Look Homeward, Angel*.[12] With an ominous blare of nondiegetic horns, this oneiric opening narrative bracket cuts straight to Max Cady, who is being released from Georgia State Penitentiary. In a dramatic wide-angle shot, with storm clouds and lightning behind him, Cady walks right up to the camera, literalizing his apocalyptic return to society.[13] For Danny, real life has already begun "to come crashing in." Her childhood memories of the family vacations on a houseboat on the Cape Fear River are of a mystical, if not mythical, time before her parents' marital problems began, and before her own transition from childhood into puberty.

Paradoxically, even during these timeless experiences Danny experienced the dread of their temporality, and thus termination ("the only thing to fear was that the magic would end").[14] These memories are the unconscious trauma within the wider familial trauma, and from the beginning narratively link with Cady's horror. The very fact that Danielle has retroactively constructed this memory of her childhood as timeless idyll already registers as unconscious acknowledgment that her childhood *has already* terminated. As early cinematic treatments suggested, the Southern idyll is a symptom of the fact that *something was already wrong*.[15] As a teenager, Danny is the only character most explicitly in transition from puberty to adulthood, and unlike her parents, she does not deny: that the past lives on, and that development, progress, and achievement (on the level of both individual and society) are never complete, easy, or without a price.

It is apt that Danielle is this film's narrator, as she is the focus of sexuality, both in her own nascent desires and in the unconscious and overt sexual attention that she receives from her father and Max Cady. Scorsese's creation of her as narrator foregrounds the psychic and subjective dimensions of her story. The film's opening bracket in which Danny suggests that the "lovely" Cape Fear River is *mystifying* in its ominous name self-reflexively begs the narrative question of just what did happen in Danny's childhood. We recall that mystifying can mean something that is designed to be mysterious or obscure, and like a biblical prophecy offers signs that must be decoded. We are prompted to ask, Was Danny's childhood the "magical world" she so lovingly recalls? When her father asks what she will write about for her homework assignment, Danny replies, "The houseboat." Sam's response is a terse "Oh, the houseboat," as he continues striking a piano key that will not sound. This silent piano key metonymically suggests repressed secrets in the Bowden family. This scene immediately follows Max Cady's violent rape of Lori Davis, and the key is silent, because Max Cady has already been in the Bowden's house to steal the piano wire. Later he uses it to garrote Kersek and Graciela (Zully Montero). Thus, the repressions of Bowden's past (whether sexual or legal) return in the avenging figure of Cady, who takes the piano's sound away as the symbolic foreshadowing of his homicidal rage.

Samuel Bowden's repression of his earlier ethical and legal transgressions (the burial of the report of Cady's rape victim's "sexual promiscuity") masks and encodes his unconscious incestuous desire for his daughter, which remain unspoken like the suggestive piano key. As her father questions her, Danny unconsciously brushes her lips with her thumb, as if recalling the kissing and thumb sucking with Cady. The emotional intensity and sudden violence of Bowden's reactions to his daughter's illicit contact with Cady betrays his unconscious jealousy, as he grabs Danny roughly around the mouth with his hand and says, "Wipe that smile off your face! Did he touch you?" His growing awareness of her pubescent sexuality is an uncomfortable one: "Put some clothes on, you're too old to be running around like that [wearing underpants]." The film displaces his unconscious incestuous desires for his child by projecting them onto Max Cady as the external sadistic threat to his family. Danielle quickly becomes the target of Cady's stalking, and, as Bowden is aware, is only one year younger than Cady's first rape victim. It becomes apparent that Sam Bowden understands this sexual threat to his daughter when he is deliberately vague about Cady's criminal history and lies to his wife, "I think it was battery" (instead of the aggravated sexual assault and battery that we know Bowden clearly remembers). Similarly, Bowden lies about his current affair to his wife and in an unconscious displacement of what could be a description of his teenage daughter, misleadingly but suggestively describes his mistress Lori Davis as "just a kid, a baby. She's just infatuated." As a monster and as a doppelgänger of Samuel Bowden, Cady becomes the displaced external figure of dread for a family already fractured by conflicts engendered by the father's ethical lapses. Embodying the threat of sexual violence to all the Bowden women, Cady substitutes for Bowden's incestuous desires, yet the real threat to the family is in the legal and sexual improprieties that Bowden already has committed.

Scorsese subtly suggests the oedipal nature of the family's tensions in an exchange between Sam and Leigh as they prepare for bed. The scene is presented in a two-shot reflection in the bathroom mirror, with Samuel Bowden's face reflected in the extreme foreground of the frame, and Leigh Bowden in the background corner, rubbing her skin in a dreamy, erotic manner (as she often does in front of mirrors). The parents fret over Danny's drug bust, as she is required to attend summer school, or risk expulsion:

> BOWDEN: Why'd they have to make such a stink, like she was on heroin or something? I mean marijuana, what's marijuana? You and I smoked a little dope in our time, and y'know in some cultures it's considered almost a sacrament—course I realize in ours it's forbidden.
>
> LEIGH (*playfully*): *Right up there with incest* and necrophilia and bestiality . . . (my emphasis)

Leigh muses hopefully, "Maybe this drama teacher from the college will get her excited about something," to which Sam replies, "Yeah, about him probably." This exchange ironically foreshadows Cady's impersonation of Danny's teacher, but also reiterates Bowden's unconscious sexual jealousy. While societal hypocrisy about drug use is being discussed here, masked beneath the sexual flirtation between them is the dread attached to the transgression of incest, which Leigh unconsciously seems to recognize is at stake in her husband's behavior.[16]

Here dread functions symptomatically as a marker of the fear of acknowledging the traumas, betrayals, and hypocrisies of the past, but also of what we know and desire, yet fear to look at and acknowledge in the present. Ethical and personal conflicts are mapped out on a grid of illicit sexual desires of all three family members; Samuel's adultery with Lori and unconscious incestuous desire for his daughter, Danny's desire for Cady, and Leigh's unconscious fantasies and vague desire for someone unknown for whom she puts on her lipstick. One night, after she and Sam Bowden have made love, Leigh is unable to sleep (and perhaps remains sexually unsatisfied). She rises to sit at her dressing-room mirror, sensually rubbing herself with cream. The mood is quiet and romantically lit with a soft blue light outside the upstairs verandah, where fireworks are exploding on the eve of Independence Day. Nevertheless, the shots in this sequence are dissonant. Beginning with the shots of the Bowdens making love, which appear as *negative* celluloid images (in the second use of this device), there is already a sense of Leigh's psychological distance, if not derealization. In addition, each shot of Leigh at the mirror is punctuated by a saturated dissolve to red or yellow, which uncannily resembles the similar negative images of Danny in the film's opening and closing brackets, and which thereby align Leigh with her daughter's oneiric fantasies and dread. Leigh's reflection, split into three images in her dressing-room mirror, also suggests the fragmentation of her former breakdown and her ambivalent and inchoate desire in the present. It is then that Leigh sees that Cady is watching their home from his perch on their wall, and in a repeated leitmotif, Scorsese accentuates her horrified gaze through a triple repetition of rapid zooms-in on Cady. The extreme low-angle shots of Cady emphasize the spectacular Fourth of July fireworks that explode in the sky behind him and underscore the apocalyptic dimensions of his threat (here understood in the grandiose, revelatory, and climactic dimensions of the word); they link and expand the threat from the familial to the national, which we will explore further below. Running outside, Leigh self-consciously wipes off her lipstick, as if suddenly defiled by the unknown watcher (later Danny will also wipe her mouth self-consciously after kissing Cady, in a parallel action which again links mother and daughter in their ambivalent desire for and repulsion to Cady). It is as if Cady's supernatural ubiquity includes the power to enter into the intimate space of the family home and to recognize Leigh's unconscious desire for someone other than her husband. The family are now in a state of siege—Cady's surveillance has become the primary threat.

Scopic Dread: Watching and Stalking

What if we don't want to see?

—Danny, in *Cape Fear* (1991)

In both cinematic versions, Max Cady embodies scopic dread; in other words, through his ubiquitous surveillance he prompts a tension in the subject between wanting and not wanting to see.[17] Thompson's film shows us repeated shots of Cady watching Nancy, remarking to her father, "She's getting to be almost as juicy as your wife." However, in Scorsese's version the threat of Cady's sexual gaze is even more extensive. In his first encounter with Sam Bowden, Cady leers at some teenage girls walking by, remarks, "Great at that age, in't they?" and later describes Danny as "always a firecracker on the Fourth of July. You're damn lucky to have her, boy." Like the original in which Cady stalks the family in a bowling alley, Cady haunts the Bowden's recreational time together. He watches the family at an ice-cream store from across the street, forcing the family to move inside, but when Sam looks again, Cady has vanished into the traffic that obstructs Sam's point-of-view shot. Later, under the pretense of returning the collar of the family dog he has poisoned, Cady gets a closer look at Leigh. When she realizes who he really is, she defiantly acknowledges his predatory gaze: "Go ahead, Mr. Cady. Take a good look. You satisfied now?" Leigh's fascination with Cady epitomizes Kierkegaardian dread, with its mixture of desire and repugnance. She acknowledges her transgressive desire: "I'd been wanting to see what you looked like, I'd been wanting to see your face. But you know now that I see you, you are just repulsive." Cady seems to sense her illicit fascination as he lowers his reflective mirror glasses and wryly observes, "I know what I see."[18] Then, unexpectedly, Danny comes out and becomes vulnerable to Cady's gaze. Immediately, Leigh screams: "Danny don't come out here!" Danny's nascent sexuality links to the horror that threatens the family, as she becomes subject to Cady's chicken-hawk gaze. Because her parents forbid Danny to look or listen, much of what she does is illicit (her reading of Henry Miller, her use of drugs, her sexual contact with Cady). Danny is told repeatedly to "go back to her room" or "not to listen" when her parents are fighting, and later, "not to look" at Kersek's corpse. Later, when she descends the staircase, she does take a forbidden look and screams, because she is the first to see the corpse of the family maid, Graciela. Trauma's bloody visibility is also underscored when Sam slips in Kersek's pool of blood and, to his horror, falls and is covered in it. Refusing *to look and to see* is no longer an option for the Bowdens.

The most stylized exposition of this scopic trope of dreadful surveillance is the Fourth of July parade that the Bowden family attends (and which does not appear in the first screen version). The wide-angle and close-up shots of the Fourth of July parade with its floats of significant moments in American military history (Valley Forge, Iwo Jima) are photographed in slow motion—and the whole scene is presented as a dizzying visual kaleidoscope of sound, confetti, flags, and faces. The mise-en-scène of the Independence Day Parade connects the Bowden family with the historical imaginary, which in the case of each iconic float represents the United States in iconic moments of its historical peril and triumph. In this way, historical and national crisis and survival is both aligned with and puts into question familial survival, and as we suggested earlier with Cady's visual conjunction with fireworks, it injects an apocalyptic dimension by linking him with the climactic and prophetic.[19] Unseen by them, Cady is on the opposite side of the parade, watching Danny and Leigh. Bowden spots Cady, and says "The son of a bitch is staring at you!" Enraged, he confronts him. As Sam and Cady scuffle at the parade, the performers on the Iwo Jima float turn their eyes to watch, further linking the familial crisis with the historical pageantry. We do not see Cady until Sam does so, but then the camera cuts away to a shot emphasizing Danny's vulnerability, lost in the crowd, she calls out "Mom?" We are not sure where Leigh is at this point, nor do we know from whose point of view we see Danny. Cady is the unseen voyeur of Leigh and Danny, until Sam's point of view reveals him to us, almost hidden in a long shot of the crowd. By alternating between privileged and restricted narration, Scorsese's editing intensifies spectatorial disorientation and the ubiquity of Cady's scopic threat.

There are similar ambiguities in what we see, particularly when the image shifts into negative form. On the night of Graciela and Kersek's murders, Sam awakens to see what appears to be Cady in his bedroom, watching him. The image we see is starkly defamiliarized—like the film's opening close-up of Danny's eyes, it is a photographic negative suggesting the unconscious flip side of vision. The negative then dissolves into a brief positive image of the same shot. However, when Sam rubs his eyes, the image has uncannily vanished, and it appears that Cady has been a nightmare. At this point in the narrative, we do not know that Cady is already in the house, murdering Graciela and Kersek, but his uncanny haunting of familial space is already prefigured in Bowden's eerie vision. Sam tells Leigh of his spatial dread, "I had the weirdest feeling he was already in the house," and it is this dream/vision that makes him realize that Cady had been in their house several times before. Accordingly, Scorsese's third use of a negative image underscores Cady's connection to

Bowden as uncanny doppelgänger, and is the celluloid trace of the Bowden family's unconscious dread.

Corporeal Dread: Body and Text

> With his long slicked-back hair, under a white yachting cap, mouth wrapped around the world's biggest cigar butt, and torso draped in a flaming aloha shirt, De Niro is a cracker from hell.
>
> —J. Hoberman, "Sacred and Profane"

Max Cady is an *Übermensch* with an agenda. He embodies all four meanings of the apocalyptic: the prophetic, the destructive, the grandiose, and the climactic. As textual special agent on a self-appointed mission, his first words in Scorsese's *Cape Fear* are "Already read 'em" (in response to the prison guard who ask him if he wants his books). With the hyperintellect of the serial killer and the hard body of fourteen years of prison workouts, his character is a constellation of class, race, Christian iconography, and textual references. Cady, in other words, is our monstrous fetish, a clichéd devil with inhuman strength and spooky ubiquity. Our first image of him is a full-frame close-up of his back, which is tattooed with a large cross holding two scales labeled Truth (holding a Bible), and Justice (holding a knife). Cady literally embodies Judgment Day; he is a walking, preaching body metaphor, covered in tattoos of biblical quotations. In separate shots we see "Vengeance is mine" (Romans) and "My Time is at Hand" (Matthew) on each arm. Close-up pans over his back and chest reveal "The Lord is the Avenger," "Time the Avenger," and "My Time is Not Yet Full Come" together with figures of the cross and the grim reaper. The observation of Lieutenant Elgart (Robert Mitchum), "I don't know whether to look at him or read him," registers both a horror and a fascination with the grotesque body— in other words, a corporeal dread. Although Cady's tattoos exoticize his body as diabolically eschatological, his function as a double of the paterfamilias also chillingly suggests that the Bowden family have their own reasons to dread Judgment Day.

De Niro's performance as Cady differs from Robert Mitchum's characterization in its physical, self-referential, and, above all, hypertextual dimensions. Cady is always ready with a prophetic reference: "Have you suffered so many things in vain?" (Gal. 3.4). His physical embodiment of theological text matches his performative embodiment of speech; he merges speech and writing. The moments of maximum horror are when Cady's speech moves into an inaccessible language, glossolalia. When he threatens Leigh with her imminent rape, he promises apocalyptic dread, or

Figure 2.3. Robert De Niro as Max Cady in *Cape Fear* (1991). © MCA/Universal Pictures/Photofest

revelation through sexual violence: "Ready to be born again, Mrs. Bowden? A few moments alone with me and you'll be speaking in tongues." At first De Niro's Cady mimics the psychological subtlety of Robert Mitchum's performance in the original. But where Mitchum's restrained sexual threat was suggested through his breaking an egg in front of Peggy Bowden, De Niro's Cady moves from thumbsucking (of Danny) to cheek biting (of Lori Davis). By shifting Cady's monstrosity to a baroque and graphically violent sadism, Scorsese adds the conventions of apocalyptic slasher horror to the psychological thriller.

Dreadful Loss and Dreaded Revenge

Buried alive in an "eight by nine" cell for fourteen years, Cady's imprisonment is the metonymic extension of Bowden's uncanny burial of a court
report, which Cady suggests might have prevented or reduced his prison
sentence. Hidden books, wills, deeds, and burials alive litter the Gothic
uncanny; they are what Schelling describes as "everything that should
have remained hidden, but has been brought to life" (Freud 345). Cady
erupts from his burial as the return of the repressed, vowing that Bowden
will "learn about loss." His key trauma in prison was rape: as he observes
wryly, "I learnt from the get go in the joint to get in touch with the soft
nurturing side of myself, the feminine side."[20] At his sentencing, his wife
and child disown Cady and have no further contact with him. Thus, as
husband and father, Cady loses his family, for which he blames Bowden.
When Sam initially offers to buy him off, Cady is insulted, "What shall
be my compensation, sir, for being held down, sodomized by four white
guys? Or four black guys? Shall my compensation be the same? What is
the formula for compensation, sir? Ten thousand dollars? . . . Hell that's
not even minimum wage!" Rape for rape, wife for wife, and child for child,
Cady promises a substitutive retribution (an eye for an eye). At the same
time, his commentary on the racial identities of his rapists also suggests that
neither justice nor retribution is racially blind. As horror collapses boundaries between self and other, both corporeal and psychic, so does Cady
seek, as Bowden's uncanny double, to take his place. In the first *Cape Fear*,
Cady's initial target is his ex-wife, whom he kidnaps, rapes, and murders,
before he turns to the Bowdens. By contrast, Scorsese's version makes the
Bowden family Cady's *only* target for retribution. Cady says,

> Good, 'cos if you're not better than me I can have what you have
> a wife, a daughter. I'm gonna teach you the meaning of commit-
> ment. Fourteen years ago, I was forced to make a commitment to
> an eight-by-nine cell. And now you're gonna be forced to make a
> commitment. You could say I'm here to save you.

Max Cady's corporeal revenge is the reenactment of his trauma and his
loss, mapped across the bodies of Bowden's wife, mistress, and daughter.
He asks Bowden, "Have you ever been a woman?" referring mockingly
to his rapes in prison, where he was "some fat hairy ugly hillbilly's wet
dream." In return, Cady's crimes are violent acts of physical and sexual
sadism: the rape of a sixteen-year-old girl, the murder of another inmate
in prison (which echoes Hannibal the Cannibal in that he bites the man's
tongue off), the poisoning of the Bowden dog, the seduction of Danielle,

the rape and cannibalistic biting of Lori Davis, and the murders of Graciela and Kersek. As Cady rapes Lori he says, "Did [Bowden] hurt you like this, 'cos what he did to me hurt a lot worse than this!" He thus enacts himself as both rapist and rape victim. In the film's dramatic climax on the family houseboat, Leigh pleads with Cady not to rape her daughter, offering herself instead. She claims a bond with Cady based on their mutual betrayal by Sam: "You see, I know about loss, Max, I know about losing time, even losing years . . . you see, we have this connection." Leigh's offer of her own body as sacrificial substitute for her daughter links the lost time of her mental illness with Cady's fourteen-year entombment, connecting the temporal economy of her loss with his trauma, but also underscoring the dread of her ambivalent connection with him.

Performative Dread

> I'm from the Black Forest. . . . Maybe I'm the Big Bad Wolf.
>
> —Cady to Danny in the theater, in *Cape Fear* (1991)

Not only does Cady embody a white fear about the underclass, he also is a master impersonator of class, race, and gender, and as part of his dramaturgy of terror, he performs multiple roles: as an innocent citizen, an accident victim, a pot-smoking drama teacher, a nuclear-power protester, Danny's father, a sympathetic guidance counselor, and, in literal drag, as Graciela, the Bowden's maid. As the above epigraph suggests, Cady is a Gothic transvestite, whose many performances collapse boundaries of race, gender, and class. Pretending to be her drama teacher, he calls Danny on the telephone and gets her to meet him at the school theater, where he waits for her on stage in a suitably Gothic gingerbread house. By his careful choice of mise-en-scène ("what better place for theater?") Cady *performs* seduction, both sexual (inserting his thumb in Danny's mouth) and textual (citing Henry Miller's *Trilogy*). Cady initiates Danny in a number of taboo acts: meeting and sharing a joint with her, giving her Miller to read, and kissing her. As we will see with Helen and Candyman in chapter 3, dread is bound up with transgression and illicit sexual desire. Just as her mother Leigh was unconsciously compelled by her inchoate desire for Cady, so Danny responds willingly. Cady's seductive instruction to Danny, to "remember you can use all those fears to draw upon and learn," underscores the life-lessons that dread and fear offer. He stages a pedagogy of erotic seduction, and Danny's naïveté, desire, and vulnerability heighten our own spectatorial dread—we don't know what Cady will do next to her.

Cady's seduction of Danny is the uncanny echo of his earlier seduction of Lori, Bowden's mistress. Lori, drunk and giggling, meets Cady "by chance" in a bar, and, in spectatorial terms, has an unbearably dreadful conversation with him. It is so agonizingly dreadful because our narrative knowledge is greater than that of Lori, so that we hear every joke as monstrous and foreboding. Cady appears affable (to her) yet sadistically threatening (to us). She tells a joke about an ex-con who meets an unmarried woman and tells him that he "hacked his wife into fifty-two pieces" (at which Cady laughs uproariously). The punch line is "She says, so—you're single?" This leads to him joking: "Well maybe I'll hack you into forty pieces." Cady tells Lori that he is an ex-con, but cleverly pretends he was imprisoned for assaulting a violent cop, "who got a tad rough with [a] lady" at a nuclear plant protest—his lie appealing in its simulated liberalism (and further problematizing the disjunction between law and criminality). A highly intelligent and literate sexual sadist, Cady warns her, "But you gotta stay sober. If you ain't sober, then you're takin' your chances, 'cos I'm one hell of an animal." The irony, of course, lies in Lori's interpretation of Cady's words as figurative, and therefore "a joke," but as Cady has already said, "You think I'm joking, but that's the truth." When they return to his home for sex and he handcuffs her, Lori still interprets his actions as performative sexual aggression, laughing, "He's a rough one." However, Cady is a literal man. Just as he embodies theological punishment in his tattoos ("My Time is at Hand"), so he also enacts the unconscious of language, such that verbal aggression becomes corporeally enacted and figurative aggression becomes horribly literalized. He bites her cheek, mutilates, and beats her, saying, "I got you now, bitch." He makes her eat her mocking words, by eating her.[21] The spectatorial dread that has been agonizingly sustained through these scenes of sexual flirtation now climaxes in an unexpectedly graphic mutilation—performative dread has now become horrifically real.

By biting Lori's skin and spitting out her flesh with contempt, Cady's cannibalism is symptomatic of his desire to consume everything that belongs to Samuel Bowden, from his mistress to his family to the law itself, and Cady's consumption of Lori's skin also points to his transgressive will to break down all (class) differences between himself and others. In the houseboat battles, Danny twice burns Cady's face, and Cady burns himself with a melting flare to show his contempt for pain. His own skin is burnt, melted, and dissolved, as the necessary step in the monstrous flesh made legible—through destruction, he becomes revelation. Like Freddy in *Nightmare on Elm Street*, he is the victim of vigilantism, and as with *Candyman* in chapter 3, the horror of that communal violence is a central part of his monstrosity. Cady's display of monstrous flesh is the corporealization of the illicit violations, direct and indirect, that he has endured. It also represents Cady's own deracinated transformation from illiterate "Pentecostal cracker" to learned autodidact, and finally to the monster who literally incarnates the return of the repressed.

In the horror genre, drag functions as the traditional signifier of gender "perversity" with the monster wearing the clothes and sometimes skin of his victims. Max Cady's horrific drag impersonation of the Bowden's maid, Graciela, recalls the transvestism of Norman Bates in *Psycho* or Buffalo Bill in *The Silence of the Lambs*. Like Buffalo Bill, Cady takes drag one step further—for Cady not only figuratively wears the "skin" of Graciela, but also adopts her clothes and hair as well, as burnings and beatings progressively strip his own skin away. Unique to Scorsese's version, Max Cady's drag impersonation of Graciela also complexifies the monster as victim and underscores the class status he shares with a Latina maid. His performance as Graciela functions several different ways. As a white man impersonating a working-class Latina immigrant, he transforms her identity into his own, but only through a violent act of appropriation over her body. Moreover, as an act of gender impersonation, his performance links cross-dressing and cross-ethnic identification with his plan to destroy the white middle-class family. As the maid, he rises up and tries to slaughter his/her class oppressors.[22] After he kills Kersek, he abuses his corpse with the same class contempt that Kersek had shown earlier toward Cady: "How do you like that, you white trash piece of shit?" Like Candyman, as we will see in the next chapter, Cady first kills those who are *too close to him*—victims marked by their class or racial difference from the white middle-class family that is his ultimate target and site of identification. Dread is the feeling triggered by the awareness that what one would like to distance oneself from is really too close to oneself. Cady destroys Kersek for his impudent disavowal of the class status they share, and at the same time is determined to destroy Bowden for daring to think he is any different from Cady. It is Cady's mastery of the law that threatens to undo Samuel Bowden and that ultimately collapses all distinctions that remain between them.

Supernatural Dread

Like John Doe in *Se7en*, as we will see in chapter 5, Cady self-consciously constructs himself as an avenging angel of God. Cady's extraordinary strength, intelligence, resilience to pain, willpower, and uncanny ubiquity, which border on the supernatural, intensify the dread of his monstrosity. After Danielle throws boiling water in his face on the houseboat, Cady's supernatural capacity to withstand pain is triumphantly evident:

CADY: Are you offering me something hot?

(Cady lights the flare and lets it drip all over his arm)

CADY: Let's get something straight here. I spent fourteen years in an eight by nine cell, surrounded by people who were less than human. My mission at that time was to become more than human. You see, Granddaddy used to handle snakes in church, Granny drank strychnine, I guess you could say I had a leg up, genetically speakin'.

Cady's grandiose preaching of revenge and retribution, aided by his reading *Thus Spake Zarathustra*, enlarges his personal grievances to apocalyptic proportions. Although Cady feels he has created himself as Nietzsche's Superman (God is dead, he is god), he more accurately epitomizes Nietzsche's notion of *ressentiment*—as a poor, white working-class man, shut out from society and power. Cady is the classic autodidact; he first learned to read and then studied the law and philosophy with equal devotion. With the completion of his prison sentence, his physical and intellectual training are at an end: "I ain't no white trash piece of shit. I'm better'n y'all. I can outlearn you, I can out-read you, I can out-think you, and I can out-philosophize you, and I'm gonna outlast you. It's gonna take a hell of a lot more than that counselor, to prove you're better than me." Just as Cady has become like Bowden in terms of his mastery of the law as weapon, so too does he demand its attendant class trappings— Bowden's white middle-class family and home ("good, 'cos if you're not better than me, I can have what you have . . . a wife, a daughter'). The bumper sticker on Cady's car ("You're a VIP on Earth, I'm a VIP in Heaven") aligns his class resentment with his Pentecostal theology.[23] Like Edmund the Bastard who seethes with fury at his inferior status and plots to betray his brother Edgar in *King Lear*,[24] Cady's prodigal reinvention of the self expands the dimensions of the threat he poses to the Bowdens. In one of the film's horror set pieces, Scorsese shows Cady following the family to the Cape Fear River by superhumanly clinging to the bottom of their car. Similarly, after enduring a beating and yet triumphing over the three men hired by Bowden to beat him, he gleefully shouts:

> I am like God, and God like me,
> I am as large as God,
> he is as small as I:
> He cannot above me
> nor I beneath him be.
> —from Angelus Silesius *The Cherubic Wanderer* (1674–5)

Legal Dread

The remake of *Cape Fear* showcases a family profoundly unstable beneath the facade of its own ethical and law-abiding fictions. As Scorsese's negative image of Cady suggests, he was always already in the house, haunting their dreams. As tensions rise, the Bowdens fight over the past—Sam's infidelities, Leigh's three-month depression, their marriage counseling, and the shift to New Essex from Atlanta. Sam tries to use the counseling as an excuse to keep his past (and present) affairs buried: "Now isn't this what Dr. Hackett talked about? *Digging* up the past" (my emphasis). His comment is an uncanny slip, unconsciously echoing his desire to keep other transgressions—whether legal or personal—in a crypt of disavowal. Cady's first attack on the family is poisoning the overdetermined figure of the Bowden's dog. In the first *Cape Fear*, Marilyn, the family dog, "couldn't bite through a doughnut." The whole family sees her death, but the narrative privileges the distress of Nancy (Lori Martin) through her eyeline matches. Scorsese makes the dog's death an offscreen occurrence, emphasizing its psychological impact on Mrs. Bowden rather than on her daughter. Leigh's tearful but melodramatic soliloquy on her dog's death, "He was winding down, like an old clock," is in keeping with her Tennessee Williams–like character, always on the verge of another nervous breakdown.[25] Scorsese replaces the female dog in Thompson's *Cape Fear* with an ineffectual male guard dog called Benjamin (who never obeys Sam), but extends this castrated impotence to Sam Bowden, who is powerless to stop Cady smoking a cigar in a movie theater.

    Afterward, Danny and Leigh admonish Sam for his ineffectual behavior in the theater. Danny says to him, "You should have just punched him out," and Leigh taunts him, "Yeah, you know how to fight dirty, you do that for a living." Sam's masculinity and identity are bound up with his legal skills, which Leigh's nickname for him ("ol' Slippery Sam") implies are rooted in manipulation and deception. (A further irony is evident in Bowden's biblical first name, Samuel; Samuel was the righteous prophet who insisted that even kings must obey the rule of God.) Ironically, rationality is at the center of the law—a discourse in which both Bowden and Cady trade. The initial battles between them occur over legal issues— harassment, stalking, trespass, assault, threats—and for every extralegal act that Bowden takes, Cady replies with a legal countermove. As the law proves inadequate to Cady's threat, Bowden's actions become increasingly irrational, violent, and illegal, in his attempts to protect his family. This conflict between justice and the law suggests the corruption in Bowden's character, which Cady has already pointed out. Bowden has transgressed emotionally (his previous adulteries and current affair with his court clerk,

Lori Davis) and professionally (his failure as Cady's attorney). When
Bowden admits to his legal colleague Tom Broadbent (Fred Thompson)
that he buried a report that could have mitigated Cady's sentence,
Broadbent lectures Bowden on his breach of the Sixth Amendment; he
says, "In every criminal prosecution, the accused shall have assistance of
counsel for his defense." In a further irony, the self-righteous Broadbent
like Bowden is also corrupt, and is further uncanny, given that performer
Fred Thompson's career as politician, lawyer, and senator has seamlessly
blended with his acting career, in which he specializes in playing public-
official roles.[26] Bowden's burial of the report about Cady's first victim is
rapidly multiplied by further legal transgressions: (1) he tries to bribe
Cady to keep quiet and leave town; (2) he threatens Cady in a café;
(3) he hires thugs to beat up Cady; and (4) he intends to entrap and kill
Cady for trespass (premeditated murder). Cady seeks a restraining order
against Sam Bowden (after being beaten by three men Bowden hired) in
a court scene that ironically foregrounds Cady's manipulation of the law,
and through casting and dialogue wryly marks the return of the past.
Martin Balsam, who played a police officer in the first *Cape Fear*, now
plays a judge who grants Cady's restraining order. He admonishes Bowden
with a deadpan citation of "our great Negro educator, Mr. Booker T.
Washington, who said 'I will let no man drag me down so low, as to
make me hate him.' " This ironic scene foregrounds the dissonance
between the words of a former slave espousing a Christian demand for
equality and justice, and their enunciation by a representative of the
white Southern judiciary, known for its racist opposition to desegregation in the sixties.[27] "In the interests of Christian harmony," the judge
orders Bowden to stay away from Max Cady, and is congratulated by
Cady's attorney, Lee Heller (Gregory Peck), who ingratiatingly compli-
ments the judge—"King Solomon could not have adjudicated more wisely,
Your Honor!"—and vows to bring Bowden to disbarment hearings for
"moral turpitude."

    Cady's escalating strategies of stalking and intimidation heighten
the Bowden family's hysteria without leaving them any protection or
solutions. His legal training serves Cady well, as he knows the laws on
trespass, harassment, assault, and blackmail and uses them to hoist Bowden
with his own legal petard. In response Bowden hires Kersek, a private eye
and corrupt ex-cop. "This is all fucked up, Kersek. The Law considers me
more of a loose cannon than Cady," he says, and, following Kersek's
advice, hires some thugs to beat up Cady. Bowden's increasing frustration
with Cady's skillful legal manipulations prompts a lecture from Kersek on
the realpolitik of the law:

BOWDEN: What good are cops and law and due process . . . ?

KERSEK: (*interrupting*) Sam, Sam, Sam, calm down, let me explain something to you. See, the system is set up to handle generalized problems like burglary and robbery. If some lone creep out there targets you for some obscure reason, the system is slow and skeptical, it's pathetic even.

Bowden keeps swinging between vigilante actions and a fading belief in the law (so central to his identity). He remarks, "Maybe 2000 years ago we'd have taken this guy out and stoned him to death, but I can't operate outside the Law. The Law's my business." Out of fear that he will get caught, Bowden takes a belated ethical turn, and refuses Broadbent's offer to get his daughter to lie in an unrelated court case. " I won't do it, it's perjury," he says, and refuses Kersek's offer of another vigilante action: "No more guys." This conflict between vigilantism and adherence to the law is one that echoes the first *Cape Fear*, in which Bowden's internal struggles pointed to conflicts over the role of the law and freedom of expression and association in the historical context of both the cold war and McCarthyism, when these very issues were at stake.[28] In Scorsese's version, the manipulation of the law by those who have class privilege is underscored when Bowden first gets the police to pick up Cady. An ambivalent symbol of the law, the ironically cast police lieutenant Elgart (Robert Mitchum) helpfully suggests to Bowden, "If he's unemployed, he's gotta have money or we'll bust him for vagrancy. We got so many ways on the books to lean on an undesirable. He'll feel about as welcome around here as a case of yellow fever."[29] Forced to disrobe and assume the position ("Spread 'em, Spread 'em") as Elgart and Bowden watch through a one-way mirror, Cady's body is at first subject to the law's controlling gaze (and one which echoes his earlier rape in prison). However, as Cady turns out to have money, the police have to let him go. In response to Bowden's frustration, Elgart gives some veiled advice in the form of a hunting allegory:

ELGART: I can't bust someone for planning to rape your wife, you're a lawyer, Mr. Bowden, you know that damn well. The way I'd handle it. Just think of this fella Cady as a tagger. The trick is to get him out of the brush. And how do we do that? You stake out a couple of your goats, and hide in a tree.

BOWDEN: What are you suggesting, Lieutenant, that I use my family as bait? And then what? I'm agonna hope that this psychopath attacks my wife and child, and then what? Blow his head off?

ELGART: I'm a law officer, it would be unethical of me to advise a citizen to take the law into his own hands. So I suppose you must have misunderstood me.

BOWDEN: I guess I must have.

ELGART: Well, pardon me all over the place.

An ironic double entendre, Elgart's rustic hunting fable metaphorically offers a plan to break the law. Bowden responds with performative sarcasm, not irony (for his meaning accords with his words), but the context demonstrates two officers of the law openly, yet secretly, discussing in uncanny language how to commit premeditated murder.[30]

Bowden finally decides to act on Elgart's advice, and with Kersek's help fools Cady into thinking he has flown out of state to attend his disbarment hearing. Cady, in another performative disguise at the airport, pretends to be a victim of a car accident, in which "his little daughter Danny" died. Under this ruse, he gets the check-in clerk to break regulations (another ethical impropriety) to confirm that Bowden was on the flight's passenger list. Thus satisfied, Cady returns to Sam's house to attack his wife and child, who are seemingly defenseless. Bowden and Kersek wait to lure Cady into the house in order to kill him in "self-defense." Yet Sam worries: "You know what really disturbs me is killing this guy—dammit, it's premeditated, it's, uh, it makes me an accomplice, an accessory, an abettor. It's also excessive force." To this the ever obliging Kersek gothically rationalizes, "The only thing excessive we could do to Cady would be to gut him and eat his liver." Here Cady's dehumanization is made explicit, as a Girardian sacrificial figure that demands ritualistic execution and consumption. Kersek ties wire to all the windows, using Danielle's teddy bear as a visual trigger of movement (and an ironic symbol of child-girl sexuality under threat, with its string of pearls around its neck), and asserts, "I'll know if the Holy Ghost is sneaking in" (but not if the devil as Cady is). The stakeout fails, ending in Kersek and Graciela's murder. Upon the family's discovery of the bodies, they flee the scene (a legal offense in a homicide), for which Bowden cites a legal defense of exceptionality in force majeure, an unforeseeable "act of God." That literally understands disaster in theological terms, and as such again suggests the apocalyptic dimensions of Cady's threat. He calls Elgart on the phone, saying "this 'force majeure' cancels all promises and obligations. So legally speaking all bets are off." The Bowdens flee to their family houseboat on the remote and haunted Cape Fear River, oblivious to the fact that Cady is under their car. By contrast, in the first *Cape Fear* Bowden *plans* to entrap and execute Cady at the houseboat, not the house, and his meticulous plan enlists the police and a private investigator. Instead, Scorsese's dramatic climax on the houseboat dramatically isolates the Bowden family in its final battle with Cady. In an earlier scene, Cady forecast the biblical significance of this final conflict, in his suggestion to Bowden to "read the book between Esther and Psalms"— that is, the book of Job. However, Scorsese's biblical intertext is ironic, for it recasts the family's ordeal, not as a lesson in faith, as with Job, but in mere survival. Sam tells Leigh that God tested Job by taking away everything he had, "even his family." Leigh muses, "I'd like to know just how strong we are—or how weak. But I guess the only way we're gonna find that out is just by going through this."

Crime and Punishment: The Mad Trial on the Houseboat

Scorsese's dramatic climax stages another innovation: on the houseboat Cady puts Sam on trial before his wife, daughter, and God, in a mock trial whose upside-down world recalls King Lear's trial on the heath. As part of this metaphoric upending, Scorsese shows Cady and Bowden hurled upside down, as the houseboat capsizes on the rocks. Cady does not blame his trial judge or prosecutor, "who were only doin' their jobs," but Bowden alone for violating his professional obligations as Cady's defense attorney. In direct address to the camera (as God), in a sermon of declamatory fury, Cady rages:

> I'm Virgil, counselor and I'm guiding you through the gates of Hell. We are now in the ninth circle, the circle of traitors—*traitors* to country, *traitors* to fellow men, *traitors* to God. You, sir, are charged with betraying the principles of all three. Can you please quote to me the American Bar Association's rules of professional conduct, canon 7?

> BOWDEN: A lawyer should represent his client

> CADY (*interrupting*):—should *jealously* represent his client within the bounds of the Law and I find you *guilty*, counselor, *guilty* of betraying your fellow man, *guilty* of betraying your country, *guilty* of abrogating your oath, *guilty* of judging me and selling me out. And with the power invested in me by the Kingdom of God, I sentence you to the ninth circle of Hell, now you will learn about loss; loss of freedom, loss of humanity, now you and I will truly be the same counselor.

Linking personal betrayal to the national and divine, Cady under-scores the apocalyptic dimensions of his retribution, "Now you will find out about loss. Now you and I will truly become the same." As Bowden's uncanny doppelgänger, Cady will now take from Bowden the privileges of his white, upper-middle-class life by raping his wife and daughter before his very eyes. Cady's scopic threat has now become Bowden's enforced specular retribution. Cady rages that Bowden's unethical actions not only are viola-tions of their professional relationship, but also are betrayals of a national order—he is "guilty of betraying [his] fellow man" and "guilty of betraying [his] country"—which recalls Scorsese's symbolic staging of the Fourth of July parade. These discursive connections are uncanny pointers to what Eric Savoy calls "a discursive field in which a metonymic national 'self' is undone by the return of its repressed Otherness" (2).

By the film's bloody climax, Bowden acts like a caveman, throwing a large rock down onto the head of Cady, in a gesture that underscores his snarling regression to a man that now uses rocks, not the law, as his weapon. He has moved far from the castrated masculinity we saw at the story's beginning, and in his brutality has indeed become the same as Cady. By contrast, in the first *Cape Fear*, Thompson's Bowden wounds Cady with a gun but refuses to kill him, instead sadistically promising his Gothic entombment: "You're gonna live a long life in a cage and this time for life. Bang your head against the walls, count the years, the months, the hours, until the day you rot!" In the remake, Scorsese uses biblical imagery that recalls the Flood in Genesis; slow-motion reverse photog-raphy of the houseboat's capsize in the river shows us Bowden and the waters flowing backward, an apocalyptic image that allegorically figures Bowden's regression and undoing. However, unlike Noah's family, the Bowdens do not survive the Flood unscathed, but are cast ashore in the post-Edenic mud. Although battered by the rock, Cady is not yet dead, but still helplessly handcuffed to wreckage in the rising Cape Fear River. He sings, "I'm bound for the promised land" and then "dissolves" into glossolalia, language inaccessible and uninterpretable, the language of "God." Bowden washes Cady's blood from his hands and watches as Cady slowly sinks beneath the rising waters. Yet like Pontius Pilate, Bowden's hand washing is to no avail, and he remains filled with dread, expecting Cady to reemerge from the river, as he has done before. The film's final shots of Leigh, Sam, and Danny staggering up from the mud are an ironic rework-ing of prelapserian myth, in which God made "man from clay."

Scorsese photographs Leigh's rise from the mud in reverse, thus adding a strange quality to her movement and underscoring the regressive logic of the scene (see figure 2.4). The bloodiness and destruction of the narrative's final scenes show this middle-class family at a point of near-complete destruction—crawling in the slime in which they are now thoroughly implicated. The final horror of violence, although so hyperbolically projected onto Cady as monster, is now internalized explicitly within the family that we see lying muddied, bruised, and bloodied through their Darwinian struggle in the floodwaters after Cady's (final) death. This portrait of a family barely intact segues into a matter-of-fact acknowledgment of the new trauma that must be repressed, in Danny's final voice-over that concludes the film. The voice-over accompanies the same negative image of her eyes that opened the film, again shifting from color to gray and white, but this time ending with a saturated bloodred filter. Danielle says,

> We never spoke of what had happened, at least not to each other. Fear, I suppose, that to remember his name, or what he did would mean letting him into our dreams. And me, I hardly dream about him anymore. Still, things won't ever be the way they were before he came, but that's all right, because if you hang onto the past, you die a little every day. And for myself, I know I'd rather live. The end.

The ambiguous conclusion to Danny's story underscores the Bowden family's desperate desire to forget the dreadful primal scene of Max Cady's violence—and that of their own—and signals a return to the repressions that have traumatized this family. Although Danny's last words, "The end," mark her authorship and survival as "final girl" (Clover 35), the destruction of Max Cady paradoxically only reproduces a generalized dread that cannot be completely contained, for he continues to haunt the family's

Figure 2.4. Après le deluge: Family in the Mud: Leigh Bowden (Jessica Lange) in *Cape Fear* (1991). Digital Frame enlargement © MCA/Universal Pictures

unconscious. The eerie fairy-tale horror of Danielle Bowden's "reminiscence" is also a fantasy of terror and desire, a tale of her—and our own—unconscious dread. If trauma is a pathology of a subject's history, through a symptomatic lack of integration into consciousness as memory, then Danny's flashbacks, memories, and voice-over are a *tempus interruptus* that have no integrated place in past or present. Like the houseboat "lost in some inlet" on the Cape Fear River, they linger outside time. In chapter 3, we will see a different form of dread emerge, moving out from one specific family to a broader consideration of genealogy, community, and myth. The unconscious dread of sexual, national, and historical traumas that remained inchoate in the haunted waters of the Cape Fear River will become narratively explicit in *Candyman*, taking historical dread to a new plane.

3

Strange Fruit

Candyman and Supernatural Dread

*C*ANDYMAN (BERNARD ROSE, 1992) is an exploration of the genesis, dissemination, and interpretation of myth, as it circulates across differing boundaries of class, race, and gender in Chicago. A cult horror film, the film is unusual in that it links a supernatural tale to the horrors of a racist past and the poverty and urban segregation of many African Americans today.[1] The story of Daniel Robitaille, a young man who was mutilated and lynched in 1890 and whose eponymous spirit haunts contemporary urban spaces in Chicago, *Candyman* foregrounds how uncanny space bears the memorial trace of repressed historical traumas rooted in an American history of racial violence and murder. As national allegory, *Candyman* foregrounds the ways in which memorial dread erupts in the topographical and mythological circulation of an urban legend that depends upon a specific ritual of incantation and invocation that is voluntary. Through the film's self-reflexive staging of the genesis, dissemination, and interpretation of an urban legend, it is also a metanarrative about the spectatorial pleasures of watching, hearing, and telling tales of horror, in which both dread and doubt are always at stake. In its meditation on storytelling and American racial violence, *Candyman* suggests that oral storytelling and, by extension, urban legends are valuable forms of historical memory, and that the price of historical amnesia will be apocalyptic ("I came for you").

Have you heard about Candyman? Well, his right hand is sawn off and he has a hook jammed in the bloody stump, and if you look in the mirror and say his name five times, he'll appear behind you, breathing down your neck.

—Unnamed student interviewed by Helen, in *Candyman*

Candyman begins with a tale of white suburban horror, as a female voice-over tells us "it's the scariest story I have ever heard, and it's totally true." Claire and Billy are the teenage characters in this tale-within-a tale set near Moses Lake in Indiana, the allegorical Midwestern and suburban locale used for the recounting of this horror story. An unseen narrator tells us that while babysitting, Clare is two-timing her boyfriend, Michael, in her decision to "go all the way" with "bad boy" Billy. In a further tale-within-the tale, Clare tells Billy the story of Candyman, erotically interweaving her tale of the "hookman" with her sexual seduction of Billy. The eponymous hookman can be summoned by reciting his name five times in front of a mirror.[2] Billy stands behind Claire as we see their reflection in a 3/4 shot in the bathroom mirror, and we hear the two teenagers say "Candyman" four times. Clare then halts the game of desire with "no one ever got past four" and tells Billy to wait for her downstairs as "she has a surprise for him." A subsequent shot shows her boyfriend, grinning with sexual anticipation as he waits on the couch downstairs. The voice-over resumes, "She looked in the mirror, and I don't know why, but she said his name the last time." In a privileged moment alone, a medium shot shows Clare in front of the bathroom mirror, as she whispers "Candyman" the illicit fifth time. When the light turns off we see Candyman (Tony Todd) suddenly appear behind her, which is followed by an abrupt cut to a low-angle shot of the ceiling (from Billy's point of view), through which Clare's blood drips. The narrator then concludes the horror story with "[He] killed her, split her open with his hook, and then killed the baby, too. And Billy got away, but soon after he went crazy." *Candyman*'s opening tale then segues into a reaction shot that reveals that the auditor of this tale is Helen Lyle (Virginia Madsen), who with fellow graduate student Bernadette Walsh (Kasi Lemmons) is interviewing students as part of her doctoral research into the urban legend of Candyman.

As the narrative unfolds, Helen and Bernadette discover that the Candyman legend is oral folklore, whose genesis is spatially linked to the Cabrini-Green projects, a poor, predominantly African American public housing complex in Chicago. Based on Clive Barker's short story "The Forbidden," which was originally set in a British working-class housing estate, the American cinematic adaptation shifts its location to the noto-rious, rundown projects on Chicago's North Side, which as the narrative reveals, is the literal space where the story of Candyman began. Within its rat-infested walls, a series of brutal murders and disembowelings oc-cur, attributed to the work of a murderous hookman known as "Candyman" who kills those who summon him. After Helen calls him by saying his name five times while looking in the mirror, Candyman embarks upon a murderous rampage, for which ultimately Helen will be held responsible as a psychotic murderer.

Mimicking *Halloween*, *Friday the Thirteenth*, and *Nightmare on Elm Street*, the first version of the Candyman myth we see is an allusion to the slasher horror film: in an overwhelmingly white suburb, a homicidal maniac threatens heavy-petting teenagers, terminating their sexual activity with death. It is the first of what will be several incarnations of the Candyman myth that the film explores: from the tales recounted by white students and black cleaners from the University of Illinois-Chicago to the poor black residents of Cabrini-Green, the film explores a tension between belief and doubt that crosses class, race, and educational boundaries. So-ciologists, workers, psychologists, students, professors, and city dwellers all have different frameworks for understanding the story of Candyman. These competing understandings, which frame or foreclose the story as myth or as "totally true," underscore the film's interrogation of dread and (dis)belief, and the different ways in which these become connected to storytelling as a form of national memory.

Candyman's credit sequence opens with aerial shots of Chicago's expressways, which thread the city in an arterial image and foreground urban space as metaphoric body. The spatial boundaries and limit-points that figure the politics of race in Chicago are suggested by the horizontal and vertical sweep of the credits over the cars on the expressway, and foreshadow the border crossings that the heroine, Helen Lyle, will later make. Accompanied by the deep organ tones and choral accompaniment of Philip Glass's rich score, which is key to establishing the film's aural and visual atmosphere of uncanny dread and menace, the second shot is an extreme close-up of bees crawling all over a honeycomb, a micrometaphor of the postindustrial city-space that Candyman haunts. This analogy to the dronelike city befits a subsequent establishing shot: a surreal image of a vast swarm of bees over Chicago's skyline. It is an eerie image of apocalyptic portent—for the city is about to be struck by a plague of biblical proportions, and it visually aligns Candyman's desire for revenge with the implication of impending disaster.[3] As a prophetic omen, the organ music and swarm of bees signal the free-floating anxiety and fear of the future that is apocalyptic dread, and that becomes displaced onto the specific dread embodied by Candyman. The apocalyptic dimensions of this dread are further underscored by Candyman's first name—Daniel—which connects Candyman to the famous prophet.[4] Metonymically signaled by the bees, he announces his arrival with an ominous voice-over:

> They will say that I have shed innocent blood
> What's blood for, if not for shedding?
> With my hook for a hand,
> I will split you from your groin to your gullet.
> I came for you.

With this voice-over and the anonymous direct address of the tale of Clare and Billy, *Candyman*'s opening narrative strategy generalizes the threat of the hookman, intentionally provoking terror in the spectator ("I came for you"), as every listener is a potential victim. In this way, the film both foregrounds and interrogates the compelling and seductive dread of telling and listening to stories of horror by playing with spectatorial fear, caught as we are between doubt and fearful belief. This tension is at the forefront in the narrative dread that surrounds the urban legend's ritual of invocation ("Say his name five times in the mirror, and he will appear behind you breathing down your neck").

Mirror Dread

I'm happy knowing that this film has had such an impact on audiences that people actually went around challenging each other to chant Candyman in front of a mirror five times. People look at mirrors a little differently after seeing *Candyman*. I'm sure there's a lot of kids that look at mirrors the way another generation reconsidered taking showers after *Psycho* came out.

—Bill Condon, Director of *Candyman: Farewell to the Flesh*

In narrative terms, Candyman threatens every eye that looks into a mirror, and every ear that hears the telling and retelling of his legend. Helen and Bernadette dare each other to look in the mirror and call Candyman's name (see figure 3.1), but like Claire in the prologue, only Helen says his name the forbidden, fifth time. Candyman's passage into the narrative is through that mirror and into Helen's home, which, as we will later see, he already haunts. The *voluntary* yet transgressive aspect of the ritual of invocation ("say his name five times in the mirror") is central to the urban

Figure 3.1. In Front of the Bathroom Mirror, Helen Lyle (Virginia Madsen) and Bernadette Walsh (Kasi Lemmons) Dare Each Other to Call Candyman Five Times. Digital Frame enlargement © Gramercy /Tristar/Columbia Pictures

legend and is therefore a definitive component of the dread in which this story is enveloped. Unlike many other horror stories, the monster in this urban legend only comes when he is called in a specific manner, and as Kierkegaard reminds us, the act of prohibition thus awakens the desire to transgress, *because we can*. The film stages both impulses, here with Bernadette halting after the fourth "Candyman"—and Helen alone saying his name the transgressive final time.

As spectators to this scene, we also look into the mirror as Helen speaks his forbidden name, and consequently we too are implicitly at risk. When Candyman first appears it is always from *behind* his victim, framed in their point of view shot in the mirror, but simultaneously he also appears to us (thus providing a jolting moment of extradiegetic vulnerability). By extension, then, Helen's transgression also leaves us vulnerable to the same potential horror. Will you be a disbeliever like Helen and reap the consequences?

At first, nothing happens to Helen. However, camera movement already suggests something spooky is afoot: the camera's tracks and zooms seem to metonymically signal Candyman's offscreen presence. Indeed the proliferation of long, narrow passages in Helen's apartment through which the camera prowls heightens the claustrophobia of a mise-en-scène in which, as in many horror films, the optically peripheral is always a threat, and in which there is a dialectical play between the seen and the unseen.

Unmotivated camera movement only points our eyes forward to the ominous bathroom mirror at the end of every corridor.

Candyman is the return of the repressed as national allegory, for the monstrous hookman brings with him a history of racism, miscegenation, slavery, and lynching—the taboo secrets of America's past and present. Candyman's lynching, torture, and murder were his violent punishment for falling in love with and impregnating a white woman. In turn, Candyman, now a supernatural entity with a hook for a hand (see figure 3.2), sadistically reenacts his torture on the bodies of his new victims. In

Figure 3.2. The Hookman (Tony Todd) in *Candyman*. © Gramercy /Tristar/ Columbia Pictures/Photofest

this way, the historical trauma of white violence against African Americans is displaced onto the supernatural formation and circulation of the legend of Candyman, and is signaled by the dread that his legend prompts. It is these historical repressions, central to the power of Candyman as dreadful specter, to which I now turn.

Strange and Bitter Fruit: Lynching

The proper subject of the American Gothic is slavery.

—Leslie Fiedler, *Love and Death in the American Novel*

The genesis of the Candyman legend is in the 1890 lynching of Daniel Robitaille, the educated and artistic son of a black slave, and the lover of Caroline Sullivan, a white woman. Pregnant with Robitaille's child, Caroline had fallen in love with the talented artist her father commissioned to paint her portrait. In retaliation, a mob organized by Caroline's father, Heyward Sullivan, captured Robitaille and then tortured and murdered him.

They cut off Robitaille's right hand, smeared his body with honey, and watched as he was stung to death by thousands of bees. A child who witnessed the lynching licked the honey, exclaiming "Candyman," which became the nickname of the supernatural figure. At the moment of his death Robitaille saw his own agonized face reflected in Caroline's mirror, thus inscribing the specular dimension of his myth. The mob then burned Robitaille's body and scattered his ashes onto the land where Cabrini-Green would one day stand. Born of torture, mutilation, and homicide, *Candyman* is a rare example of the horror genre's interrogation of historical lynchings.

Lynchings were a distinctly public and spectacularized act of violence, accompanied by a monstrous carnival atmosphere. As historical research and photographic evidence have demonstrated, white men, women, and children were both participants and spectators at public lynchings, where souvenir photographs and even body parts and organs of the victims were hawked.[5] Described in a voice-over by Helen's supervisor, Professor Purcell (Michael Culkin), and shown in partial flashback in the film's sequel,[6] we discover that Robitaille's lynching occurred in the post-Reconstruction period of the 1890s, after the reinstitution of Black Code Laws (1865–66), Jim Crow practices, grandfather clauses, and the "redemption" of the Southern states signaled a significant retreat from the partial gains of the Civil War. Historical studies by Sandra Gunning and by Stewart Tolnay and E. M. Beck have demonstrated that there were unprecedented increases in lynchings and white-led riots between 1890 and 1920, most notably those in Wilmington, North Carolina (1898), New Orleans (1900), and Chicago (1919) (Gunning 23; Tolnay and Beck, 17–54).[7] Between 1882 and 1930, 2,805 black men, women, and children were victims of lynchings. The peak years—1890, 1892, and 1893—gave the decade the sobriquet "the bloody nineties." Lynchings frequently involved extensive bodily torture, including flaying, castration, dismemberment, and branding of the victim, so that the graphic violence of *Candyman* becomes one form of historical memory of the extraordinary violence against African Americans.[8]

Gunning points out that lynching and mutilation symbolically feminized African American men, thereby undoing the mythical threat of the hypersexualized black male body of paranoid racist fantasies (Gunning 34). In "The Anatomy of Lynching," Robyn Wiegman has suggested that white torture and dismemberment of the black male body was a corporeal exchange, in which the defeated Confederate South remasculinized itself (446). In Robitaille/Candyman's case, the torture of the black male body is condensed and displaced. Instead of the historical castrations of black men falsely accused of the rape of white women, Candyman's right hand (the hand with which he paints) is symbolically sawn off—a metonymic castration. The violence of Candyman's lynching is recalled through the corporeal dread produced by a "hook jammed in the bloody stump" and a weapon that uncannily reenacts his own dismemberment across the bodies of his victims ('I will split you from your groin to your gullet"), and which in turn becomes the memory trace of the primal torture. His hook also penetrates the victim from behind (a metonymic stand-in for sodomy) ripping upward, disemboweling, and causing massive damage to the victim's body. He now tortures and violates his victims, just as he himself was castrated and violated by the white male mob.

Linked to this violation, extensive references to scatology and human waste in the source story, film, and sequels suggest the larger sexual displacements operating in the narrative.[9] The film suggests that in the repression of historical violence, the return of the repressed has its own corporeal insistence in the dirty secrets of bodily functions. In fact history becomes embodied, which one character in the sequel (*Candyman: Farewell to the Flesh*, 1995) suggests is "because history is alive, it isn't always pretty. It eats, and excuse me for saying, shits." When Helen goes into Cabrini-Green, she notices mysterious graffiti (such as "Sweets to the sweet") written everywhere. The phrase "Sweets to the Sweet" is also written in excrement in Cabrini's public toilets, where we learn through a flashback that a mentally disabled child was castrated, ostensibly by Candyman. A young resident named Jake, whom Helen befriends, explains that the boy's penis was found floating in the toilet, and laconically observes that he was "better off dead. Can't fix that." Opening a toilet marked with an arrow at the site of this castration, Helen unleashes a swarm of bees. Here the film links excrement and urine, the waste products of the excretory system, with the forbidden black penis. Candyman's name also alludes to the historical role of slave labor in the production of luxury goods like sugar in the West Indies[10] and is also echoed in the shrinelike altar of sweets wrapped in razor blades that Helen will find in Candyman's secret lair. Consequently, the phrase "Sweets to the Sweet," excrement, bees, and the black penis are all linked together through the mise-en-scène, and the structuring absence that connects them is the punishment of castration.

This castration is an allegorical sodomization of the black male body by white men, in retribution for the racist fantasy of the rape of a white female (Robitaille's impregnation of Caroline). Just as the film displaces Candyman's castration onto the mutilation and dismemberment of the hand with which he paints, so in turn he displaces his own bodily violation by castrating the body of his black victim. The mutilated bodies of both Candyman and his victims thereby embody historical trauma and, like the urban legend and the bees, murals, and graffiti that form part of his lair at Cabrini, become another form of memorial dread. Further, the film binds trauma to mise-en-scène by suggesting that Robitaille's lynch-murder and nonburial (his dispersal by ashes) establishes the spatiotemporal linkage with Cabrini-Green, which as an uncanny space becomes historically haunted.

Cabrini-Green: "Little Hell"

Bernard Rose's choice to shoot *Candyman* on location in the notorious (and now demolished) Cabrini-Green project was a decision that foregrounded the contemporary intersections of race, poverty, and violence implicit in the film's historical myth by addressing extradiegetic spectatorial awareness of the notoriety of the real space in the years immediately preceding the film's release.[11] At its peak in 1962, it was the second largest project in Chicago, with fifteen thousand residents living in eighty-one high- and low-rise buildings on seventy acres, and Cabrini-Green had a high-profile history of violence. In the nineteenth century the Cabrini-Green area was named "Little Hell" and was a center for poor European immigrants: German, Irish, Swedish, and then Sicilian (Reardon). Through its history of successive poor and immigrant populations, Cabrini-Green is an overdetermined microcosm of the history of American racial politics and segregated urban space.

In the nineteenth century, Chicago was a center for industrialization and transportation, and a principal site of immigration for both foreign and native-born, fleeing slavery or poverty. Professor Purcell's story of Robitaille's life tells us that Daniel's father, a former slave, moved to Chicago like thousands of other African Americans in the Reconstruction period (and later as part of the Great Migration). In part determined by the train lines that ran from the Mississippi Delta region to the Midwest (and the route of the Underground Railroad), many former slaves sought work in the textile mills and factories of Northern industrial centers like Chicago. Purcell tells us that there Robitaille's father "had amassed a considerable fortune from designing a device for the mass-producing of shoes after the Civil War," thus genealogically connecting Robitaille to an American history of slavery, industrialization, and internal migration. In this way, the story of Daniel Robitaille and his family alludes to multiple historical dislocations, from the Middle Passage that brought Robitaille's ancestors to the United States, to his father, the ex-slave's migration north to Chicago, and finally, to the dismemberment and nonburial of Robitaille himself, its own form of corporeal diaspora. As Robitaille lacks either a tomb or monument,[12] he inhabits Cabrini-Green, itself the uncanny ruins of home with its crime, drugs, and poverty.

In the early part of the twentieth century, the Great Migration, the movement of over 5 million African Americans from the South to the North, increased pressure on the housing market in Chicago. Before World War II, Chicago was almost exclusively segregated across a North/South divide, with the majority of African Americans living on the South Side. The near North Side, where Cabrini-Green was located was initially integrated, with 75% of its families white, but by the 1990s, the project and area were 90% black.[13] Cabrini-Green was part of the postwar development of public housing that began with Franklin Roosevelt's creation of the Federal Housing Authority in 1937 as part of the New Deal. In 1942, Mayor Edward Kelly dedicated the Francis-Cabrini row houses; these were followed by the Cabrini Extension in 1959, and the William Green Homes in 1962, with other large Chicago projects like Henry Horner (1957) and the Robert Taylor Homes (1962) also being built.

Cabrini-Green's design was part of a postwar "tower in the park" model of high-rise public housing, influenced by the modernist architects Corbusier and Van der Rohe. Constructed with the aim of solving the problems of nineteenth-century urban overcrowding and poverty, high-rise projects like Chicago's Cabrini-Green became new sites of squalor. The large, open, concrete spaces that surrounded the high-rise projects and that physically isolated the buildings from their surrounding communities gave rise to the term "vertical ghettos," (and they have led to similar problems in the impoverished, largely second-generation North

African immigrant projects where the Parisian riots of the summer of 2005 began). According to Anthony Vidler's study of the architectural uncanny, the "cement honeycombs" of modernist public housing embodied an uncanny domestic alienation, for the home was no longer a house (65). Ironically, his honeycomb metaphor for this architecture is itself uncanny, as it points to the figure of the bee, the agent of Robitaille's brutal death, and one also bound up with the etymological history of *heimlich*.[14] Not only are bees uncanny agents in making something secret, as in sealing wax (*Heimlichkeiten*), but the film's swarm of bees over Chicago's skyline also suggests the metonymic return of the repressed, in Candyman's return to Cabrini. What has been repressed bears the burden of endless repetition, and so Candyman returns to haunt those who now live in an *unheimlich* simulacra of home (the projects), where once Robitaille himself could find no home (the North). The film suggests that as the historical site of Robitaille's murder and scattered ashes, Cabrini is a haunted trace of the racial politics of public policy, which foregrounds the ways in which dread erupts in the topographical and mythological circulation of horror.

The history of Cabrini-Green is a microcosm for the formation and persistence of racially segregated urban space from the nineteenth century to the contemporary era. There were three distinct periods in the formation of segregated black ghettos in Chicago, with the first period consolidating in the early part of the twentieth century. Historical research has demonstrated the ways in which public housing played a key role in the formation of the second ghetto in the fifties and sixties.[15] John Hagedorn has observed that the "high rises, universities and highways also functioned as walls between a growing African-American population and the Loop and white ethnic communities." He also points out that the University of Illinois-Chicago (which features prominently in *Candyman*) was "located to protect the Loop's western flank from eastern expansion of the west side ghetto, just as the Robert Taylor Homes and Dan Ryan Expressway attempted to stem western expansion of the south side Black Belt" (Hagedorn 8). The expansion of the Loop in the nineties, which brought the demolition of parts of Cabrini-Green and the Robert Taylor projects, ironically spurred another formation of segregated space, as residents were dispersed to already segregated areas further south and west. In each period, justification for urban renewal appealed to white fears about increasing violence and crime, with many critics calling it "Negro removal" (Hagedorn 4).

Bernard Rose's decision to shift Clive Barker's tale from its original British setting to a contemporary, urban, and African American space, enabled him to examine the connection between race and urban space in the United States, and *Candyman's* recurrent aerial shots visualize the spatial dimensions of the class and race divisions with which the story is engaged. The first and most important border is that dividing Chicago into north and south in a de facto line of racial segregation. Cabrini-Green is in the predominantly white, near North Side of Chicago, but in a segregated black demographic pool adjoining wealthy white areas.[16] From the film's opening credits, Bernard Rose shoots the projects with high-angle long shots, which accentuate the spatial isolation of its "Red" and "White" buildings (see figure 3.3) in a sea of surrounding concrete parkways. The second key border is the specular relationship between Cabrini-Green and Helen's expensive condominium, the slyly named Lincoln Village, which Helen discovers is a mirror image of Cabrini-Green, and which she discovers was originally built as a project before its subsequent gentrification.[17] Helen tells Bernadette that Lincoln Village was converted to condominiums because "the city soon realized there was no barrier between here and the Gold Coast," to which Bernadette agrees, adding, "Unlike [at Cabrini-Green] where you've got the highway and the L Train to keep the ghetto cut off." Drawing attention to another uncanny spatial connection she shares with Candyman's home, Helen shows Bernadette that just like Cabrini-Green, her bathroom mirror has a secret passage behind it that

Figure 3.3. Cabrini-Green "White" Towers featured in *Candyman* (1992). © Photo Courtesy of Ms. Ronit Bezalel, 2001.

leads into the adjoining apartment. The secret history of Lincoln Village's construction as public housing and its specular doubling of Cabrini, although repressed, have now come to light, and they foreground the ways in which uncanny space bears the trace of historical memory in *Candyman*.

Uncanny Traces: *Locus Suspectus*

Filmic fragmentation of bodily unity finds its paratextural complement in the textual fragmentation of architectural unity.

—Anthony Vidler, *The Architectural Uncanny:*
Essays in the Modern Unhomely

As chapter 1 discussed, the familiar and the unfamiliar often form a complex interrelationship that evokes the uncanny in those strange yet familiar things that prompt dread. The uncanny was a domesticated form of terror experienced in the uneasy shift between the *Gemütlichkeit* of home and the uneasy presence of something alien, which S. S. Prawer describes as "our common dread of something unknown, something on which one does not look, a dread of the possibilities of one's own being, a dread of oneself" (122). Prawer points to an element of Kierkegaardian dread, which is not a fear of something specific (such as a monster) but instead suggests an uneasy sense of possibility and choice that, for Helen Lyle, ultimately points back to herself.

Through the uncanny figure of the doppelgänger or double, *Candyman* suggests that Helen Lyle is a reincarnation of Caroline, Robitaille's original lover. Just as Helen realizes the uncanny relationship between her apartment and Cabrini-Green, she begins to understand her historical connection with Caroline Sullivan when she stares at a mural of Candyman's lynching in his inner sanctum in Cabrini-Green. Her point-of-view shot slowly zooms in to show us Caroline in the mural, while we simultaneously hear the return of Phillip Glass's music-box leitmotif, a recurrent element in the score, accompanied by Candyman's oft-repeated voice-over: "It was always you, Helen—it was always you." From the frequent repetition of phrases (be my victim, be my victim) to the necessary repetition of the ritual of invocation (say his name five times), *Candyman* suggests that historical trauma engenders a compensatory economy of repetition and return, and that dread erupts in the face of this repetition. The relationship between Helen Lyle and Candyman is uncanny, not only because she doubles Caroline Sullivan, Robitaille's lost and forbidden lover (as her reincarnation), but ultimately because she will become Candywoman, by appropriating his supernatural powers and his very weapon, the hook. When she crosses over into Candyman's mythic realm upon her fiery death in a bonfire at the film's conclusion, Helen has both supplanted him and become him, the two of them forever tied in an alliance of myth. Through the uncanny repetition of Helen for Caroline, Candyman wishes to finally reunite with the lover and family he lost with his own death. As he holds her in the flames, he alludes to the repetition of his own corporeal consumption ("Our bones will soon be ashes and we shall never be separated again"), suggesting that the path of familial reintegration always is mediated through horror's violent narrative of corporeal dismemberment.

Spatial Dread

Like all horror films, Candyman foregrounds the specific fear of death through its multiple, untimely, and violent enactments. Candyman's particularly graphic means of dispatching his victims ("I'll split you from your groin to your gullet") foregrounds a dread not only of death and the supernatural, but also of castration, dismemberment, and mutilation, or corporeal dread. In addition, Candyman engages with specific sociocultural dread, a dread that the film suggests crosses class and race boundaries, yet is dominated by a white middle-class paranoia about black criminality. It does this through the fear of specific spaces, from the notoriety of Cabrini-Green projects themselves ("The gangs hold this whole place hostage"), to specific sites such as Ruthie-Jean's apartment and the public toilets, which the film suggests remain haunted and taboo because Candyman killed there. These spaces are feared by Bernadette ("I heard a kid got shot there the other day"), who repeatedly warns Helen about the project's crime, drugs, and gang violence, thereby reiterating Cabrini-Green's spatial dread and its real-life extradiegetic notoriety. This lack of spatial safety is echoed by Cabrini's own residents, for as Jake warns Helen, "You're crazy walking here on your own. It ain't safe around here." From the fear of specific spaces, dread extends to a fear of border crossing, as foregrounded in the frequent aerial shots showing us Helen crossing eight blocks from her home in Lincoln Village to the projects. Naively fearless in her unconscious racial privilege, Helen responds to Bernadette's fears about going to Cabrini-Green for research by retorting, "Okay, let's just turn around then, let's just go back and we can write a nice little boring thesis regurgitating all the usual crap about urban legend. We've got a real shot here, Bernadette—an entire community starts attributing the daily horrors of their lives to a mythical figure."

Indeed, Helen never questions her own sense of entitlement to go where she wants. Despite the fact that no one has ever invited her to Cabrini-Green, she proceeds to enter the projects, undeterred by their dangerous reputation. She boldly photographs the graffiti that line the hallways of Cabrini-Green as well as murder-victim Ruthie-Jean's abandoned apartment, and the public toilets. All these intrusions into various public and private spaces at Cabrini-Green suggest her ideological assumptions about space as a white, middle-class woman. Anne-Marie McCoy (Vanessa Williams), a young black Cabrini resident, echoes Bernadette's pleas: "You don't belong here, lady, you don't belong going through people's apartments and things." As Helen is photographing the toilets where the young boy was castrated, she is surprised by the leader of the Overlords gang, who carries a hook for a weapon and calls himself Candyman. By using his name, the gang leader appropriates some of the legend's power in order to instill fear and dread in the local community. Again, Helen assumes that her academic status will guarantee access and immunity wherever she goes. This is revealed in her bizarre offer of her academic business card to the gang leader: "I'm from the university!" He responds, "Hear you been lookin' for Candyman, bitch? Well you found him," and beats her unconscious with the hook. We then cut to a series of close-ups of black men, each repeating in a monotone, "Hear you been looking for Candyman, bitch." A subsequent wide shot reveals that the men are in a police lineup, after which Helen identifies her assailant. Through editing, the uncanny repetition of black faces and voices self-consciously underscores the racist interchangeability of the criminalized black man in the white imagination.[18] Yet the narrative remains ambiguous: was the castrated child the victim of the false Candyman, because, like Helen, he had stumbled onto the gang's territory? Why then was the boy castrated? Alternatively, did Candyman kill the child?

Helen's overweening ambition is a key component of her personality. "We're going to be published!" she exclaims with delight to Bernadette. Helen wishes to beat her husband, Trevor (Xander Berkeley), and her mentor, Professor Purcell, at their own game of academic interpretation, and this ambition leads her to transgress boundaries. Helen has made an exciting link between her doctoral subject, the urban legend, and a recent murder in Cabrini-Green, as we see her hunched over a microfiche, pausing on a newspaper headline "Who Killed Ruthie-Jean? Life in the Projects." Hypothesizing that the formation of an urban legend is rooted in the material conditions of a specific urban community, she excitedly reveals her discovery at a dinner with Bernadette and Purcell. Although Helen's ambition is to "bury Purcell" (as she proudly asserts to her teacher), it turns out he has already researched and published a paper on the Candyman legend, as he triumphantly proclaims: "Cabrini-Green—Candyman country? You should read the paper I wrote on it, oh, ten years ago." It is then that Purcell narrates the story of Daniel Robitaille. As a voice-over, his

tale continues as we cut to close-ups of Helen's face accompanied by
sounds of the lynching of Robitaille. Structured through Helen's point of
view, the prolonged reaction shot of her face, coupled with the asynchro-
nous sounds of Candyman's terrified cries, suggest that she *sees* and *hears*
the primal scene of torture. Photographed with muted lighting and a soft
filter, Helen appears to have an uncanny, quasi-hallucinatory memory for
these events, as if she had been there. In addition, the lighting on her face
suggests her unconscious erotic fascination with and repulsion to this
story, a romantic dread that will shortly be fulfilled.

Fascinated—indeed, obsessed—with Robitaille's story, Helen returns
to Cabrini-Green. Climbing through a hole behind a bathroom mirror in
Ruthie-Jean's apartment, she discovers Candyman's secret lair. Helen enters
this interstitial space, like that of the mirror, through a hole in the wall.
A zoom out of the reverse angle reveals the hole to be a virtual Hellmouth,
a giant mural of Candyman, with his mouth wide open, through which
she enters (see figure 3.4). It is a sexual and oral image: for just as Helen
(and academia) has consumed Candyman's myth, she must in turn, be
consumed by him ("be my victim"). The visual style of the mise-en-scène
underscores the film's romantic and Gothic themes. The cinematographer Anthony B. Richmond designed the lair as "architectural Gothic,"

Figure 3.4. Helen Enters Candyman's Lair through His Mouth in *Candyman*
(1992). Digital Frame enlargement © Gramercy/Tristar/Columbia Pictures

with low-key lighting, graffiti-covered windows resembling stained glass, and frescos depicting Candyman's lynching (Gramercy Pictures, *Candyman* 5). Helen discovers a shrine with offerings to Candyman, including sweets with razor blades, which gothically invoke both Halloween and urban legends about violence toward children.[19] Near the shrine she finds Candyman lying on a bier, a recumbent Dracula, who welcomes her with delight: "Helen, you came to me! " A tall, handsome man, dressed in a long fur coat, Candyman embodies the paradoxical qualities of corporeal dread, for beneath his beautiful exterior is a cadaverous rib cage (revealed when he opens his coat), in which thousands of angry bees swarm.

This body horror is typical of Clive Barker's work, which Paul Wells suggests not only "emphasizes the protean nature of the body and identity, but readily draws together issues of eroticism and brutality" (91). Candyman embodies the compelling yet repulsive elements of dread for Helen (and for us), for he is both pitiless killer and passionate lover, repulsive monster and handsome artist. Dancing with Helen he kisses her tenderly yet sadistically, murmuring, "The pain, I can assure you, will be exquisite," for his mouth is filled with bees. Helen's embrace with Candyman becomes a diffusely lit oneiric romance, where the camera spins dizzyingly as they dance. A gauzy filter makes her face glow like an old-fashioned movie star, and the change in lighting and makeup heightens the scene's romanticism, echoing the cinematography of the earlier scene in which she listened to Purcell's tale of Robitaille. Diegetic waltz music seems to have transported them back into the past as Daniel Robitaille and Caroline Sullivan, in a romantic fantasy of what was lost.

Psychotic Dread

Candyman first appears to Helen in a parking garage, whereupon she promptly faints. A cryptic narrative ellipsis then ensues, as we cut to Helen as she wakes up in a pool of blood. Mysteriously, she finds herself in Anne-Marie McCoy's apartment in Cabrini-Green, which she has previously visited. The blood belongs to Anne-Marie's dog, which lies decapitated on the floor—and Anne-Marie's baby, Anthony, is missing. There Helen is arrested by the police at a particularly incriminating moment (in a similar way to the manipulative opening of *Dolores Claiborne* described in chapter 4), as she struggles violently over a kitchen cleaver with Anne-Marie (who believes Helen has killed her child). The film's restricted narration offers a number of different narrative possibilities to the spectator: has Helen become psychotic, killing Anne-Marie's dog and kidnapping Anthony? Alternatively, is Candyman responsible for these crimes? Could the other crimes at Cabrini-Green (the murder of Ruthie-Jean and the castrated boy) actually be the violent acts of the gang leader of the Overlords, the "false" Candyman? The ellipses in the narrative when certain murders occur also allow for the possibility that Helen blacks out, and that in fact, she is the psychotic author of the crimes; yet the narrative does not clarify these ellipses, nor privilege any of these alternative narrative possibilities.

Yet *Candyman*'s narrative structure also privileges spectatorial identification with Helen and a belief in the hookman through cinematic interpellation and identificatory editing. Along with Helen, his hypnotic baritone also seduces us to become part of his congregation. Indeed, the narrative shifts between Helen's rational dismissal of the Candyman myth and the growing dread that he exists. This oscillation between supernatural (marvelous) and realist (uncanny) explanations is exemplified by Todorov's category of the *fantastique*, and is epitomized by the ambiguous events in stories like Henry James's *Turn of the Screw*. Todorov distinguished three kinds of horror. First, there is that which is apparently supernatural but proves to have a natural explanation; second, there is the marvelous, or the truly supernatural; and third, there is the *fantastique*, the doubtful hesitation between the realist and the supernatural (41–58). Like Todorov's interstitial category of the fantastic, Freud's uncanny is also liminal, as "the representation of a mental state of projection that precisely elides the boundaries of the real and unreal in order to provoke a disturbing ambiguity, a slippage between waking and dreaming" (cited in Vidler 11).

This ambiguity is epitomized when Helen is hospitalized as criminally insane and assumed to be responsible for the murder of her friend Bernadette. A psychiatrist, Dr. Burke, interviews Helen and shows her a surveillance videotape of a scene that we had seen earlier in the narrative, when Candyman appeared to her. The videotape reveals to Helen's (and our) horror that Candyman is *not* there, contradicting the earlier scene in which we witnessed Candyman floating above Helen as she lay in a hospital bed in restraints. Through the authority of the video recording, the narrative now suggests that what we saw before (the appearance of Candyman), was false, and in fact was Helen's psychotic vision. This is the place where the spectator is left, shifting between the pathology of Helen and the terror of the myth made real. Consequently, the narrative may be unreliable—it may be the visual product of Helen's psychotic overidentification with Candyman. By extension, when Candyman is visible to us, our vision may not be trustworthy and may imply an unconscious spectatorial identification with Helen's psychotic subjectivity.

Are we now confronted with the horror that ambiguous editing and narrative ellipses may have suggested: that Helen did indeed kill Anthony, the dog, or Bernadette? Now the narrative's atmosphere of dread shifts from the fear of a supernatural monster to more troubling implications— the uncertain boundaries of identity, memory, and volition. We shift from object dread to existential dread. Discomforted by the videotape's implications, Helen argues, "No matter what's going wrong, I know one thing— that no part of me, no matter how hidden, is capable of that." Unconvinced of her apparent psychosis, Helen offers to prove her sanity by summoning Candyman in the ritualized form. The narrative holds this ambiguity for a moment, as nothing seems to happen in response to Helen's invocation of Candyman. This narrative dread is literally then murdered, as Candyman smashes through the window and promptly disembowels her psychiatrist. This violent scene underscores the threatening "truth" of the myth, with its visceral implications for all disbelievers (and spectators).

Academic Disbelief

> Candyman isn't real. He's just a story, you know, like Dracula, or Frankenstein. A bad man took his name so he could scare us, but now that's he's locked up everything's going to be OK.
>
> —Helen Lyle, in *Candyman*

From the opening of *Candyman*, the narrative credibility of the myth and how it culturally circulates are always at stake. The metatext of Candyman is the interpretation of myth, and of the tension (and violation) of the spectatorial contract to believe. When, as part of their research into the urban legend, Helen and Bernadette hear variant and contradictory versions of the Candyman myth from their white undergraduate students, their reaction shots reveal their cynical disbelief. Like the story of Billy and Claire that opens the film, suburban variants of the legend circulate among the students ("The babysitter just roasted the kid like it was a turkey or something"). Henrietta Mosely and Kitty Culver, two cleaning women at the university, overhear Helen's student interviews and add their own naive confirmation of the myth of Candyman: "Yeah it's true, I read it in the papers" (Kitty claiming authority for her tale by referring to its source, her cousin, who lives at Cabrini-Green).

At first, as a white academic, Helen colonizes a figure from African American folklore—the boogeyman—and turns it into a sociological reading of crime, class, and race. Helen's interpretation of the Candyman story is shaped by her husband, Trevor, a professor of sociology at the university who lectures on urban legends, explaining them as "modern oral folklore" and "the unselfconscious reflection of the fears of urban society." Like the specular relationship between Cabrini-Green and Lincoln Village, the University of Illinois-Chicago, which Helen attends, is also a mirror image of itself. In a rotating establishing shot (which occurs twice in the film), the shape of the university auditorium recalls a specular Rorschach image, which in turn suggests the psychoanalytic paradigm with which the Sociology Department interprets urban legends. Largely a white space, we know that the university has been an important historical boundary in the racial politics of Chicago's housing segregation, acting like the Expressway and the Loop as a barrier between white and black segregated communities. Helen threatens Candyman's discursive authority through her academic research and by instilling doubt in the Cabrini community. In talking with Jake, she dismisses the story of Candyman as a Gothic fairy tale: "you know, like Dracula, or Frankenstein." However, those who deny Candyman respect or belief are punished, for as he says to Helen, "You were not content with the stories and so I was obliged to come." Candyman acknowledges that his existence is dependent on the fears and faith of "his congregation." Having lost his body so completely to torture and burning, he has recuperated his profound loss of self through the immortality of myth. He whispers this existential plea to Helen: "Why do you want to live? If you had learned just a little from me, you would not have begged to live. I am Rumor. It is a blessed condition, believe me. To be whispered about at street corners, to live in other people's dreams, but not have to be."

The Congregation of Believers

> Our names will be written on a thousand walls, our crimes told and retold by our faithful believers. We shall die together in front of their very eyes and give them something to be haunted by. Come with me and be immortal.
>
> —Candyman, in *Candyman*

The battle between Candyman and Helen is a struggle over discursive ownership, to see who will control the myth. Ironically, Helen gains the fame and attention she desires, not by publishing her findings on the Candyman story, but through a different level of notoriety. Arrested for the kidnapping of Anne-Marie's baby, and later for Bernadette's murder, Helen is besieged by press and TV cameras, and hospitalized as a psychotic killer.[20] After Helen escapes from the mental hospital, she returns to discover her husband repainting their apartment at Lincoln Village (Trevor's new grad-student girlfriend, Stacey, and a fresh coat of pink paint have supplanted her). "It's over" are her final despairing words to Trevor. A long shot of Helen, thinly dressed in her stolen nurse's uniform, follows as she stands alone on a bridge looking out over the frozen river in Chicago. In voice-over, we hear Candyman's seductive and mellifluous tones: "They will all abandon you . . . All you have left is my desire for you." With this quasi-Christological voice-over, Helen is alone in her own Garden of Gethsemane. In this key turning point in the narrative, Helen realizes that she has nowhere left to turn except toward Candyman. Indeed, Candyman's existence as immortal myth and the dread that surrounds him is one from which Helen can no longer separate herself; she has finally become part of his "congregation, the community of believers" (this Christian discourse will be expanded in the sequel's use of Mardi Gras and Lent). Originally unwelcome and uninvited in the projects, Cabrini-Green ironically now becomes the only home to which Helen can return.

Tonight our congregation will witness a new miracle.

—Candyman, in *Candyman*

As she wanders through Cabrini-Green, Helen hears a baby crying and realizes that Candyman has placed Anne-Marie's baby, Anthony, in a woodpile, which is ready for a bonfire the next day. While the Cabrini-Green community had already planned to hold a bonfire,[21] it subsequently turns into a communal ritual to destroy Candyman. Woken by the noise Helen makes as she digs through the bonfire to find the baby, Jake's point-of view shot spies Helen's hand, poking up through the rubble and holding a hook. Jake assumes that the hook belongs to Candyman and calls his neighbors to start the bonfire that will ultimately kill both Candyman and Helen in a ritualized auto-da-fé. There is a Christianized dimension of sacrifice in Helen's final act, for she dies in the bonfire in order to save the baby that she allegedly kidnapped. After killing Candyman by plunging a wooden stake through his heart, and with her scalp on fire, Helen struggles out of the fire with the baby, and then succumbs to her burns.

In the film's epilogue, Anne-Marie and Jake lead a long procession of Cabrini-Green's residents into the graveyard where Helen's burial takes place. A high-angle overhead shot shows this procession winding through the cemetery to her grave site, where Trevor, his girlfriend, and Purcell are Helen's only mourners. A low-angle shot from within the grave shows Jake throwing Candyman's hook (in slow motion) onto Helen's coffin. We cut to Helen inside the coffin, where her pale white corpse lies as still as Snow White (the privileged shot transforming the casket into a kind of glass coffin through which we can see). The abrupt clang of the hook as it hits the coffin, coupled with the long take of the inside of the coffin, suggests that Helen's burial is an uncanny one, and that at any moment she could suddenly wake—and in a supernatural sense, she will. For the community of Cabrini-Green, and especially for Jake (the child as symbolic carrier of the myth), the ritualized return of Candyman's hook to Helen's grave symbolizes the passing of his supernatural powers to her. Helen has moved from writing about and photographing the myth to becoming a new chapter in the legend—as Candywoman.

The film's epilogue shows Helen's postmortem revenge in which she returns to punish her adulterous husband. As Trevor sits alone crying and thinking of Helen, he unwittingly says her name aloud as he looks into the bathroom mirror. At the sound of his fifth "Helen" she appears, holding a hook: "What's the matter, Trevor? Scared of something?" Helen's long blonde hair has vanished into a marcelled short bob; she has become a kind of *Bride of Frankenstein* flapper-girl in a marked transformation from her fairy-tale appearance in the casket shots. After Helen has split Trevor "from his groin to his gullet," his girlfriend, Stacey, walks in from the kitchen, holding a knife. When she sees his bloodied body, she starts to scream hysterically. Thus, the narrative comes full circle, ending with a new trauma: a brutal murder with a hysterical woman as a convenient suspect. The film's final shot tracks in on another scarred mural in Cabrini, showing a haloed white woman. This image is ambiguous—is it Caroline, Robitaille's original lover? Alternatively, is it Helen? Candyman's uncanny words tell us, "It was always you." The portrait has a strong resemblance to the iconographic style of Victorian stained-glass images of saints, and like Joan of Arc, Helen's bonfire martyrdom is the genesis of her own myth. In saving Baby Anthony's life, there is a suggestion that Helen redeems her earlier academic exploitations. Yet her gruesome revenge on Trevor (his corporeal evisceration) undercuts this portrait of angelic sacrifice. She gleefully embraces her supernatural powers, and we expect to hear from her again.

Candyman's narrative interrogates the various interpretations of the story of the hookman, from Helen's sociological interpretation of the urban legend through contemporary socioeconomic conditions, to the narrative's elliptical suggestion that Candyman is the psychotic projection of Helen's own overidentification with the myth. It sketches how the psychotopographies of Chicago bear the historical traumas of racism and the history of lynching in America, which then reemerge in the dissemination of the urban legend of a monster. The film foregrounds an atmosphere of dread whose roots are historically and spatially located in an American history of racial violence, but which become displaced onto both the dread of a supernatural figure and white middle-class anxieties about race, dystopian urban spaces, and contemporary crime. Moreover, *Candyman*'s self-reflexive interrogation of storytelling both recognizes and plays with extradiegetic dread through its constant and uneasy shift between both spectatorial doubt and fearful belief in an urban legend. Hybridizing the conventions of the Gothic fairy tale, slasher horror, historical romance, and urban realism, *Candyman*'s different versions of the story of the hookman critically interrogate the reception and transmission of horror as "myth," but unlike most horror, foregrounds historical racism as a continuing cultural crime.

In the next chapter, "*Dolores Claiborne*: Memorial Dread," we shift away from the broad historical scope of Candyman's interrogation of racial violence to the more intimate focus of a hybrid melodrama/thriller. The film's investigation of two mysterious deaths and the alleged crimes of an eccentric woman named Dolores Claiborne joins the classic interpretative strategies of the detective story with melodrama's traditional explorations of mother-daughter relationship in a story that is ultimately about family secrets of incest and domestic violence, and whose repression is signaled, as with *Candyman*, by spatial and memorial dread.

4

Dolores Claiborne

Memorial Dread

W HEREAS *CANDYMAN* AND *CAPE FEAR* construct an atmosphere of dread from repressed secrets rooted in the national and historical public spheres, the narrative focus of *Dolores Claiborne* (Taylor Hackford, 1995) becomes more circumscribed. As a hybrid that blends elements of social realism, murder mystery, and courtroom drama with melodrama's explorations of mother-daughter relationships, *Dolores Claiborne* explores the traumatic impact of domestic violence, incest, and sexual abuse and how these traumas lead to repressed secrets and murder. The film tells the eponymous story of the professional and personal life of an eccentric middle-aged woman (Kathy Bates), who becomes the suspect in two deaths that occur many years apart: the first, of her abusive, alcoholic husband, Joe St. George (David Strathairn), in 1975; and the second, of her wealthy employer, Vera Donovan (Judy Parfitt), in the narrative present. The film explores the question of Dolores's moral and legal culpability for these two deaths, as well as her estranged relationship with her adult daughter, Selena St. George (Jennifer Jason Leigh), who has returned to their small home on Little Tall Island in Maine after eighteen years away, in order to help in her mother's defense in the Donovan murder inquiry. We will explore how Dolores's and her daughter's separate and conflicting understandings of several distressing events in the familial past reveal the ways in which dread is bound up with personal

83

memory, and is produced by uncanny spaces that recall the historical crimes committed in them.

Adapted from Stephen King's eponymous best seller,[1] the film's narrative has two principal story lines. The first focuses on Dolores Claiborne and her family, including her relationship with her husband, and her psychologically damaged daughter, who live together in an isolated community on Little Tall Island. The second story line is Dolores's relationship with Vera Donovan, for whom Dolores has worked for twenty-two years as a cleaner and servant in Vera's summer home on the island. The narrative moves repeatedly between events in the present—events in the embittered relationship of Dolores and her adult daughter as they deal with a legal investigation into Vera Donovan's death—and their flashback memories as they recall the events of the summer of 1975, when Dolores's husband died. These flashbacks eventually reveal that Joe had been sexually abusing Selena. After Dolores tells Vera about Joe's actions, Vera encourages Dolores to kill him, and discloses that she has murdered her husband, wryly observing that "an accident Dolores, can be an unhappy woman's best friend." Dolores follows Vera's advice, and kills Joe in an "accident"—she causes him to fall into an old well near the St. George house at the very moment an eclipse darkens the whole island in the summer of 1975. Afterward, Dolores continues to work for Vera and takes care of her as she descends into senility and old age. After Vera commits suicide by throwing herself down the stairs, Dolores is suspected of her murder, and is persecuted by Detective Mackey (Christopher Plummer), who has long suspected Dolores murdered her husband but has been unable to prove it.

As a feminist melodrama, *Dolores Claiborne* does not show the victimization of the family by an outside figure, as we saw in the other case studies, yet like them it suggests that dread is nonetheless to be found within the family, revealing that the (symbolic) monster is the familial patriarch. Moreover, the film suggests that what ultimately replaces the fractured family are the desiring relationships between three women—Dolores Claiborne, Selena, and her employer and eventual friend, Vera Donovan. Depicting these relationships helps the film explore a broad range of social issues affecting women that second-wave feminism has raised as political concerns, and that critical response to the film widely recognized.[2] From domestic violence to sexual abuse, and from gender discrimination to psychological trauma, the film depicts the suffering that Dolores and Selena endure, and the resourceful steps that mother and daughter take to survive these traumas. Once the province of the women's picture, in the last thirty years melodrama has largely migrated to television, where it has turned into made-for-TV movies. Influenced by this televisual genre and the conventions of the classical Hollywood melo-drama and woman's picture, *Dolores Claiborne* shows the ways in which the effects of trauma alter one's sense of identity, agency, and subjectivity, and produce dread.

This chapter explores how traumatic memory about familial secrets of incest, violence, and murder become conjoined with uncanny space, which in the narrative refers to the St. George house, the Donovan mansion, and the island ferry as the traumatic archives where these acts occurred. The result of this confluence is not simply the theatricalization of the uncanny, but the emergence of a particular form of resistance to the past, or *memorial dread*. As the introduction outlined, Kierkegaard's understanding of dread was centrally concerned with radical freedom. This absolute choice implies a commitment to ethics, which in turn would seem to distinguish between the voluntary and the involuntary action (e.g., between murder and self-defense), but as *Dolores Claiborne* shows, social reality demonstrates ways in which this distinction is not so clear-cut. With regard to domestic violence, there is a large gray area in which the voluntary and involuntary blur, and this gray area is both a social problem and the narrative domain of melodrama. This blurring not only complicates issues of culpability, but also of memory, for the trauma of sexual abuse and possible violent responses to it may resonate long after the event(s) themselves, and often work against subsequent attempts at justification, explanation, and rationalization. Consequently, memorial dread is a marker of the ambivalence, anxiety, and apprehension involved in *remembering*—that is to say, it refers to the resistance to remembering and acknowledging the past traumas, betrayals, and secrets that one already (albeit sometimes unconsciously) knows. The spectator's journey of discovery into the circumstances surrounding the deaths of Vera Donovan and Joe St. George initiates a complex temporal movement between past and present, and parallels the psychological dread that Dolores and Selena feel in remembering that past. By means of the spatial uncanny these memories reemerge, bringing with them the knowledge that Selena and Dolores, in different ways, have dreaded to confront.

Memorial Dread and Uncanny Space

You don't seem to remember much of anything, do you?

—Dolores to Selena, in *Dolores Claiborne*

Like *Cape Fear*, *Dolores Claiborne* opens with a series of lap dissolves of murky waters—this time of the sea surrounding Little Tall Island in Maine.

A crane shot moves from the sea to a low-angle establishing shot of the Donovan mansion, which is perched on a hill overlooking the ocean. Subsequent dissolves take us closer to the house, and from the front door into the interior. This is where we see ominous shadows of Vera and Dolores on the staircase, in what appears to be a mortal struggle in offscreen space. The film's opening sequence adopts the generic strategies of a horror or thriller by suggesting that the house is haunted by a violent crime. It does this through restricted narration and manipulative framing and editing, in which we see the shadows of Dolores and Vera's offscreen struggle prominently cast on a staircase. Deliberately ambiguous, the opening scene makes it appear as if Dolores has thrown Vera down the stairs (we hear Vera say "Please, Dolores"), and we only discover later that Vera in fact has attempted to commit suicide. The Donovan mansion, so peculiarly an extension of Vera's obsessive personality, is a dreadful space, because it holds the secret of the events that the restricted narration of the film's opening withholds from us. Like Selena we ask, "What happened in that house?"

After Vera's death, Dolores moves out of the Donovan mansion, in which she had been living for many years, and back into the decrepit house in which the St. George family used to live. There she is joined by her daughter as they await the coroner's inquest. The simply furnished house in which Dolores and Joe once lived is almost a ruin, and (to Selena's frustration as a journalist), no longer has a working telephone line. Selena resents the poverty and lack of technology in her mother's home—and metaphorically connects this absence with the distance in their own relationship: "The lines go both ways, mother." Even before entering the old family home, Selena dreads her old home: "Spooky, ain't it?" comments Dolores, who advises her to go inside, because "the longer you stand here, the more boogery you're gonna feel." Like Cabrini-Green in *Candyman*, this house is haunted by past events and trauma, but unlike the public housing project, the St. George house is a private space and freestanding house, underscoring the familial melodrama's more circumscribed focus on the private and psychosexual.[3]

The narrative's highly restricted and manipulative opening withholds from the spectator the answer to all our initial questions, but the increasing frequency and length of the flashbacks that follow suggest the pressure that the past exerts on the memories of the characters. With formal distinctions in color and cinematography, the film's interrogation of past and present events is narrated through fourteen subjective flashbacks. Taylor Hackford and the cinematographer Gabriel Beristain gave each time frame a completely different visual tone by using two different film stocks. For the present-day sequences (set in 1993), a cold blue filter, a predominant gray color scheme, and muted lighting were used to evoke the bleak quality of winter in northern Maine, as well as the barren nature of the story's present-day relationship between mother and daughter. The drab visual sterility of the present is an isomorphic register of the psychological damage that Dolores and Selena carry. Flashbacks to 1975, when the St. George family were still together, are in summery, warm tones and form an ironic contrast to the violent events that will unfold in this temporal sequence. Like the cinematography in *Cape Fear*, *Dolores Claiborne*'s saturated color functions as a visual strategy that is patently artificial, defamiliarizing the past and calling attention to its differential status in the narrative.

Hackford's formal choices shift between or simultaneously show past and present, either by cutting between Dolores's point-of-view shots in color (the past), and her reaction shots in blue filter (the present), or by combining color and blue filters in the same image. In fact, the film does not adopt the conventional flashback of Hollywood cinema but instead uses the formal devices of the avant-garde; at the beginning of each sequence in which the narrative segues into the past, there are two temporalities *simultaneously* depicted of both past and present. These flashbacks literalize the simultaneous merging of past and present in Dolores's memory, in that they combine the color cinematography of the past with the cool lighting of the present, and through digital compositing and motion-controlled photography they merge the two temporalities in the same frame. Here the seamlessness and apparent transparency of the transitions from present to past are enunciated through dissolves from gray-blue to full color *while* the camera pans—that is, Hackford avoids the option of a cut. By moving within the spatial parameters of the frame, his continuous camera pans unite with Dolores's dialogue and voice-overs and shift us into the past, by linking space and time in a visual continuum enabled by digital effects.[4] At the same time, these transitions also literalize the emotional and psychological continuities between past and present in their spatiotemporal dimensions. With one exception, these innovative flashbacks are Dolores's memories, which become lengthier and more complex in structure as the narrative progresses.

The first brief flashback begins with Dolores standing outside the house, looking out over the bleak winter landscape. In a match dissolve, Dolores's point of view shifts to color as we see a search party discovering the well in which Joe St. George's body lies. Dolores sees her thirteen-year-old daughter (played by Ellen Muth) and yells, "Selena, get in the house right now." Abruptly we cut back to the present, with the adult Selena responding, "I *am* in the house." Here, as *locus suspectus* or uncanny space, the house immediately triggers the emergence of repressed memories. For both Dolores and Selena, *being in* and *getting in* the house marks the onset of memorial dread. As Dolores begins to talk with her daughter inside the house, increasingly frequent flashbacks intercut with the present. As mother and daughter sit drinking, Dolores's second flashback is prompted when Selena asks Dolores why she killed her father. We then cut to Dolores's point-of-view shot of Joe, who enters the house and walks around behind the present-day Selena as she talks. This extended flashback is an important one, as it is our first view of Dolores's husband, and our first indication that he was a violent alcoholic. The frequency and peculiar suddenness of these flashbacks gives them a certain hallucinatory quality, and conveys the concrete physical presence of Dolores's memories, which the film materializes through the mise-en-scène. Point-of-view shots, graphic matches, and dissolves form narrative segues into the past, and foreground the mise-en-scène as memorially haunted, for in Dolores's mind, the past literally lives on in this uncanny ex-home.

Melodrama

The relationship between Dolores Claiborne and her daughter, Selena, squarely places the film within the classic territory of the familial melodrama, which had its cinematic roots in the films of D. W. Griffith and rose to prominence with Vincente Minnelli, Otto Preminger, and Max Ophuls in the forties, and Douglas Sirk and Nicholas Ray in the fifties.[5] Characteristic features were a complex and overdetermined mise-en-scène, a narrative focus on the bourgeois family, and a concern with the relationship between intimate emotions and social issues. Hollywood continues to make such melodramas with films like *Kramer vs. Kramer* (1979), *Marvin's Room* (1996), and *A Thousand Acres* (1997). *Dolores Claiborne* is also an example of the maternal melodrama, in which mother-daughter relationships are dramatically central. Moreover, in the relationship between Dolores and Vera the film is also an example of the women's picture, a genre first developed in the early thirties and eventually subsumed within melodrama, and which focused on personal relationships between women. Borrowing thematic and ideological concerns from all three traditions, *Dolores Claiborne* adds the restricted and manipulative narration of the thriller and the suspenseful staging and editing of the horror film, and in this complex hybridity exemplifies what I call the postmodern melodrama.

Marriage

Invoking the familial melodrama, *Dolores Claiborne*'s jigsaw narrative begins by building a gradual portrait of the troubled marriage of Dolores and Joe. In Dolores's flashback, we see that Joe has started drinking again, and is physically abusive to her. Returning from work one day, Joe comes inside the house and switches on the television. As he bends over the refrigerator to get a drink, a shot from Dolores's point of view shows us that his pants are split up the back. When Dolores calls his attention to this fact, Joe at first seems to be humorously self-deprecating. He "moons" Dolores in his underpants, saying, "Look, D, a big old smiley moon. Wanna see the dark side? Yeah, I guess it is pretty funny."[6] Suddenly, in response to her laughing comment, "I hope you haven't been walking around all day like that!" he hits her with a large piece of firewood. In the narrative, violence is always sudden, overwhelming, and unexpected, and typifies the "too soon" of trauma. This abrupt violence also becomes one of the ways in which the film blends the conventions of the thriller/horror with the familial melodrama. In addition, through associational imagery, Joe's "mooning" also foreshadows the apocalyptic day of the eclipse when Dolores will finally enact her revenge, and kill him under the cover of darkness.

Joe is a fisherman who also works odd jobs, cleaning and repairing boats for a company his father once owned. Uneducated like Dolores, Joe does not share her ambition for their daughter to have a different life (later he steals Selena's college fund for liquor). Joe's economic position has clearly declined, and he has lost what little assets he once owned, we assume through his drinking. This extended flashback reveals Joe's resentment and verbal abuse of Dolores. As he looks at a childhood photo of her and himself, he rants that he "married down," blaming Dolores for his economic and personal failures. His verbal abuse and constant references to his mother suggest the unconscious oedipal dimensions of his relationship with her: "My mother warned me you'd let yourself go—fat ass, lousy cooking." When Dolores breaks a plate, he yells, "Goddam it, that better not be one of my mother's dishes." As Strathairn has described his character, "He had to be an effect, a kind of operatic larger-than-life image in the lives of both the mother and daughter" (Castle Rock Entertainment 4–5). Several hours later, after Dolores recovers from the traumatic blow that Joe gave her, she hits him with a plate of food and threatens him with an axe. Then, throwing the axe into his lap, she calls his bluff and dares him to kill her—"All I ask is that you do it quick, and don't let Selena see the mess once it's over"—saying that she will never let him hit her again, "or one of us is going to the boneyard." Dolores's warning also prefigures the day of the eclipse when Joe will try to strangle her, and she keeps her promise and kills him.

Sacrificial Mothers and Ungrateful Daughters

From *Way Down East* (1920) to *Madame X* (1966) the maternal melodrama foregrounds suffering and sacrifice, in which there is an intimate relationship between the mother's class and her relationship with her daughter (classically staged in *Stella Dallas* and *Mildred Pierce*). Daughters in the maternal melodrama are associated with social progress and class ascension, and in *Dolores Clairborne*, Selena, a Vassar graduate and successful professional journalist in New York, has moved as far away as she can get from the poverty and working-class world of her mother. Often presenting an obstacle to her child's social ambitions, the denial of her own desires and identity becomes the price the mother must pay for her child's success. Indeed Dolores's suffering and sacrifice are suggested in her sorrowful first name. Like the eponymous heroine in King Vidor's 1937 classic *Stella Dallas*, Dolores Claiborne is a woman who has sacrificed everything for her daughter's future, and this comes with no small cost to her relationship with Selena.

The representation of social unconventionality is another typical element of melodrama. David Thorburn describes it as a "hunger to engage or represent behavior and moral attitudes that belong to its particular day or time, especially behavior shocking or threatening to prevailing moral codes" (qtd. in Byars 18). In the film, Dolores's provocative personality is this social unconventionality. Selena has left behind the poverty and isolation that she experienced as a child, and is embarrassed by her mother's idiosyncrasies, dialect, and working-class status as a servant. With her tenacious toughness, will to survive, and clipped Maine accent, Dolores is a woman of few, if astringent, words. Detective Mackey insults Dolores by mocking her class: "If you'd feel more comfortable, you can use the back stairs."[7] Whereas Stella Dallas's excessive and cheap jewelry is a source of embarrassment for her daughter, Dolores's earthy, colorful language (she calls a detective "Mr. Grand High Pooba of Upper Butt-crack") and strong-willed personality seem self-destructive to Selena when Dolores is under suspicion of murder.

Why is every story do or die with you?

—Dolores to Selena, in *Dolores Claiborne*

Now living in New York, Selena is a professional investigator, a journalist who specializes in exposés of official corruption and malfeasance.[8] Dolores has proudly kept a scrapbook of Selena's press articles, including interviews that she conducted with Richard Nixon and Jean Harris (a studied reference to another husband-killer). Estranged from her mother because she believes Dolores has killed her father, Selena identifies with Joe and uses his patronymic, St. George (while her mother has changed her name back to Claiborne). Ironically, given her profession as an investigative journalist, Selena is reluctant to delve into the secrets of her family's past. She refuses to hear any derogatory remarks about her father, whom she idealizes, and instead is obsessed with a "big story" she wants to cover in Phoenix. Detective Mackey sends a fax to Selena about her mother being taken in for questioning in Vera Donovan's death, and later tells her, "There's a little more to this than what you've read in the paper." Selena reluctantly leaves her investigative scoop in Phoenix, even though her boss suggests that "there will be other stories, better stories."

Ironically, the comments of both Mackey and her editor foreshadow the traumatic familial and personal secrets that Selena will subsequently uncover with her mother. The first night she returns to the old family home, Selena provocatively asks Dolores why she killed her father. When her mother does not respond and angrily gets up from the table, Selena self-reflexively acknowledges her own interrogatory training, dryly remarking, "Oh, tough question I guess. Occupational hazard. Don't feel bad, Ma, I asked Jean Harris the same thing once." Selena is under no illusion about familial happiness, sarcastically remarking, "Let's not pretend that we're in some goddam Norman Rockwell family reunion here" just as Dolores's flashback begins. This conversation underscores the ways in which mother and daughter differ in their memories and interpretations of the past, and further suggests the irony of Selena's blindness, in light of her professional identity as an investigator. Through privileged narration, Dolores's second flashback then introduces the spectator to our first view of Joe, in a scene in which his violence and alcoholism is revealed, and to which Selena remains oblivious.

As the flashbacks reveal, the "big story" that Selena ultimately will uncover is her own past and the secrets of what really occurred on the day of the eclipse in 1975. Selena's selective amnesia about the events of that summer is closely tied to the narrative mystery of her mother's criminal responsibility. Her reluctance to see her mother and her eighteen-year absence from the island are motivated by the fact that she has repressed her sexual trauma, and because Dolores acts as a narrative trigger for unlocking these memories. Selena has also repressed the details surrounding her father's death, displacing them onto a dread of her mother, whom she regards as a monster and also believes is her father's murderer. But beneath Selena's dread of her mother's guilt is a greater dread, a dread that her suspicions *will be confirmed*, by remembering the reason *why* Dolores killed her father: that Dolores killed Joe, in order to *protect* Selena from further sexual abuse at his hands. Consequently, Selena's repression of her sexual abuse and of her father's culpability as her abuser is at the root of her dread. In addition, her dread is intensified by the unconscious guilt she feels because she was the specific catalyst to her father's murder.

Consequently, mother and daughter have different relationships to memorial dread. Selena's repression is rooted in the trauma of sexual abuse, which has led to profound amnesia and denial. Her knowledge of what really happened is firmly sequestered in her unconscious, only emerging when she returns to the scene of the crime. By contrast, Dolores's reluctance to remember and acknowledge the past is partially rooted in her stubborn and recalcitrant personality. At the same time, Dolores's memories of the past and the reasons that motivated her actions toward her husband, together with her estrangement from her daughter, are part of the masochistic sacrifice that Dolores feels is the price she paid for her daughter to have a better life. Reencountering her daughter and living with her in the family home under the conditions of a legal crisis (the inquest) now trigger the reemergence of repressed memories. Her memories are more readily accessible than Selena's, as thirteen out of the fourteen flashbacks in the narrative belong to Dolores.

Selena's repression of her father's sexual abuse is unconsciously turned back onto herself and her own body. Addicted to pills and alcohol, the adult Selena unconsciously shares her father's addiction, complexifying her identification with the aggressor (she even drinks the same brand of Scotch whiskey, Black and White).[9] Dolores recognizes this parallel, as she remonstrates with her daughter about her drinking as they sit together in the St. George house the first night of Selena's return. Dolores responds to Selena's retort, "Believe me, I know my limit," with "Yeah, don't that sound familiar. I've seen my share of drunks, that's all I'm saying." Selena has become a form of the living dead: dressed all in black, and self-mutilating, she is all but embalmed. As Dolores hears the phone ringing (which we know has been disconnected in the present), a sound bridge signals another flashback. Dolores now remembers when thirteen-year-old Selena deliberately slashed her throat with a Christmas ornament, the initial event in her nervous breakdown. This act of self-mutilation was triggered by a prank phone call, in which local boys taunted Selena by asking her, "Did you help your ma kill your dad?" This memory is triggered by a similar event in the present, when some local boys drive their Jeep around the house, yelling to Dolores, "You goddam murdering bitch, how many more people are you gonna kill before they put you away?" which only reduces Selena to tears again. In these ways, Selena's traumatized response to the stress of her father's death, and the events surrounding it in both the past and present, only reinforces her certainty of her mother's culpability.

What might be described here as a binding of trauma to representation or scene: in order for this return to the scene of the crime to take place, time must be converted to space, act into scene; cause into effect, act and fantasy, perception and representation must change place.

—Mark Seltzer, *Serial Killers: Death and Life in America's Wound Culture*

Like Helen Lyle in *Candyman*, Selena crosses boundaries into uncanny space; when she catches the ferry to the island, she is crossing a boundary back into her childhood past. The ferry is the space where her father sexually abused her, and in a flashback within a flashback, also the place where Dolores first confronts her about her moodiness and failing grades, and guesses that sexual abuse is the cause. Noticing that Selena is wearing her paternal grandmother's locket around her neck, Dolores suddenly understands its significance, crying out, "Oh my god, has he been touching you?" Thirteen-year-old Selena panics and slaps her mother, and we abruptly cut back to the present with Selena shouting a further denial of these events with "You bitch." Angrily rejecting Dolores's claims of abuse, she shouts, "I remember you hitting him, that's what I remember." Consumed with the memorial dread that her mother's claims of sexual abuse provoke, Selena storms out of the house, intent on leaving the island.

Selena has been in flight all her life, either literally (by leaving her mother and the island) or metaphorically (by dissociating from her body though pills and self-mutilation). As she drives to the ferry, she discovers that her mother has left an audiotape in her bag, and she listens to it. The tape returns us to the moment when Dolores suspects sexual abuse. To Dolores, Selena's possession of the locket appears suspicious as it is one of Joe's prized possessions from his mother. The metonymic power of the locket is clarified if the viewer recalls that Joe has made much of the fact that Selena resembles his mother. One of the earlier flashbacks has already shown us Joe caressing Selena's hair, observing, "There's that St. George smile. Don't you look just like my mother." Later he describes Selena to Dolores as "a goddam tease." Marked by his constant references to her, Joe's incestuous desires for his mother unconsciously motivate his abuse of Selena, or so the film intimates. It makes explicit what *Cape Fear* merely hints at—Samuel Bowden's unconscious desire for his daughter, Danny. Unlike *Cape Fear*, however, *Dolores Claiborne* adds an oedipal dimension to the trauma of incest and does so through the symbolic maternal locket.

Like Danny in *Cape Fear*, Selena stubbornly holds on to her illusions about her childhood, until her repressed memories reemerge as she catches the ferry to leave. When she buys a cup of coffee, she suddenly remembers her father buying her cocoa when she was thirteen, triggering her first flashback of her father's sexual abuse. This marks the first time when Selena has complete access to the events of the past. Like Dolores's flashbacks, the past again becomes physically simultaneous with the present, and digital effects make Joe and the young Selena appear within the same physical space of the shot as her present-day self. She then watches a scene unfold in which her father makes her thirteen-year-old self fondle his penis. Warned by her father that "this is our little secret," Selena immediately represses what has happened. Photographic special effects subtly accentuate the dread of Selena's involuntary memories by making the background seem to spin 360 degrees behind her, while the foreground remains static. However, now that Selena has crossed over into the spaces of her past (the St. George house, the ferry), the spatial insistence of these memories can no longer be resisted, and her repression starts to crumble. She flees inside to the restroom, where another moment of subjective de-realization occurs.

When Selena sees her reflection in a restroom mirror on the ferry, to her horror she sees her reflection as her body *facing away from her* (see figure 4.1), as if she were standing behind herself. There may be a visual reference here to René Magritte's *Reproduction Prohibited* (1937). The mirror becomes a site of dread, for her dissociated self-image visually embodies Selena's past trauma. Instead of seeing her reflection, she stands behind a doubled figure of herself, in an uncanny moment. As we know, the uncanny figure of the double points to an intellectual uncertainty about the boundaries between self and other, in what Freud has described as "the urge to defense which has caused the ego to project that material

Figure 4.1. Selena St. George and Mirror Trauma in *Dolores Claiborne* (1995). Digital Frame enlargement © Castle Rock/Columbia Pictures

outward, as something foreign to itself" (358). *Candyman* suggested one such reading: that Helen was the uncanny double of Caroline, and also would go on to double Candyman's mythic function in her supernatural afterlife. When Helen stood in front of the mirror and chanted Candyman's name, and he appeared behind her, national-historical trauma was condensed into that one shot. That is to say, the mirror is the space in which Candyman was first entrapped when he was lynched (he sees his image in Caroline's mirror as he dies), it is the space he haunts, and it is the space from which he can be summoned when the subject performs the incantatory ritual. By contrast, in *Dolores Claiborne* Selena's trauma is sexual and familial, rather than national, and therefore her mirror image is ontogenetic and not phylogenetic (that is, it relates to the individual rather than to the national).

The image is even more complicated than a simple specular doubling, for as Selena's reflection faces away from her, it reflects a profound alienation. Literally obscene, or "off the scene," the image is an aggressive attack on the viewer, for it dehumanizes Selena and turns her reflection into an image of horror. Here the mirror image invokes dread because it is an obviously impossible image; her body no longer produces a reflection, but stands behind another self. It embodies Selena's own historical response to sexual abuse and visualizes it as profoundly dissociative. The mirror image also articulates a tension in the subject between wanting to see and not wanting to see, and Selena's dread resides within this ambivalence. Recalling chapter 1's discussion of trauma, we remember that the frequency of symptoms constituted by sight (the flashback, the hallucination) point to a scopic legibility of trauma, even as its meaning may remain inaccessible in consciousness. Here Selena's flashback has produced an alienated specular image, in the same way that cinematography and special effects previously produced a mise-en-scène that merged dual temporalities and enabled Selena's past and present selves to be in the same space. Continuing this temporal investigation into traumatic events from the past that underscore its atmosphere of dread, the film now takes up the relationship between Dolores and Vera Donovan, and the role that this relationship played in the events that led up to Joe St. George's death.

Work: The Suffering Body

Bearing certain narrative resemblances to *Imitation of Life* in its representation of a bond between two women across class (if not racial) differences,[10] the film emphasizes the suffering and exploitation that have been the hallmark of Dolores Claiborne's working life. The film's feminism focuses on professional and personal relationships between women and, in particular, the unusual cross-class bond that forms between an arrogant rich socialite, Vera Donovan, and her stoic, blunt-speaking employee, Dolores. As mentioned, Vera owns a vacation home on the island, to which she and her husband repair each summer, and there she employs Dolores as her maid and housekeeper. Vera's obsessive-compulsive personality demands absolute fidelity and attention to detail. As she says to Dolores in her job interview, "This house has a number of rules," subtly anthropomorphizing it as an unconscious extension of herself. The tubs are to be scrubbed and sheets ironed daily, with fresh cut flowers placed everywhere. Subtle touches of Vera's controlling personality and compulsive obsessions are frequent: she remonstrates that sheets are to be hung with "six pegs, Dolores, not five, six pegs." As Dolores notes, "I don't know where she got her ideas from, but I do know she was a prisoner of them."

In Dolores's job interview, she tells Vera that she has worked since she was thirteen years old, first for her father, and then for the Devereaux Hotel. The film's fourth flashback centers on the personal and working relationship of Vera and Dolores and is triggered when Selena looks in horror at her mother's hands, which are cracked and calloused by years of hard work. Subtly suggesting the film's blend of horror and melodrama, Dolores acknowledges that her hands are "spooky." As she wryly observes, "If you wanna know somebody's life you look at their hands; that's what twenty-two years of Vera Donovan will do to you," underscoring that her life has been shaped by her class and her sacrificial dedication to both Vera and Selena. Dolores takes Vera's job and works long hours to save $40 a week for her daughter's college education, so that Selena can leave the island and the poverty and isolation of her parents' lives. For Dolores it was "three square meals of bitchery every day:"

Her voice-over takes us into a flashback where she is hanging out the washing:

> I took it, I knew what kind of hell it would be (*laughs*). Hell ain't something you get thrown into overnight. Nope, real hell comes on you slow and steady as a line of wet winter sheets, snot leaking off your nose, your hands so cold and dry, you'd start wishing they'd go numb. It's only December. You know by February that skin's going to be cracked so bad it'd break open and bleed if you'd clench a fist. But you go on to the next and the next and before you know it, those sheets stretch out twenty years.

The harshness of Vera's demanding regime has meant that she has had a large turnover in her servants. Vera's obsessive regime of housecleaning represents a challenge in submission and tenacity for Dolores, who has few economic alternatives. Indeed Vera's sadistic and controlling rules show that Dolores's endurance as her dogged servant is built on suffering and humiliation, themselves classic components of a woman's lot in melodrama. In fact, in epistolary British literature, the figure of the (female) servant abused by a (male) master was a genre convention.[11] *Dolores Claiborne* both uses and reinvents these conventions by making both master and servant female and de-sexualizing the relationship, and yet laying the groundwork for the two women's future emotional closeness.

Female Relationships

> Husbands die every day, Dolores. Why, one is probably dying right now while you're sitting here weeping. They die and leave their wives their money. I should know, shouldn't I? Sometimes they're driving home from their mistress's apartment and their brakes suddenly fail. An accident, Dolores, can be an unhappy woman's best friend.
>
> —Vera, in *Dolores Claiborne*

A more intimate relationship between the two women has its beginnings in Dolores's collapse into tears at work one day. She tells Vera that her husband has been molesting her daughter, and that he has stolen her hard-earned savings of the preceding eleven years that were earmarked for Selena's education, and money that Dolores was going to use to escape from him and the island. Vera's initial response is a hostile one: "Well, don't look at me, Dolores, all my money's tied up in cash." However, as the scene progresses Vera's hard manner begins to soften, and she becomes more empathetic and intimate, saying, "I insist that all women having hysterics in my drawing-room call me by my Christian name." This marks an important shift in their relationship from one divided by class to one in which they share confidences about their marital problems. It is at this point that Vera's pivotal role in the subsequent narrative is foreshadowed. She acknowledges a gender bond that ultimately outweighs their class difference: "It's a depressingly masculine world that we live in, Dolores."

Vera reveals that her marriage to Jack Donovan is also an unhappy one. She has discovered that he has been having an affair, and it soon becomes clear his death in a car crash was no "accident." Like John Doe and Detective Mills, discussed in chapter 5, Vera becomes an instructor in the art of murder. She suggests that Dolores kill her husband, in order to protect herself and her daughter from his abuse, remarking acerbically, "an accident Dolores, can be an unhappy woman's best friend." By also killing her husband, Dolores's crime alludes to a rich history of such narratives in the classical women's melodrama. The film's characterization of the psychology and motivation of Vera and Dolores points to the ideological threat posed by women who kill, and the public fascination with the transgressive spectacle that these crimes reveal. In other words, women who murder call into question normative and essentialized gender roles for women as wives, mothers, or daughters. [12]

Bitches and Witches

> Sometimes Dolores, sometimes you have to be a high-riding bitch to survive. Sometimes, being a bitch is all a woman has to hold on to.
>
> —Vera, in *Dolores Claiborne*

As an outsider in a very small community, Dolores is shunned, and subject to gossip and verbal abuse ("Killed anyone recently, Dolores?"). Vandals have spray-painted "bitch" on the St. George house, and drive around the house shooting guns. Dolores does not give a damn about the islanders' belief that she is a murderer, and freely describes herself as a "bitch," also using the term to describe Vera. Vera self-mockingly uses the term about herself, as she revels in her reputation as a notorious employer. While waiting to be interviewed for the job, Dolores overhears Vera taunting one applicant (who flees in tears), "Look on the bright side, dear, you may not have gotten the job, but think what fun you'll have telling your friends *what a bitch* (my emphasis) Vera Donovan is." Conventionally a pejorative term for women, its specific usage by Vera and Dolores also suggests that a bitch is a woman who is transgressive because she refuses traditional gender norms. As misogynistic epithets, the semantic slippage between bitch and witch is also subtly suggested in both Dolores and Vera's characterizations; indeed, one reviewer described Kathy Bates's performance as "wip[ing] away all signs of self-pity . . . choosing to play her instead as an impenitent witch with the mouth of a stevedore" (Hinson). [13]

From the film's ambiguous and misleading opening almost until the conclusion, the narrative withholds the true status of Dolores's actions, increasing spectatorial dread around her monstrosity. This ambiguity is furthered when Dolores asks Selena "Hand me that axe," using it not as Faye Dunaway did in *Mommie Dearest* (Frank Perry, 1981) to hack away at rosebushes, nor as Joan Crawford did in *Strait-Jacket* (William Castle, 1964) to hack away at her husband's adulterous head, but to smash a vandalized window of the St. George home. [14] This image of Dolores with an axe underscores her defiant personality (and makes us recall her earlier use of an axe to threaten Joe, after he beat her). As Dolores breaks the window with the axe, her reflection remains unnaturally frozen for a few seconds before it shatters, and this peculiar moment likewise foregrounds the ambiguity of Dolores's sudden and violent act. Like Lizzie Borden, who also wielded an axe, a homicidal woman who takes up weapons is an image of transgressive femininity of long provenance, binding pathology with violence and situating it as unnatural. The iconographic image of a woman with an axe, together with its cinematic antecedents, increases the ambiguity around Dolores's character as a suspect in two deaths. Dolores's smashing of a window in the house goes beyond its mere narrative function of attacking the graffiti that pathologize her as killer. As the reflective surface of a part of the family home, the window is both a physical and emotional barrier between mother and daughter, and an entry point into their shared traumatic past. Hackford underscores the symbolism of this smashing by holding Dolores's reflected image for a split second, after the axe smashes the window.

Dolores's transgressive personality is also subtly linked to witchcraft through the narrative's lunar symbolism. The *Malleus Maleficarum* and other works that described the characteristics of witches suggested that their power was at its greatest at midnight, and especially under a full moon. The moon was also a female symbol in Greek and Roman mythology and was under the guidance of Diana and Venus, respectively. Aligning her murder with this feminine lunar imagery suggests that Joe's death signals a (temporary) eclipse of patriarchy. In addition, it aligns Dolores with a rare, yet natural, event as a figure of dread. Indeed Detective Mackey's warning to Selena that "the next eclipse is due in '96—she gets away with it this time, she might actually have another chance to kill again, before she's through," figures Dolores's alleged criminality as a monstrous and apocalyptic force of nature. Like Max Cady's ominous arrival in New Essex in *Cape Fear*, and Candyman's descent onto Chicago in *Candyman*, Dolores becomes a figure of apocalyptic dread. Detective Mackey's implication that Dolores's violence may recur like the eclipse reminds us of Kierkegaard's understanding of dread as a fear of the future, mediated by the past. Infuriated by his suspicion that Dolores got away with her husband's murder, Mackey believes that Dolores will keep on killing.

The Eclipse

Through a series of incremental flashbacks, the narrative takes us further and further back in time, to Joe St. George's death and to the eclipse, when day turns to night with the movement of the moon between the sun and earth. In Dolores's thirteenth flashback, the story's privileged narration now gives us access to that mysterious day's events and, by implication, to the ethical imperatives under which she acted. The film shifts into the full color of the past, when Dolores has just discovered that Joe has stolen all her wages. This theft, together with Dolores's discovery of Joe's sexual abuse of her daughter, serves as a narrative turning point, which leads directly toward his death. Dolores confronts Mr. Pease, the bank manager, for letting Joe withdraw her entire savings account without her knowledge, and underscores the film's feminist critique: "It's 'cos I'm a woman, ain't it? If it'd been the other way around, if I'd been the one passing off a fairy story how I'd lost a passbook and asking for a new one, if I'd been the one drawing out what took eleven years to put in, you would have called Joe."

Later that same day Vera hosts a party to celebrate the eclipse but lets Dolores go home early, with the suggestion that she tend to her husband's removal: "I want you to go and share this remarkable experience with your husband." Vera's implicit direction to kill is connected to the timing of the eclipse—"Oh, I'll have my eclipse. I'm sending you home, Dolores"—and underscores its apocalyptic dimensions as a destructive, grandiose, climactic, and revelatory moment. Vera gives Dolores some reflector boxes with which she and Joe can watch the sky. These devices work through the mediation of mirrors in order to protect the viewer from a direct gaze at the blinding sun. Later when Joe tries to look at the eclipse through the viewing device, he fails, because he is literally "blind" drunk. Joe's alcoholism thus subtly underscores his castrated status: as abusive father and husband, and inadequate economic provider. Freud's reading of E. T. A. Hoffmann's story "The Sandman" presents a scenario in which the uncanny fear of going blind is ultimately about the fear of castration (Freud 352). Freud's tale of the eponymous figure of dread who tears out children's eyes and feeds them to his owl-like children suggests that the Sandman is uncannily doubled by the enigmatic Coppelius and the itinerant optician Giuseppe Coppola—and that all three men are displaced forms of the fear of the father's castrating powers. *Dolores Claiborne* links castration and blindness/looking to the eclipse, which paradoxically, both discloses and hides. Looking at the moon in the sky while driving home, Dolores plans to cater to Joe's every whim that afternoon; and she begins by giving him food and (most importantly) a bottle of his favorite Scotch. Then she confronts him about his abuse of their daughter, and deliberately enrages him by calling into question his masculinity and suggesting he is already castrated:

> DOLORES: I wonder [if your barbershop buddies] are going to think you're such a stud when they find out the only ass you can get your hands on belongs to your thirteen-year-old daughter.

JOE: I don't know what you're talking about.

DOLORES: Really? Then how come you look like the devil just reached in and grabbed those little raisins you call balls . . . So you can just go fuck yourself. That is, if you can get that limp old noodle of yours to stand up. The only thing you're gonna get is a long stretch in Shawshank Prison for child molesting!

Her trap laid, she runs through the garden, leading Joe to chase her toward the empty well shaft. She jumps over the wooden well cover which is rotting away, and Joe falls through it. Dolores knows his cries for help will go unaided, because all of the neighbors are out in the harbor watching the sky. Under the cover of the eclipse, Joe's disappearance will not be noticed until the next day.

The eclipse effect is an example of *intempesta nocte*, a paradoxical moment of dread when the visibility of the domestic home and garden in daylight has been transformed into the darkness of night (Freud 341). The darkness provides the cover for Joe's fall into the secret space of the shaft (which has been accidentally uncovered by Dolores earlier) in another example of the uncanny, or that which has been buried but has come to light.

The eclipse is further uncanny, not only because it transforms day into night, but also because it leads to a temporary burial alive of Joe (he

Figure 4.2. The Eclipse in *Dolores Claiborne* (1995). Digital Frame enlargement © Castle Rock/Columbia Pictures

is left in the shaft to die of blood loss and shock). Editing transitions and the graphic composition of the shots reiterate the thematic importance of the lunar imagery, as we see a sequence of shots graphically matched through their circular design. At near-maximum eclipse, the first shot of this sequence is of Dolores standing over the shaft looking down at her husband. In this low-angle shot, a presumed eye-line match from Joe's point of view frames Dolores with the moon behind her; it has nearly covered the sun (see figure 4.2). The second shot is a plan américain of Dolores shining her torch down the shaft, and the third and fourth shots are graphic matches of the circular shape of the well mouth (a high-angle crane shot looking down followed by an extreme low-angle shot from Joe's point of view looking up at Dolores). The final shot is a graphic match dissolve to the sun disappearing completely behind the moon. Then, in voice-over, we hear Dolores: "The eclipse lasted six and a half minutes. They said it was some kind of record. It was a hell of a lot more than a thunderhead passing across the sun. It was beautiful." Dolores's ability to master the darkness—indeed, to use it to control Joe—aligns her act of murder with natural forces and marks the symbolic sunset of patriarchal power in her life. In this way, the eclipse becomes a moment of apocalyptic dread, because it destroys (Joe's death), it reveals (the sexual abuse has come to light), it is grandiose (as a global natural event), and it is climactic (it ends Joe's power forever).

Mediated through female iconography, the eclipse sequence also functions uncannily in that it is the visual cover for the trap that Dolores lays for her husband and the metaphoric punishment for his crimes (sexual abuse and theft) that have recently come to light. With its saturated colors and dramatic intensity, the stylized artificiality of the eclipse sequence suggests what Jackie Byars has elsewhere described as the tendency of melodrama "to give material existence to the repressed" (17). With its rich saturated reds, pinks, and orange, the hyperbolic stylization of the lunar eclipse (itself a complex quadruple-exposure of three different spaces created through special effects) also echoes the stylized cinematography of *Cape Fear*.[15] The eclipse stands out as a marker of memorial dread, and its literal darkness is a metaphoric analogy for the psychological and emotional darkness with which Selena and Dolores have struggled in their repression of the past. Scopic dread reflects the play between withholding and revealing, just as the eclipse simultaneously darkens (the sky, daylight) yet reveals (the death of Joe). Like that of dread, the eclipse is paradoxical, in that it is a scene of literal darkness (masking Dolores's crime) and yet marking the point of maximum narrative disclosure.

In other words, what the film's restricted narration has withheld from us (and Selena) for most of the story—the circumstances of Joe's death—are finally and fully revealed. Like the flashlight that Dolores shines down the well onto Joe's body, it brings to light what her daughter had repressed and leads directly to Selena's memories of sexual abuse on the ferry. We then shift to the manipulative scene that opened the film, when Dolores was found holding a rolling pin over a dying Vera. We now hear dialogue that the film's restricted narrative opening omitted in its shots of struggle between them on the stairs. We now hear Vera beg, "Please Dolores . . . will you help me die? Don't let me die in some hospital, Dolores, help me die now." Sick and incontinent, Vera has thrown herself down the stairs, in what ultimately turns out to be a successful suicide. The flashbacks have revealed three key secrets: first, that Dolores did kill her husband; second, that she did so to protect her daughter; and third, that she did not kill Vera. After Selena recalls this abuse, the memorial dread of the St. George family's repressed secrets has finally been broken, and the film's flashbacks are over.

The narrative returns us to the present day, where a coroner's inquest into Vera Donovan's death will mark the reconciliation of mother and daughter. Dolores's taped confession prompts Selena to go directly to the inquest to act as her mother's advocate. At the film's beginning, Dolores hadn't recognized Selena, because they had been estranged for so many years, and when she first met her, she assumed her daughter to be her attorney. Yet now Selena embraces the role of defending her mother in earnest. As Selena and Detective Mackey argue before the judge, claims and counterclaims emphasize emotional claims over legal argument, foregrounding the ways in which melodrama privileges feelings and personal insight. Mackey challenges Selena for not visiting her mother and Vera for years, and Selena counters by arguing, "We both spent the last eighteen years prosecuting this woman." She also turns to her mother and asks her why she put up with the harshness of her low-paid job with Vera for so long, and then answers her own question by foregrounding the two women's personal relationship: "These two women loved each other. These two women were together for twenty-two years. My mother spent the last ten years caring for Vera twenty-four hours a day, 365 days a year, for $80 a week." It turns out that Vera has willed her multimillion-dollar fortune to Dolores. An even greater narrative surprise is that Vera secretly drew up this will eight years before her death. Mackey believes this gave Dolores a motive to kill Vera, but Selena counters this with a personal observation that acknowledges the role that repression has played in her own life. Referring to her sexual abuse, she observes, "I think people can keep secrets for a lot longer than eight years."

Consequently, this scene marks the full melodramatic register where the *display* of the new emotional bonds between mother and daughter now control the narrative. Defeated by the zealousness of Selena's defense, Detective Mackey's plan to bring Dolores to trial for Vera's death fails, and Selena and her mother leave the inquest together, emotionally reunited. The conventions of the detective story and courtroom drama now give way to melodrama, in which Selena's previous recall and acknowledgment of familial trauma can now produce catharsis and emotional solidarity. Dolores's secret actions on the day of the eclipse and Selena's repressed memories of her father's abuse are unfurled and produce a reconciliation of mother and daughter. Unlike the traditional conservative ending of the women's picture, this film is a feminist allegory that reveals patriarchy as the real divider between women, and overcomes this through the newfound emotional intimacy of mother and daughter. In fact, *Dolores Claiborne* is in some ways an answer to the classic maternal melodrama *Stella Dallas*. It provides a similar portrait of maternal suffering and sacrifice, but also offers an optimistic resolution to the mother/ daughter relationship. By uncovering Selena's repressed memories of her father's sexual abuse, Selena's dread of her mother is dissipated, and although both mother and daughter still part at film's end, there is a sense that this separation is no longer a permanent one.

Like Cape Fear, Dolores Claiborne is a melodrama that centers on the dysfunctional family, foregrounding the ways in which lies and repressed secrets from the past haunt the family in the forms of spatial and memorial dread; and like *Candyman*, it uses mirrors as spaces in which historical and personal traumas are represented. Although *Dolores Claiborne*'s conclusion is one in which a family transcends the trauma that has initially divided it, in the next chapter, "*Se7en* in the Morgue: Dystopian Dread," we turn to a narrative in which a serial killer effects the complete destruction of the family, and in which trauma can neither be repressed nor surpassed.

Se7en in the Morgue

Dystopian Dread

You know this isn't going to have a happy ending—not for us.

—Detective Somerset, in *Se7en*

THROUGH ITS BLEAK PORTRAIT OF a metropolis beset by random, arbitrary, and endless violence and apathy, *Se7en* (David Fincher, 1995) suggests the complete *absence* of a future. Instead, the film is set in a perpetual present tense, understood in terms of serial, repetitive trauma. Without markers of time or place, Fincher's city is allegorically both nowhere and everywhere, prompting our own spectatorial anxiety. At the same time, through a stylistic homage to forties' architecture, its neo-noir mise-en-scène visually recycles the past. Either way, *Se7en*'s metropolis brackets any sense of future possibility, and exemplifies dread's ambivalence and fear of the future.

In response to this meaningless violence, a serial killer acts as an apocalyptic agent of catastrophe; he is on a self-appointed mission of violent attrition, which will purge society of all its sins. *Se7en*'s narrative follows the murderous trail of a killer known only as "John Doe" (Kevin Spacey), who carries out a series of murders that are based on the Seven

Deadly Sins. Over seven days, seven murders that "punish" victims who are guilty of each deadly sin reveal themselves. These murders are designated Gluttony, Greed, Sloth, Lust, Pride, Envy, and Wrath. Only seven days from retirement, Detective William Somerset (Morgan Freeman) and his junior partner, Detective David Mills (Brad Pitt), are assigned to investigate this series of crimes. After five murders, John Doe unexpectedly turns himself in to the police, promising to reveal the location of his last two victims. Doe leads the detectives out of the city to a deserted location, where a mail truck appears, delivering in a box what turns out to be the decapitated head of Detective Mills's pregnant wife Tracy (Gwyneth Paltrow). Doe confesses that he envied David Mills's ordinary life, and that Tracy's murder was the enactment of Doe's own sin, Envy. The gruesome revelation of Tracy's murder is the culminating act in John Doe's plan, which is to encourage Detective Mills to "become Wrath" (the final deadly sin), violate his duty as an officer of the law, and execute Doe in the film's climax—which Mills subsequently does. Arrested for murder, the film ends with Mills driven away by the police as a saddened Detective Somerset watches.

Like *Candyman*, *Se7en* foregrounds social anxieties about urban crime and random violence, but also displaces them onto the mystified figure of the serial killer. In response to the metropolis's sin and corruption, John Doe's murderous trajectory through the Seven Deadly Sins proffers meaning and purpose in an overdetermined narrative of crime and punishment, turning crime into a textual apocalypse. Preaching through his crimes, John Doe enacts an apocalyptic allegory with messianic implications for society, and ultimately for one specific man and family (David and Tracy Mills). Like Candyman and Max Cady, John Doe's actions embody the dual meanings of the apocalypse; that is, he both destroys (through murder) and reveals (through preaching). *Se7en* splits the concept of dread into a host of smaller categories. Like anxiety, dread is an intense and ambivalent relationship with something that terrifies (a monster, a serial killer, the violence of urban crime), but it also produces an inchoate and indeterminate anxiety that has no object. *Urban dread* is not only the anxiety produced by the random, meaningless crimes that beset the unnamed metropolis in which the story is set, but also a more diffused and nonspecific sense of claustrophobia, entrapment, and pessimism. *Se7en* also foregrounds *scopic dread*, or a fascination and repulsion with what is seen and unseen, staged through the spectacle of grotesque bodies that John Doe leaves behind, and climaxing with Tracy Mills's head in a box. In other words, wanting to see ("What's in the box?"), yet dreading what Doe might reveal to us, epitomizes dread's paradoxical mixture of desire and repulsion.

Se7en's atemporality or sense of endless repetition, together with the eschatological narrative that John Doe follows, prompts a dread epitomized by the narrative's pessimistic conclusion—that is to say, one in which there is no way out, and where the subject is powerless to act in the face of Doe's complete and absolute narrative mastery. Like Helen Lyle who chooses to perform the ritual of invocation in *Candyman*, Detective Mills is directly inserted into John Doe's criminal masterwork—a metonymic stand-in for our own manipulation in horror narratives that we cannot predict, and therefore dread. At the end of the film, a voluntary choice confronts Detective Mills (whether to kill Doe or not), in a scene that stages *moral dread*. As Kierkegaard reminded us, dread gives rise to the anxiety-provoking urge to do something *because we can*, and the consequences of this choice in *Se7e*n bring about suffering to those who exercise it, or are affected by it. By murdering Detective Mills's wife, John Doe constructs the conditions under which he knows Mills will succumb to his wrath, and thereby complete Doe's crime series. However coercive these conditions may seem, Mills's actions are still voluntary, yet the appalling conflict of rage and duty that confronts and ultimately confounds Mills is what constitutes moral dread. Consequently, this chapter suggests that the effect of *Se7en*'s unexpected and horrific conclusion only reinscribes dread—which, even after Mills's summary execution of the serial killer, can never be eradicated.

Urban Dread

For murder though it hath no tongue, will speak with most miraculous organ.

—*Hamlet* 2.2.589–590

The madness of desire, insane murders, the most unreasonable passions—all are wisdom and reason, since they are a part of the order of nature. Everything that morality and religion, everything that a clumsy society has stifled in man, revives in the castle of murders.

—Michel Foucault, *I Pierre Rivière, Having Slaughtered My Mother,*
My Sister and My Brother . . . A Case of Parricide
in the Nineteenth Century

With Darius Khondji's silver retention process, dark and moody cinematography, and rainy urban mise-en-scène,[1] *Se7en*'s setting is a neo-noir moodpiece in a city that is no place, but far from utopian. Art design makes the city space purposively anonymous, with no details in the street signs, costumes, police cars, or helicopters to identify the metropolis's name, location, or temporal setting. The anonymous mise-en-scène allegorizes the postmodern city through its representation of urban crime, intrusive sound, and the ever-present threat of violence. Paradoxically, the city remains not only outside of time in its allegorical nonspecificity, but also trapped within an endless temporal loop of stasis and repetition, in which corruption, violence and sin recur day after day after day, revealing a world of apathy, cynicism, and hopelessness in which there is no sense of a future. In this way, it is symptomatic of postmodern millennialism, a continuous end-time in which both the future and the past are bracketed. The continuous present of the postmodern of which Francis Fukuyama and Fredric Jameson have written (although from very different ideological positions) is one in which there is no hope for fixed meaning, in which narrative mastery is impossible, and in which the future is understood only in the recycled terms of the past.[2] These are all elements of apocalyptic dread, which in *Se7en* is constituted by an ahistorical theological narrative (the Seven Deadly Sins) that displaces the inchoate anxieties of social conflict, urban crime, and sudden change onto the fear of figures like the serial killer.

Seven days away from retiring, Detective Somerset looks forward to leaving the city and moving to a quiet home in the country that he has bought.[3] He is a quiet, scholarly, methodical man, and an unmarried loner. Somerset invites us to share in his cynicism and bleak view of the state of the world as he goes about his work. He despairs of life in the city, where crime is repetitive and bizarre, and a search for meaning seems to be futile. His boss tries to talk him out of retiring, and Somerset responds with this story: "A guy's out walking his dog at night, gets attacked. His watch is taken, his wallet. While he's lying on the sidewalk helpless, his attacker stabs him in both eyes. . . . I don't understand this place any longer." The captain replies, "It's the way it's always been."

The film opens with Somerset investigating a domestic "crime of passion," in which a wife has murdered her husband. Looking at a blood-splashed wall he muses, "Just look at all the passion on that wall." He asks the cops on the scene "Did the kid see it?" to which a detective replies, "You know, we'll all be real glad when we get rid of you Somerset, you know that? It's always these questions with you. Did the kid see it? Who gives a fuck?" Similarly, Detective Mills later asks the massage parlor owner at the Lust crime scene, "Do you like what you do for a living? These things you *see*?" (my emphasis). Like the scopic dread in *Cape Fear*, *Se7en* similarly presents the act of seeing as dread-infused and closely tied to trauma and the horror of the visible. Although virtually all John Doe's crimes are committed offscreen, police photographs, autopsy scenes, and representations of the grotesque body (especially with the Gluttony and Sloth victims) intensifies our dread of what *is* visible. John Doe's crime tableaus are so horrific and extraordinarily unusual that they prompt Detective Mills to ask Somerset, "Honestly, have you ever *seen* anything like this?"

Not unlike Detective Mackey in *Dolores Claiborne*, Somerset is a compulsive perfectionist, proud of his success rate in solving crimes: "Those other cases were taken as close to conclusion as humanly possible." When he is confronted with Doe's initial crimes, he despairs and says, "This can't be my last duty. It's just gonna go on and on and on." This is to suggest that *Se7en*'s atmosphere of apocalyptic dread not only is associated with an inchoate terror of ubiquitous crime in a dystopian space, but also, most importantly, with hopelessness ("It's the way it's always been"). Time itself becomes as endlessly cyclical as the crimes that Somerset confronts every day. Somerset's association with time is underscored by his use of a metronome as a device whose measured tick (exactly seven times in each shot) both soothes him and blocks out the roar of the city's terrors. Midway through the story he will smash this metronome, and by the narrative conclusion he will have given up on his determination to retire and escape to the country. All hope for the future has died with the arrest of David Mills, the young detective who was to have replaced Somerset. Here, then, dread is no longer mediated by the historical traumas of what has happened in the past, as we saw in *Cape Fear*, *Candyman*, and *Dolores Claiborne*, but by the complete absence of any possibility of change in the endlessness of trauma in the present.

Detective Mills's wife, Tracy, also shares Somerset's deep unhappiness with the city and sense of hopelessness about the future. A schoolteacher, she confides to Somerset that the condition of the inner city schools are "horrible," and that she longs for she and her husband to return to their original home, somewhere "upstate." The rumble of subway trains that pass by every ten minutes overwhelms even the Mills's apartment, an apparent refuge from the city. Here the train is no longer a utopian means of escape from the city, but another figure of entrapment. Like *Candyman* and *Cape Fear*, the family home is profoundly vulnerable to the predations of the killer or monster, and ultimately will be the space where John Doe will kill Tracy. Confiding in Somerset, Tracy tells him that she is pregnant, but that she is seriously considering having an abortion, as she doesn't wish to raise a child in this city. Somerset responds by telling her about a relationship he once had with a woman who also got pregnant, and whom he convinced to get an abortion. The result of this decision led to their breakup and to his failure ever to marry. Somerset's (literally) abortive relationship and Tracy's subsequent murder (together with that of her fetus) suggests the film's conservative ideology, in that it aligns abortion as both cause and symptom of urban malaise, and subtly links abortion to the film's apocalyptic sense of no future.

It is the Mills family who will be drawn into Doe's master plan and who, like the Bowdens in *Cape Fear*, are specifically under threat, in this case because their "normality" makes John Doe enraged with envy ("I tried to play husband . . . it didn't work out . . . Because I envy your normal life, it seems that Envy is my sin"). The destruction of the Mills family is the culminating act in John Doe's apocalyptic work, as a serial killer for whom homicide becomes a theological response to sin. By using a medieval allegory of the Seven Deadly Sins, Doe embodies dread as a deeply conservative fear of the future. That is to say, if Doe considers that contemporary society is sinful, and if this sin is always already marked by original sin as the defining human condition, then for Doe, social change is impossible, the future is absent, and history can only be understood in the form of eschatological narratives drawn from the Bible.

Apocalyptic Dread and the Serial Killer as Agent of Catastrophe

> The demonic serial killer functions as an aspect of a catastrophic form of apocalypse that has lost much of its millennial optimism and instead is characterized by despair, not necessarily for the individual, but for the society.
>
> —Philip L. Simpson, *Psycho Paths: Tracking the Serial Killer Through Contemporary Film and Fiction*

> It is terrible to be alone with the judge and avenger of one's own law. It is to be like a star thrown forth into empty space and into the icy breath of solitude.
>
> —Friedrich Nietzsche, *Thus Spake Zarathustra*

Catalyzed by the Academy Award success of *The Silence of the Lambs* (Jonathan Demme, 1991), and capitalizing on the trial of real-life serial-killer Jeffrey Dahmer, the serial-killer film became a prolific and commercially successful subgenre of the crime film in the nineties, a subgenre that continues to this day.[4] Between 1983 and 1985 (with the trials of Ted Bundy and Henry Lee Lucas) the serial killer first emerged as a social problem in the public sphere, and there were congressional hearings into serial crime in 1986.[5] Seizing upon the public fascination with notorious serial killers in the news, early entries like *Manhunter* (Michael Mann, 1986) and *Henry: Portrait of a Serial Killer* (John McNaughton, 1990) had already appeared before Demme's film. The repetitious nature of the serial-killer film cycle subtly mimics the powerlessness of representation to explain individual or social violence. If the serial killer presents an epistemological crisis—in other words, acts as a figure that is essentially unknowable or inexplicable (in terms of motivation)—then the anxiety provoked by this crisis is foreclosed by a turn to Gothic mystification. It is easier to understand what Jeffrey Dahmer is if we explain him in terms that are familiar from Gothic representation: as a monster, a vampire, or a Jekyll-and-Hyde personality. Consequently, popular representations of the serial killer draw upon archetypal figures of horror—the vampire, the devil, the wolfman, the sorcerer, and the cannibal. This resort to super-natural and mythological models is evident even in the nomenclature of real-life serial killers, from The Hunchback (Ted Bundy) to the Vampire Rapist (Wayne Boden), the Angel of Darkness (Randy Kraft), and the Dracula Killer (Richard Trenton Chase). Further, the representation of serial homicide parallels the seriality of commodity production and its stimulation of the desire for, and pleasure in, repetition. The compelling and repulsive elements of the fictional serial killer, whether it be in the cultured, gentlemanly Hannibal Lecter or in the spookily clever master-planner John Doe, both embody the paradoxical elements of dread and are intensified by the sensational and florid characterizations that fore-ground the serial killer's godlike hyperintelligence, strength, insight, and ubiquity. Both fascinated and repelled by them, we dread the serial killer because, in reality, they are occult.

Apocalyptic elements underwrite the mythic function of the serial killer as homicidal master. Philip Simpson understands the neoprimitivist, apolitical serial killers of *Kalifornia* (Dominic Sena, 1993) and *Natural Born Killers* (Oliver Stone, 1994) as apocalyptic in the restricted sense that their violence is destructive rather than revelatory (181). As Mallory says in the latter film, "I see angels, Mickey. They're comin' down to us from heaven. And I see you ridin' a big red horse. And I see the future." By contrast, *Se7en*'s John Doe typifies what Richard Tithecott calls the warrior knight, in that he constructs himself as a messianic and punitive agent of God ("I did not choose, I was chosen"), transforming his monstrous actions into prophetic purpose (150). If we recall that one of the obsolete meanings of the word "monster" derives from the Latin *monstrum*, which refers to a divine portent or warning in the form of something extraordinary or un-natural, John Doe is a monster who embodies apocalyptic dread because he enacts the Last Judgment through his crimes. Through his homicidal ser-mons on the seven deadly sins, John Doe wants his crimes to stand as warnings for the sins of modernity. As an apocalyptic agent of catastrophe the serial killer brings about the revelation of God's words. As Somerset says about the serial killer's murderous plan, "This is all about atonement for sin, and the murders are like forced attrition."

Philip Jenkins has argued that the source material for serial killers' fantasies is preeminently the Bible, "especially the Book of Revelations, the imagery of which has enormous appeal" (qtd. in Tithecott 141). The ascetic detective Somerset is the first to recognize that John Doe "is preaching," and that he has adopted the Seven Deadly Sins as a homicidal allegory. According to Lloyd Spencer, allegory depends on the reader's grasp of an implied interpretive context—that is, "the representation becomes allegorical when its internal coherence or 'compellingness' is seen as secondary to its rigor in representing or signifying something of a quite different order"—demanding a high degree of "optical awareness" in the reader/viewer (62). Like the serial killer's individual homicides that form the stations of his criminal trajectory, allegory overdetermines each individual murder, linking it to a temporal sequence. Allegory is also "destructive," because it transforms the natural into the theatrical, artificial, and reified, and this is what John Doe does—he commodifies death by transforming the grotesque body into a theatrical prop for a theological memento mori. John Doe adopts the sensational formula of the seven deadly sins because, as he says to Somerset, "Wanting people to listen, you can't just tap them on the shoulder anymore. You have to hit them with a sledgehammer, and then you'll notice you've got their strict attention." Doe is extremely aware of his public audience, who will "puzzle over and study and follow his work forever," and in this sense he understands his work as an allegory that teaches and instructs.

The Seven Deadly Sins developed out of Hellenic Mithraic mythology and Zoroastrian beliefs in which the number seven was a mystic symbol. Seven also has numerological significance and apocalyptic resonance, as it recurs over fifty times in various symbolic groupings in Revelations (Dyer 8).[6] Like the Seven Deadly Sins, apocalyptic literature such as the apocryphal Apocalypse of Peter in the early Christian era had a particular pedagogical focus on sexual (mis)behavior, and prefigured the voyeurism, scatology, and sadistic tone of the later medieval work *Visions of Tundal* (1149) and *Thurkill* (1206), where hell was the setting for the punishment of sin. In her study of the iconography of hell in Western art, the historian Alice Turner recognizes the centrality of the family as dramatis personae in the narrative of crime and punishment in the Seven Deadly Sins: "Family values were critical. The vengeance for betrayal is fierce: aborted children blind their mothers with fire; abused children watch their parents mangled by beasts; disrespectful children and disobedient slaves are tortured; 'lapsed' virgins are torn to pieces; fornicators are cruelly punished, as are homosexuals" (84).

Turner's observation locates the ideological imperatives of Christian sin as rooted in the reinforcement of social hierarchy and the pathologizing of sexuality and difference. Transgression *within* the family threatened social hierarchy, and so the Seven Deadly Sins were a means of social control for the Catholic Church, whose temporal power in turn depended upon its cautionary tales of eschatological judgment. Dramatized in the peripatetic morality plays that starred Satan, Death, and the Sins as leading characters, the Seven Deadly Sins had a repressive function, for women were consistently linked to *vanitas*, and Jews were associated with greed (through usury). The plays also reflected homophobia, misogyny, erotophobia, and disgust for the body as part of the Pauline influence in the Catholic Church.

Gnosticism, which understood the world as in the grip of the devil and the body as inherently evil and gross, and Manichaeism, which saw the world as a struggle between good and evil, also influenced medieval understandings of the Seven Deadly Sins. This complex genealogy forms the background to the allegorical texts—Dante's *Inferno* and *Purgatory*, Chaucer's *Canterbury Tales*, Thomas Aquinas's *Summa Theologica*, and Milton's *Paradise Lost*—that John Doe reads and that Detective Somerset in turn consults. Just as *Cape Fear's* Max Cady refers to Dante's ninth circle of hell, so Doe alludes to a literary and theological canon that frames his narrative of crime and punishment, as with the citation he leaves from Milton's *Paradise Lost* at the Gluttony murder scene: "Long is the way and hard, that out of Hell leads up to the light." Both Max Cady and John Doe see themselves as messianic agents of retribution, both conceive their missions in explicitly Christian apocalyptic terms, and both turn their attention to a particular family that they both desire to have and wish to destroy. In this ambivalent relationship of desire and rage, Cady and Doe both embody dread. As spectators we also feel dread in our fascination with the exotic spectacle of the serial killer, and a simultaneous fear and repulsion, which their actions provoke.

In opposition to the city's "random" violence and meaninglessness, John Doe adopts the Seven Deadly Sins as an allegory that proffers both theological judgments and solutions for contemporary malaise. Like Travis Bickle in *Taxi Driver* (Martin Scorsese, 1976), Doe oozes with contempt for junkies and prostitutes, and sees himself as on a purgative mission.[7] As he sneers to Somerset and Mills: "We see a deadly sin on every street corner, in every home, and we tolerate it. We tolerate it because it's common, it's—it's trivial. We tolerate it morning, noon, and night. Well, not anymore. I'm setting the example."

His *j'accuse* implicates the spectator in a social indictment that will become literal in his later manipulation of Detective Mills. Skillfully enraging the detective, Doe's commentary also invites the detectives to acknowledge their own antipathy toward the victims: a greedy lawyer, an obese man, a vain woman, a diseased prostitute, and so on.

> MILLS: . . . I thought all you did was kill innocent people.

> DOE: Innocent? Is that supposed to be funny? An obese man, a disgusting man who could barely stand up. A man who if you saw him on the street, you'd point him out to your friends so they could join you in mocking him. A man who if you saw him while you were eating, you wouldn't be able to finish your meal. And after him, I picked the lawyer, and you both must have secretly been thanking me for that one. This is a man who dedicated his life to making money by lying with every breath that he could muster to keeping murderers and rapists on the streets.

> MILLS: Murderers?

> DOE: (*ignoring*) A woman . . .

> MILLS: Murderers John, like yourself?

> DOE: (*interrupting, louder*) A woman so ugly on the inside that she couldn't bear to go on living if she couldn't be beautiful on the outside. A drug dealer, a drug-dealing pederast, actually. And let's not forget the disease-spreading whore. Only in a world this shitty could you even try to say these were innocent people and keep a straight face.

Doe invites common social prejudices against greedy lawyers ("you both must have been secretly thanking me for that one") and the morbidly obese ("a man who . . . if you saw him while you were eating you wouldn't be able to finish your meal"). Doe's murder of a model (for the sin of Pride) and a prostitute (for the sin of Lust) also reveal his contempt for women ("the disease-spreading whore"). Reactionary in his choice of victims, Doe does not question normative notions of beauty or desire, nor their relationship with particular gendered bodies, and so he does not question his own loathing. As he systematically starves Victor (Sloth) to near death over a year, he methodically photographs the decline of his victim's body, as it metamorphoses into a corpselike state. Samples of the victim's urine and feces are placed next to his living corpse, as if the victim were a laboratory experiment on the effects of torture. Kept alive by antibiotics, his body is hideous and near-skeletal—and in a doctor's words, his mind is "mush." With all consciousness gone, as a doctor dryly observes "he's experienced about as much pain and suffering as any one I've encountered . . . and he *still has hell* to look forward to" (my emphasis). The final part of the doctor's comment also suggests a conservative agenda to which the film slyly appeals, inviting spectatorial disgust for pederasts and addicts. By turning the bodies of his allegorical victims into object lessons, Doe allegorizes his own resentment, but also implicates a society from whose prejudices he draws. Through the marketing and consumption of the film, Hollywood plays it both ways; it invites us to identify with John Doe's moral outrage and disgust, but at the same time it offers us the exotic spectacle of illicit or prurient behavior.

Corporeal Dread

The serial killer is a metonym for what Mark Seltzer calls the "pathological public sphere"—that is, he stands in for a culture that celebrates trauma as entertainment and spectacle (21). As part of what Seltzer calls this "wound culture," the serial killer exemplifies the graphic puncturing of the public sphere through private bodies.[8] Through his systematic eviscerations, mutilations, and dismemberments, he turns the bodies of his victims inside out, for maximum visibility. From the murders of Gluttony to Lust and Sloth, Doe suggests that the corporeal excesses and desires of contemporary society set the stage for sin, and he punishes these excesses and desires by making these bodies' internal corruptions visible. Each crime is brutal in its corporeal particularity: an obese agoraphobic is force-fed to death (Gluttony); a lawyer is forced to cut a pound of flesh from his own body (Greed); a "drug-dealing pederast" is systematically starved into a coma and near death over a year (Sloth); a prostitute is impaled on a knife-dildo (Lust); a model is mutilated and chooses suicide over ugliness (Pride); a detective murders an unarmed defendant (Wrath); and Doe himself kills and decapitates Tracy Mills (Envy). Doe's own homicidal practice mutilates and transforms the bodies of his victims (he explodes Gluttony, dissects Greed, starves Sloth, mutilates Pride, and punctures Lust). Similarly, John Doe's journals reveal his compulsive interest in the body, and in particular, his interest in the grotesque, abnormal, eviscerated, or dissected body.[9] In part a reflection of Christianity's contempt for the body as the vessel of sin, Doe's fascination with the body and with making its sinfulness visible embodies a dread that articulates both meanings of the apocalypse: destruction and revelation. Like a memento mori, Doe's actions have a teaching purpose—and in this way, corporeal dread becomes spectatorial dread.

Anonymous Dread: The Serial Killer as "Minus Man"

If we catch John Doe and he turns out to be the devil, I mean if he's
Satan himself, that might live up to our expectations, but he's not the
devil, he's just a man.

—Detective Somerset, in *Se7en*

They appear like the normal average guy that lives next door to
you. It's only when they do their periodic killing that they're really
quite abnormal.

—Dr. Harvey Schlossberg, psychologist,
Serial Killers: Clues to Madness (ABC, 1991)

Whereas Max Cady and Candyman's apocalyptic arrivals are marked in
their respective narratives through prophetic natural signs that can be
decoded, John Doe is an interpretative dead end (he has no identity, past,
name, or fingerprints), which only intensifies the dread of his crimes,
which are potentially endless and unalterable. His library ID card lists his
name as "Jonathan Doe," a variant of the traditional governmental nomenclature given to unidentified bodies.[10] Doe's eradication of his own
identity is total. By cutting off his own fingertips Doe erases himself from
social existence and becomes a tabula rasa (the police can find no social
security number, identifying papers, birth certificate, or fingerprints in his
apartment). By contrast, in *Cape Fear* Max Cady is a textual body; he is
covered with tattoos of biblical quotations. In other words, John Doe's
monstrosity hyperbolically literalizes the dread produced by the anonymity and illegibility of real-life serial killers as the "abnormal normal."
(Seltzer 7). *The Stepfather* (Joseph Ruben, 1987) satirizes these social
anxieties by exaggerating the horror that lurks beneath the mask of familial normality. For if the serial killer appears ordinary, even banal, Doe's
adoption of his pseudonym enacts a dread of the normal *as* pathological,
which is in contrast to the Grand Guignol tradition of Gothic monstrosity offered by Hannibal Lecter in *The Silence of the Lambs*. The Gothic
representation of serial killers like Lecter has, in Philip Jenkins's terms, "the
critical social function [of] defining conventional morality and behavior, by
providing a *ne plus ultra* against which normal society readily finds common
ground" (112). By contrast, John Doe's effacement of his own identity
transforms himself into an allegory of Everyman and epitomizes the public
dread of real-life serial killers' anonymity and ubiquity. Prompting dread,
the serial killer presents a problem of knowledge to the law and psychiatry
(notwithstanding the diagnostic and classificatory attempts of both profes-
sions), because he or she is both insane and rational.[11]

OFFICER: Is it true what they're saying?

CLARICE STARLING: Huh?

OFFICER: [that] he's some kind of a vampire?

CLARICE STARLING: They don't have a name for what it is.

—The Silence of the Lambs

Narrative Dread

The Murder and the narrative were consubstantial.

—Michel Foucault, *I Pierre Rivère, Having Slaughtered My Mother,*
My Sister and My Brother . . . A Case of Parricide
in the Nineteenth Century

As the categorical nature of the serial killer is the retroactive creation of a body of work that occurs serially and cumulatively, the serial killer has an intrinsic narratological relationship with time. Cause and effect, sequences, foreshadowing, clues, surprise, red herrings, and closure are all at play in the killer's narrative, in a dialectic of endlessness and finality. Robert Ressler, a former detective in the FBI, has claimed that he invented the term "serial killer" (in preference to the seventies' nomenclature of "stranger killing"), coining it through an analogy to film serials. Ressler's memory of the repetitive, interrupted nature of the serial with its traditional cliffhanger ending reminded him of the parallel temporal dimension of serial killing. He also suggested that narrative interruption not only was a device for spectatorial frustration (catalyzing a compensatory desire to return to the theater), but also only a temporary fix for the killer, which he describes this way: "The very act of killing leaves the murderer hanging, because it isn't as perfect as his fantasy. When the Phantom is left sinking in the quicksand, the viewer has to come back next week . . . After a murder, the serial murderer thinks of how the crime could have been bettered" (Ressler and Shachtman 32–33).

Se7en structures its tale of John Doe's Seven Deadly Sins through seven crimes over seven days, and like the last seven days of Revelations, John Doe's apocalyptic purpose is intensified with each day and each new crime, in a kind of miniseries of dread. Moreover, each of the Seven Deadly Sins are individual examples of John Doe's diegetically a priori narratives of torture and murder; each narrative is of specific duration, and the spectator only sees the corpse as end result. Standing in for each Sin is the plethora of textual and photographic documentation of each crime's duration and execution that John Doe leaves behind. For example, as Doe progressively feeds and tortures the Gluttony victim to death, he enacts the first murder for an indeterminate yet extended period. As Somerset describes it:

> The killer put a bucket beneath him, kept on serving. Took his time, too. The Coroner said this could have gone on for more than twelve hours. Victim's throat was swollen, probably from the effort. And there was definitely a point when he passed out. That's when the killer kicked him, and he burst. When you want somebody dead, you drive by and shoot 'em. You don't risk the time it takes to do this, unless the act itself has meaning.

John Doe also took time out to purchase more cans of spaghetti to force-feed the man. The forensic autopsy of Gluttony's body reconstructs the details of the murder's process and duration, and is another example of the film's use of the grotesque body to sustain spectatorial dread. (See figure 5.1.)

In the case of Sloth, the crime took exactly one year to perform, with the victim, Victor, kept alive by intravenous saline, morphine, and antibiotics to bring him precisely to the point of near death (as documented in Doe's fifty-two weekly photos left at the scene). Doe's serial photographs of this tableau of sustained starvation are like individual frames of film that record this particular mininarrative. The torture of the lawyer Eli Gould (Greed) occurred over a long weekend, from Friday to the following Tuesday, as he slowly bled to death from the pound of flesh he was forced to cut from his own body. In the case of Pride, Doe tortured and mutilated a model, "cut[ting] off her nose to spite her face,"

Figure 5.1. Autopsy of Gluttony in *Se7en* (1995). Digital Frame enlargement © New Line Productions

leaving her to choose suicide over permanent disfigurement, and so Pride is also the author of her own death through an overdose of pills. (Written in blood in her bathroom are Doe's words: "I did not kill her. She was given the choice.") For Lust, Doe uses a specially designed dildo-knife as his murder weapon. At a further remove, he does not use the killer dildo personally, but forces a man to wear it and kill with it, thus acting as the stage manager, playwright, and director of the homicidal scene. In the case of Envy, the murder of Tracy Mills occurs at some indeterminate time over several days, when her husband is busy with the crime investigation that leads him to stay away from the house. Finally, with Wrath, Mills's execution of John Doe is catalyzed through the a priori murder of Tracy Mills and is the culminating act to Detective Mills's increasing rage over the previous seven days. In each case, the victim's body is literally the agent of his or her own death, whether through starvation, or through its inverse, force-feeding. Finally, by the elaborately planned insertion of Mills into Doe's temporal scheme, Envy's punishment results in Doe's own death. By making John Mills a narrative and temporal agent ("Become Wrath, David. Become Vengeance"), John Doe writes the script for his own execution.

For John Doe, the nameless city in which he lives is a communal tableau of sin, and it is only through his own elaborate staging of crime and punishment that he can counter his own sense of psychic disintegration. Yet as Detective Somerset adroitly points out to Doe, his sadistic pleasure contradicts his messianic purpose ("If you were chosen—that is, by a Higher Power, if your hand was forced, it seems strange to me that you would get such enjoyment out of it"). Indeed, Doe also takes a certain narcissistic pleasure in anticipating his postmortem notoriety upon the completion of his crime narrative: "People will barely be able to comprehend, but they won't be able to deny. . . . I can't wait for you to see—I really can't. It's really going to be something." Although Doe claims that he is a mere instrument of God's will ("I'm not exceptional—this is, though—what I'm doing—my work") he unconsciously feels he becomes God, and by casting himself in his own morality play through the sin of envy, he inscribes himself as both author and narrative subject. Rather than serving as a warning of the day of Last Judgment, Doe's violence attempts to hasten, if not become a form, of the apocalypse itself.

John Doe's complete narrative mastery is another form of *Se7en*'s construction of dread, in that it shows that Doe foresees, controls, and preordains the future. The film's penultimate scene, in which Doe talks with Detective Mills and Somerset as they drive out of the city, intensifies the atmosphere of anticipatory dread. Whereas the detective's solution of the crime traditionally brings closure to the narrative, here *Se7en* subverts the formula, because midway through the crime series John Doe mysteriously gives himself up to the police. In retrospect, we understand that the blood with which he is covered is that of Tracy Mills, but at this point, our knowledge is as partial and delayed as that of the two detectives. As dread is bound up with knowledge, the film suggests that the failure of both Mills and the wiser Somerset to anticipate Doe's final two crimes (Envy and Wrath) means that Doe remains the master narrator.

Further, John Doe's mastery of the future (in the form of his plans for Detective Mills) and the complete illegibility of his plan for both detectives and viewer help produce the film's unrelenting atmosphere of spectatorial dread. *Se7en* intensifies the conventions of the thriller and mystery genres, which play with the viewer's desire to know and to see; earlier on the phone Doe taunted Mills (and the spectator) by acknowledging this narrative desire: "I feel like saying more, but I don't want to ruin the surprise." His adoption of a narrative series of seven sins that synchronize with the seven days of the narrative only intensifies this desire, because as Richard Dyer notes, "We want to know and see the pattern, and the film in turn knows that we do" (32). As the two men prepare to leave the city with Doe on a search for his final victims, Detective Somerset warns his partner, "If John Doe's head splits open and a UFO should fly out, I want you to have expected it."[12] Our desire to anticipate Doe's homicidal conclusion is forestalled by the unexpected introduction of Mills into the crime sequence. The film's shocking final scene in which Tracy Mills's head arrives in a box embodies the dual meanings of apocalypse—which up to that point had been withheld from us. That is, with her head comes destructive violence (decapitation) and revelation (Doe and Mills are guilty of sin, as are we all) of dread.

Discursive Dread

In *Se7en* the act of murder is inextricably linked to its own allegorical representation—in fact, becomes a *discursive* as well as physical phenomenon. As artist, the serial killer uses the body of his victims as text, which the detective-critic (and viewer) must in turn interpret and decode. Doe is also a collector, as he takes trophies as mementos from each murder victim. These trophies form a collection of *Kunstkabinett* or cabinets of curiosities, one for each sin.[13] Recognized through his signature or authorial function, the serial killer's defining attribute is style—whether in the manner of the killings or ritualized modus operandi, homicide figures the serial killer as a postmodern producer through his repetitious masterpiece. Historical serial killers (like Dennis Rader, aka BTK, or Bind-Torture-Kill) have engaged in the construction of their own homicidal personae through letters to the police, diaries, journals, and, in recent years, also through video cameras and Web sites, for they are characterized by compulsive "graphomania and technophilia" (Seltzer 73–78). This self-representation has a feedback relationship with popular culture and cinematic representation, such that the serial killer operates as a metaphoric clone of societal consumption and reproduction. Mills's response to Doe—"You're no messiah. You're a movie of the week. You're a fucking T-shirt at best"—points to the celebrity status of crime in popular culture, and suggests that John Doe's serial narrative will be little more than cultural ephemera in the public's short attention span. At the same time, this scene self-reflexively calls attention to Hollywood's practice of commodifying and selling the apocalyptic dimensions of the serial-killer narrative ("You're no messiah") of which *Se7en* was a highly successful example.

> Ted Bundy, Henry Lee Lucas, Charles Manson, John Wayne Gacy, John Christie, Denis Nilsen, Peter Kürten, Gilles de Rais, Jeffrey Dahmer, Joel Rifkin, Kenneth Bianchi, Ed Gein, Angelo Buono, the Boston Strangler, the Hillside Strangler, the Yorkshire Ripper, the Lipstick Killer, the Coed Killer, the Green River Killer, the Zodiac Killer, Son of Sam, Jack the Ripper, the Lovers' Lane Shooter, the Preppie Murderer, the Corridor Killer, the Night Stalker, the Interstate Killer.

Indeed, as celebrity *Übermenschen*, serial killers often become known by a pop trademark, either tabloid-created, as with the Zodiac Killer, or the Yorkshire Ripper, or self-authored by a signature tag such as Son of Sam or Jack. These tags also name the killer as celebrity author of a specific form of performance, connected to method, victim, or mise-en-scène; their nomenclature is synonymous with their crime as murderer/protagonist, as their identity usually remains unknown until they are caught. Sometimes they are signified by synecdochic locale, such as the Hillside Strangler, the Green River Killer, the Boston Strangler, or by a social tag, such as "the Preppie Killer," "the Coed Killer." Their fictional names intertextually echo earlier discursive forbears. For just as the Yorkshire Ripper echoes Jack the Ripper, serial-killer nicknames remind us of the reiterative commodification of serial killing.

John Doe epitomizes the textual proliferation, circularity, and repetition of the postmodern condition. *Se7en*'s stylish opening credits, which accompany the Nine Inch Nails track "Closer to God," suggest that the erasure of his identity enhances his messianic purpose.[14] In a series of quick-cut extreme close-ups, we see Doe's hands assembling text and image, using scissors and cellophane, and even sewing his journals by hand. The journals contain photos of crime scenes, photographic negatives, Polaroids, X-rays, a CliffsNotes™ diagram of Dante's *Inferno*, photos of s/m bondage and autopsies, clippings from surgical texts, and instructional manuals in police procedure, forensics, and firearms analysis. In this, Doe is the archetypal postmodern bricoleur, assembling cultural ephemera and constructing mixed-media art. He has a compulsive desire to document and map his crimes—his cavernous apartment is filled with thousands of journals "in no discernible order," each filled with microscopic writing in which he pours out his rage at the world. In the face of this mountain of texts (two thousand journals, each with 250 pages), Somerset despairingly remarks that there is *too much* evidence: "If we had fifty men reading in twenty-four hour shifts it'd still take two months." This tidal wave of data stands in for the film's broader reflection of a postmodern anxiety about *too much* representation, in which textuality like crime is also endless and unmanageable; as Somerset despairingly sighs, "Even the most promising clues usually only lead to other clues . . . so many corpses pile up unavenged."

In the face of John Doe's constructed anonymity, Mills and Somerset's pursuit of him also raises broader political questions about the relationship between technology, identity, and privacy, and draws attention to the disciplinary function of technology and its use by the law in the digital era. Somerset tells Mills about an illegal FBI scheme that involves surveillance of reading records in public libraries: "If you want to know who's reading *Purgatory* and *Paradise Lost*, and *Helter Skelter*, the FBI's computers will tell us. Could give us a name." Mills remonstrates that, in addition to being illegal, the scheme is conceptually flawed ("could get a name of some college kid writing a term paper on twentieth-century crime"). Nonetheless, the two detectives use the illegal data that subsequently leads them to John Doe's address. After Detective Mills breaks into his apartment, the detectives bribe a junkie to give them a legal pretext for breaking and entering without a warrant. This narrative point is an allegory for the state's use of technology for the purposes of monitoring and social control. Although the film was released in 1995, it ironically foreshadowed the state powers enabled by the Patriot Act (2001) after 9/11, which enabled the government to view patrons' reading records in libraries and to "sneak and peek" into citizens' homes without their knowledge.

Doppelgänger Dread

Since the battles of Sherlock Holmes and the slippery Moriarty, detectives and criminals have matched wits in a tactical game of move and countermove. However, as the film *Manhunter* suggested, the detective is always vulnerable to overidentifying with the killer. This vulnerability is produced by the psychological insight, if not empathy, that the detective needs in order to construct a behavioral profile of the killer. *Se7en* suggests that Detective Somerset and John Doe are psychological doubles and are contrasted with the impulsive, emotional John Mills. Where Somerset is cool, analytical, and cynical, Mills is impulsive, emotional, and idealistic. Like Detective Somerset, John Doe is "methodical, exacting, and, worst of all, patient," and shares his literary education as well as his disgust with society's apathy, violence, and corruption. Like Somerset, Doe is also responsible for the "death" of a fetus. Like Doe, Somerset lives a life of monastic solitude, in which he is dedicated to his work. After Somerset smashes his metronome, he turns to using a switchblade for dart practice when he cannot sleep. This switchblade even causes some passing interest in the narrative, when his partner Mills asks him, "Where did you get that?" It is this same switchblade that Somerset will later use to cut open the box in which Tracy Mills's head lies. Midway through the case, Mills and Somerset sit drinking at a bar, discussing the broader philosophical issues that the case has brought up for them. Somerset says in despair, "I just don't think I can continue to live in a place that embraces and nurtures apathy as if it was virtue." Somerset is saddened that all people want to do is "eat their cheeseburgers, play the Lotto, and watch television." John Doe shares Somerset's contempt for society's banality and apathy, as one of his journal entries reveals: "What sick ridiculous puppets we are / and what a gross little stage we dance on / What fun we have dancing and fucking / Not a care in the world / Not knowing that we are nothing / We are not what was intended." Doe also writes of an encounter with a stranger who came up and made small talk with him, "My head began to hurt from his banality . . . I suddenly threw up all over him. He was not pleased and I couldn't stop laughing."

When Mills and Somerset go to Doe's apartment, and a gun battle and a chase ensue between the detectives and the killer, Somerset and Doe are dressed almost identically in overcoats and hats, while Mills's costume visually separates him from them. In the ensuing chase scene, crosscutting between Mills, Somerset, and Doe, long shots, and lighting make it difficult to tell the difference between Somerset and Doe. Indeed the visual similarity between the detective and killer's costuming underscores their shared intelligence, erudition, and personal control. In other words, as uncanny doppelgängers, Somerset and Doe draw attention to the permeable boundary between self and other and the ambivalent dread that the serial killer provokes as the "minus" man.[15]

Dread of Familial Dismemberment

When John Doe gives himself up at the police station, he looks at Somerset and says, "I know you," but this remark and his connection with Somerset remain unexplained. This hint at the interchangeability of Somerset and Doe is paralleled by Doe's desire for David Mills's family, a desire (like that of Max Cady in *Cape Fear*) that is based on substituting oneself for the family patriarch. As Doe says to him, "I tried to play husband. I tried to taste the life of a simple man. It didn't work out." John Doe reorders the traditional sequence of the Seven Deadly Sins, for which the culminating sin is usually pride.[16] Instead, Pride becomes the fifth sin in Doe's schema, with Doe's Envy and Detective Mills' Wrath forming the final two sins. Even the mixture of text and number in the film's title subtly draws attention to Doe's choice of Envy as his final sin, and suggests the personal importance that the Mills family plays for Doe. Just as Max Cady demanded retribution from Samuel Bowden in *Cape Fear* ("Good, 'cos if you're not better than me I can have what you have . . . a wife, a daughter"), John Doe changes the trajectory of the Seven Deadly Sins from the broader social critique of the first five murders to the personal and familial focus of the concluding two. By extension, Doe's acknowledgment of his own sin of Envy also implicates the viewer, whose apathy and indifference to sin he has already condemned.

The final scene in the desert outside the city intensifies the dread that has been building over the seven days of the narrative. Like Hitchcock in *North by Northwest* (1959), Fincher exploits the incongruity of the setting. Darkness, rain, and the dreariness of the city have dominated the narrative, but in the final scene the setting is now one of light and maximum visibility. Paradoxically, this final scene also becomes one of scopic dread, which, we recall, is the ambivalent resistance to seeing what one fears, yet already knows. The horror of the film's denouement is Doe's revelation that he has killed the pregnant Tracy Mills (". . . she begged for her life, and for the life of the baby inside of her"), and the revelation of Tracy's pregnancy (which Detective Mills was not yet aware of) is a further indication of Doe's complete narrative control. Given that Tracy's murder is the catalyst to Mills's murder of Doe, it is especially significant that neither Mills nor the spectator ever see her (other than in flashback) in this scene. At exactly 7:07 p.m. a truck unexpectedly appears from nowhere and delivers a box to the detectives. Only Somerset looks in this Pandora's box and acquires the forbidden apocalyptic knowledge (because it reveals through violence) denied to both the viewer and Mills. Our spectatorial dread is intensified by his physical recoil and cryptic comment, "John Doe has the upper hand."

Whereas Doe's five earlier crimes have left behind tableaus of trauma, the final two murders that complete his masterwork produce a new trauma. It is only the spectator's slowly dawning realization about the contents of the box (which parallels that of Mills) that gives the climax its unexpected horror. This is to say, if the dread of the serial killer lies partly in the anonymity and banality epitomized by John Doe, it is also paralleled by the scopic dread of what remains unseen. Somerset warns Mills away from the box, for its contents are too terrible for sight (as spectators we only see a few strands of her hair). This is the only victim whose body is denied to the spectator, for in the previous five deadly sins we had sustained visual access to the grotesque bodies Doe left behind. Here the monstrosity of Doe's literal dismemberment of Mills's family remains hidden, yet its metaphoric dismemberment becomes increasingly apparent. A quick flashback of Tracy appears, intercut with Mills's horrified face, as he slowly realizes that she is dead. She now exists only in his memory, and it is Mills's realization of this that leads him to finally pull the trigger. When Mills shoots Doe, he also destroys his earlier idealistic belief in his own capacity to make a difference, for now all he can do is carry out what Mills already wants him to do. Consequently, *Se7en*'s final scene encompasses a dread that shifts from corporeal violation to professional and familial destruction, for Mills's wife, child, and future have been destroyed.

Unlike the family in *Cape Fear* in chapter 1, Detective Mills and his wife do not survive. The absence of hope and a future for the Mills family underscores the way in which existential dread has paradoxically reemerged, even at the moment of the serial killer's execution. Somerset's despairing warning to Mills that "if you kill him he will win" has indeed come true, and this hopelessness is further underscored by the line "if I only had a future" in "The Heart's Filthy Lesson," which plays over the concluding credits. Just as Helen could choose whether to call the hookman the forbidden five times in *Candyman*, and Pride could choose suicide over disfigurement, Mills's final act is a *voluntary* choice, exemplifying dread. The protraction of this scene as Mills points the gun at Doe, and yet hesitates, suggests the conflict between his obligations to the law and his personal desire for vengeance, and it is the radical freedom that is dread that enables this agonizing conflict. At the same time, Doe's command to "become Vengeance, David. Become Wrath" recasts Mills's *personal* rage and grief in *apocalyptic* terms, shifting from the familial to the biblical. Yet Mills has been so skillfully manipulated by Doe that his act seems to be helplessly predetermined. The consequences of Mills's decision to choose rage and retribution are arrest and imprisonment, with the film ending on a deeply despairing (and classically noir) note. Somerset returns to work with his quiet final observation, "Ernest Hemingway once wrote, 'the world is a fine place, and worth fighting for'—I agree with the second part."

Se7en is a sustained portrait of apocalyptic dread in which the rain never ends, in a perpetual present of continuing trauma. The story of a messianic serial killer who designs a series of stylized homicides that draw upon a theological narrative of catastrophe offers an apocalyptic sermon that both destroys and reveals. The spectatorial and narrative dread that the serial killer engenders is partly a function of "abnormal normality," or the banal anonymity epitomized by the name John Doe. Through his serial repetition, compulsive textuality, and resistance to narrative comprehension, the serial killer is a provocative figure of postmodern culture. Answering social anxieties about the dread of the endless, arbitrary, or meaningless event, John Doe turns murder into an eschatological series, and through his own death produces closure and triumph in an act of narrative mastery. Doe's homicidal allegory is a narrative of social contempt that decries the meaninglessness, arbitrariness, and triviality of crime, rewriting it as sin, and ultimately punishing the nuclear family for this. In the destruction of Detective Mills's pregnant wife, career, and future, the film suggests that there is no transcending of trauma for the family, and that all that will live on is Doe's apocalyptic lesson ("he's preaching to us.") By casting Mills in his master narrative (a role that Mills also accepts), Doe brings about his own death. Yet this death only serves to shift spectatorial dread from the serial killer back out to a broader existential dread, in which the search for meaning and closure are impossible in a desolate world.

In the next chapter, about *Signs* (2002), a film made after the shift into the new millennium, we will see the continuity and intensification of dread after 9/11. Like *Se7en*, dread is connected to familial crisis, and as the chapter will suggest, the dread of unseen forces embodied in supernaturally perfect crop circles is an externalization of the already existing crisis within the familial patriarch, Graham Hess. Unlike *Se7en*, however, the survival narrative of *Signs* offers a conservative narrative framework in which faith unifies and restores the family and its patriarch at a moment of global crisis.

6

Signs of the End of the World

Apocalyptic Dread

M. NIGHT SHYAMALAN'S *SIGNS* (2002) is an extended exploration of the atmosphere of dread in its story of the ominous appearance of crop circles on an isolated family farm. As with his other films, *Signs* reveals Shyamalan's mastery of the horror and mystery genres. Self-consciously appropriating the fin-de-siècle's anxiety about the year 2000, it showcases not only an apocalyptic form of dread, but also a specifically millennial one, dramatizing an eschatological desire to perceive and decode signs. It is the story of the ominous appearance of crop circles on an isolated family farm owned by the Hess family and an extended exploration of the atmosphere of dread. From Nairobi to Jerusalem, crop circles across the globe seem to be the harbinger of an apocalyptic end of days, with the isolation of the story's restricted setting only intensifying its atmosphere of dread. Although the circles turn out to be the beginning of an alien invasion, this chapter suggests that as with *End of Days*, *The Seventh Sign*, and *Stigmata*, the film's "signs" are ultimately a catalyst for addressing a crisis in faith, and are the key to leading the Hess family to survival. Through its atmospheric soundtrack, aerial photography, and skillful editing and framing, the invasion narrative in *Signs* becomes less important than its sustained visual and aural exploration of inchoate dread.

Like many horror films from *The Birds* to *Night of the Living Dead*, the Hess family undergoes a survival narrative, or a story in which a group of characters undergoes a crisis that tests their individual and

127

collective capacity to survive. The film constructs an atmosphere of spatial and aural dread in response to an underlying trauma of familial loss. The repression of this trauma leads to both narrative dread—the anxiety that violence is random and arbitrary—and to memorial dread, or the fear of remembering what one already knows, yet has repressed. Finally, scopic dread or the fear of seeing (and believing) attaches to the crop circles and to the alien invaders who have created them, and points to the close psychological connection between familial trauma and global crisis. Like the cycle of theological and demonic films that appeared in the late nineties, *Signs* is an emblematic case study of apocalyptic dread, because it brings together the nuclear family, religion, and a feeling that the world is about to end.

Grieving over the death of his wife, Colleen (Patricia Kalember), which occurred six months before, the former Episcopalian minister Graham Hess (Mel Gibson) has renounced his profession and belief in God. He lives on a farm surrounded by large cornfields in Bucks County, Pennsylvania, with his children Bo (Abigail Breslin) and Morgan (Rory Culkin), and his brother Merrill (Joaquin Phoenix), a washed-up minor-league baseball player. Suddenly mysterious crop circles appear in the fields behind the house, and the family soon learns that these circles are appearing all over the world. Thousands of UFOs then appear across the planet, and it seems that the crop circles somehow are connected to this alien invasion. The film blends science fiction with horror, as the family barricade themselves within their home, where aliens besiege them. Morgan has several asthma attacks and nearly dies. Then, one day, the aliens mysteriously depart as abruptly as they had arrived; but one alien is left behind, which captures Morgan. The family accidentally discovers that ordinary water burns the alien, and they kill him and rescue Morgan. In the process of this crisis Graham Hess rediscovers his faith, because he remembers his wife's dying words "to swing away," and in hindsight believes these words to be a prophetic sign from God that has saved his family.

From the film's opening shot, the relationship between family and faith is figured as central to the narrative. The first shot looks out the window from the Hess house onto the family backyard, where we see a barbecue, empty swings, and a picnic table, all of which metonymically stand in for the absent family. The second shot is a close-up of a framed photo of the Hess family, with Graham (wearing a minister's collar), his wife Colleen, and their children. Hess wakes up and moves into the frame of the family portrait, which is on a table next to his bed. The mise-en-scène also subtly points to what is absent—the shadow of a cross that has been removed from his bedroom wall reminds us of Graham's lapse in faith. Hess strains to listen and moves through the house, picking up children's toys as he goes. Something is wrong, and the child's screams that we suddenly hear confirm the anxiety-ridden tone of the film's opening score. Graham and Merrill run outside into the cornfields to find out what is wrong, and they discover the first of what will be several crop circles that appear around the farm.

The opening shots of the film and the mise-en-scène represent the *absent presence* of a number of key elements: the absent family (metonymically signified by the deserted objects in the backyard), the deceased mother (in the portrait), the absent children (whose screams point to offscreen space), Hess's absent clerical collar and cross (whose traces are in the photo and on the wall), and finally, the apparently empty crop circles (in fact, the corn is not cut, but bent over to create circular patterns of large open spaces). Shyamalan changed the design of the Hess home from the traditional stone farmhouses of Bucks County, Pennsylvania, to an iconic wooden American farmhouse, and further underscored this iconicity in its red, white, and blue paint scheme, thus aligning the family with the national and global crisis of the crop circles. Later, when the family consults one of Morgan's books on extraterrestrial invasion, they see a painting of a farmhouse that bears an uncanny resemblance to the Hess home. Graham observes, "Looks a little like our house, doesn't it?" to which Bo agrees, remarking, "Same windows." Consequently, the dialectic of absence/presence in these opening scenes already begins to construct an atmosphere of dread, suggesting that all is not well in the family, and that this crisis is not only domestic, but also global.

Dread-ful Atmosphere

Signs creates a profound sense of *spatial dread*, or what I have suggested in the preceding chapters are the feelings provoked by haunted spaces that bear the traces of repressed personal or national traumas, and that continue to torment the family. This spatial dread is conveyed through a number of formal strategies, including the use of extreme high-angle crane or aerial shots that usually begin on the ground and then gradually zoom out to provide a "God's-eye" view of the crop circles. This shift from the micro to the macro scale accentuates the minuscule scale of the characters as human beings, and subtly suggests that there is some unseen deity who seems to watch over human events. The use of wide-angle lenses and tight framing distorts the perceptual field and foregrounds the importance of peripheral vision and the dread of offscreen space, while elements in the extreme foreground threaten by their spatial proximity. The threat of what may lie in offscreen space, and of what is barely glimpsed, enhances the sense of spatial dread, and is intensified by James

Newton Howard's score. Shayamalan asked Howard to cite other famous horror and science-fiction soundtracks, and his composition for the opening credits alludes to the five-note motif of *Close Encounters of the Third Kind* (Steven Spielberg, 1977) and the agitated string ostinato of *Psycho* (Alfred Hitchcock, 1960). This musical intertextuality is but one element in the film's rich array of generic allusions to prominent science-fiction and horror films of the fifties and sixties.[1] Added to the score is the careful manipulation of diegetic sound that, from agitated dog barks to the screams of children, accentuates the dread of what cannot be immediately seen. Through sound, ordinary devices become ominous; for instance, the mysterious crackles and clicks we hear over the baby monitor that Morgan uses as a radio are actually the sounds of the aliens as they communicate with each other.

The narrative's revelation of the first crop circle is a masterful combination of these elements and becomes a guiding motif. When they hear the distant screams of the children, Graham and Merrill run through the cornfields that surround the family farm, and the brusque sound of the cornstalks that impede their progress dominates the soundtrack. In addition, Shayamalan uses cornstalks that are eight or nine feet in height and completely block the protagonists' point of view, intensifying our own spectatorial anxiety. Point-of-view shots and swish pans align the camera completely with the restricted point of view of the characters, and the agitated caw of crows suggests that something is disrupting the natural order. Graham and Merrill come across an open path that bisects the fields like a tunnel, and in a long shot we see the little girl, Bo, standing in the distance. When Graham runs up to her, she says rather cryptically, "Are you in my dream, too?" Her father responds, "This is not a dream," although the heightened visual and aural quality of the film's opening scene is indeed like a nightmare. Graham then finds his son, Morgan, and walks up to him. In a carefully blocked two-shot, Graham faces his son in profile while Morgan faces the camera, staring intently offscreen, and says, "I think God did it." Graham reaches out and pulls Morgan's face into profile to look at him directly, and asks him, "Did what?" Then, in a matching gesture, Morgan pulls his father's face to the right so that he looks in the same direction offscreen, staring directly into the camera. All of this occurs in one long take. Then beginning with a 3/4 shot, we see Graham and Merrill slowly walk right up to the camera, where Graham pauses, and in close-up swallows, as he stares in apprehension. A third shot follows of a close-up of Graham's boots, which shows him slowly walking over bent stalks of corn, with the accompanying sounds of his tentative, crunching steps. A long shot shows us the dogs in the middle of a huge circle in the field. The fifth shot finally zooms out into an aerial

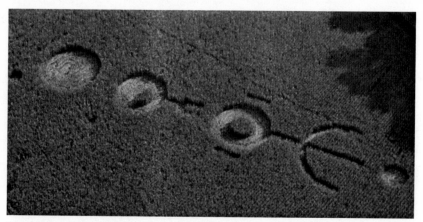

Figure 6.1. Crop Circles as *Signs* (2002). Digital Frame enlargement © Touchstone/Buena Vista Pictures

shot that reveals the pattern of the crop circle as it dwarfs and envelops the four family members. (See figure 6.1.)

The spatial and aural dread conveyed by the surrounding crop fields that wave ominously in the wind and the aerial shots that suddenly reveal the huge scale of "impossibly perfect" crop circles epitomize the mise-en-scène's careful construction of an ominous atmosphere. On the way into town for a family outing, we hear, before Graham turns the radio off, a caller's suggestion that the crop circles "are signs, intended to be seen from the sky." The subsequent aerial shots offer a distant perspective of the family as they drive down the streets of town, not unlike the aerial shots of the Loop in Chicago that begin the opening credit sequence of *Candyman*, discussed in chapter 3; such shots underscore the ways in which the mise-en-scène in both films constructs dread. These aerial shots subtly suggest the visual perspective of the aliens who descend from above to plague the family, town, and planet. At the same time, the aerial shots also suggest the family's ultimate comforting belief that someone is watching over them, and that that someone is God.

Signs

The film's title calls attention to the narrative's self-reflexive concern with the interpretation and decoding of evidence, which, as the introduction suggested, is typical of eschatological hermeneutics; that is to say, there is a concern with finding and decoding *signs* that foreshadow the end of the world. Borrowing the paranoid subtext of fifties' science-fiction cinema, and seventies' conspiracy films, and aligning them with the millennial eschatology of the nineties, the film dramatizes a broad range of community responses to the crop circles that beset the town and surrounding countryside. The film's tone often shifts between a painstaking and incremental buildup of an atmosphere of fear and anxiety and a comedic mocking of American conspiracy theories about extraterrestrials. For example, one day Graham and his family go into town to run errands and have a pizza lunch. While Graham waits to pick up Morgan's asthma prescription, Tracey Abernathy (Merritt Wever), the pharmacy dispensary technician, wants to confess to him, even though he demurs and reminds her he is no longer a minister. Tracey reflects the townspeople's disquiet and rapid turn to understanding the crop circles as signs of the apocalypse. She worriedly says to Graham, "All this stuff on TV, two girls came in talking about the end of the world. I'm just a little scared." With the Hess family, the town's friendly police officer Caroline Paski (Cherry Jones) watches breaking news on the television of a widespread outbreak of crop circles all over India, and asks herself, "What in God's name is going on?" Meanwhile, the bookstore owner who sells Morgan a book about extraterrestrial invasion says that everything that is happening is a "bunch of crock" and "horse manure." He insists that the appearance of the crop circles is an advertising scam designed to sell soda, and claims that he has counted twelve soda ads since the news coverage began, thus foregrounding that television is also a text whose signs can be decoded.

Graham Hess's young children, Morgan and Bo, are convinced that the circles are signs of "extraterrestrials," and after purchasing "Dr. Bimbu's" book on UFOs, they quote from it chapter and verse. Morgan is convinced that the sounds he hears on the baby monitor are "a code" and that the clicking sounds we hear are those of the aliens' voices. Merrill disagrees, saying, "Morgan, this crop stuff is about a bunch of nerds who never had a girlfriend in their lives. They're like thirty and they work up little codes together, and they analyze Greek mythology and make up secret societies, where other guys who never had girlfriends before can join in. They do stupid crap like this to feel special. It's a scam. Nerds were doin' it twenty five years ago—new nerds are doing it again." Meanwhile, television commentators refer to the spate of crop circles that first appeared around the world in the seventies and eighties and that subsequently turned out to be hoaxes. (From them Shyamalan drew his central concept for the film.)[2] Some callers to a radio station insist that the aliens are not there to conquer the earth, but to "harvest the humans," while others insist that it's all just the work of "copycats." Meanwhile, when Merrill goes to an army recruiting station in town, he gets into a conversation with the military officer there. In a drily comedic scene with deadpan delivery, Officer Cunningham (Ted Sutton) interprets the crop circles in the paranoid framework of a military invasion.

CUNNINGHAM: I've got it all figured.

MERRILL: You do?

CUNNINGHAM: I've had two separate folks tell me there've been strangers around these parts last couple of nights. Can't tell what they look like, 'cos they're staying in the shadows, covertlike. No one's been hurt, mind you, and that's the giveaway.

MERRILL: I see.

CUNNINGHAM: It's called probing. It's a military procedure. You send out a reconnaissance group, very small. Check things out. Not to engage but to evaluate—the situation—evaluate the level of danger—make sure things are all clear.

MERRILL: Clear for what?

CUNNINGHAM: For the rest of them.

This scene parodies the xenophobia and insularity that lurks behind this small, rural community's fear of outsiders ("there've been strangers round these parts"). Moreover, this xenophobia is also suggested by the way in which the bookstore owner's wife says she kept the store's one book on UFOs (which had come by mistake) for "the city folks." Officer Cunningham's observation that you "can't tell what they look like" suggests an anxiety about identification and outsiders. If the aliens cannot be recognized as such (in fact, they do have camouflage abilities), then they could be anybody, and consequently, as in *Invasion of the Body Snatchers* (Don Siegel, 1956) (which Shyamalan specifically has acknowledged as a source), could take over humans, one by one. The scene also parodies the long-standing paranoid tradition in American culture that has been the subject of films including *The Manchurian Candidate* (John Frankenheimer, 1962), *Seconds* (John Frankenheimer, 1966), *The Parallax View* (Alan J. Pakula, 1974), *Conspiracy Theory* (Richard Donner, 1997), and *The X-Files* (Chris Carter, TV series, 1993–2002; film, Rob Bowman, 1998). At the same time the scene also foregrounds paranoia as another form of reading and interpreting signs. Many of these paranoid narratives bring together wild-eyed theories about government cover-ups, alien abductions, or body "probing," emblematized by the classic conspiracy theory that an alien aircraft crash-landed in Roswell, New Mexico (a theory alluded to in *Independence Day*). This paranoid compulsion to find prophetic signs of the end-times is a central component in apocalyptic dread.

Gossip, rumor, hypothesis, and the plots of Hollywood movies are all ways in which the town frames its fears and anxieties—as Merrill says, the alien invasion is "like *War of the Worlds*." Morgan solemnly states that the aliens "wouldn't use our technology or use airborne weapons," because "the aliens know we would then use nuclear weapons, thus making the planet useless for their purposes." Graham Hess refers to the town veternarian Ray Reddy's theory (in a cameo by Shyamalan) that the aliens "don't like water," when he suggests that the family go to their summer home on a lake. To which Morgan retorts that this "sounds made up" (although Morgan's own theories about the aliens come directly from the plots of fifties' science-fiction narratives). Officer Cunningham's paranoid, xenophobic theory is comically paralleled by another scene in which Officer Paski comes to question the Hess family after the initial appearance of crop circles on their property. In another deadpan scene, she asks the Hess brothers for a description of a mysterious figure they glimpsed on their roof the night before, asking them if they have seen any "strangers" around, and mentioning that there were reports of a strange woman in town who was seen "cursing" when a cigarette machine did not have her particular brand. Paski wonders if the figure the Hess brothers saw at night on their roof could be this woman. Yet the comedic portrait in *Signs* of paranoia and its liberal critique of xenophobia temporarily disguise the conservative agenda of the film, which, in its dialectic of rationality and faith, will ultimately privilege religious belief.

Signs understands the global crisis in binary, if not Manichaean, terms, offering simple either/or choices: it is either aliens or a scam. In the words of the "Columbia university professor" (Clifford David), "There are only a limited number of possibilities: either this is one of the most elaborate hoaxes ever created or basically it's for real." This paranoid binary thinking is the very thing critiqued in *The Day the Earth Stood Still* (Robert Wise, 1951), in which human beings respond violently to aliens who come to warn them that their nuclear arms race imperils their own planetary existence. In that invasion narrative, human paranoia about the aliens' malevolent intentions leads to tragic consequences. Similarly, Morgan summarizes Dr. Bimbu's book on extraterrestrials as follows: "There are two possibilities: either the aliens are friendly and are making contact in the spirit of exploration" or "they are hostile and looking to harvest earth for its resources." (This latter possibility points ahead to the aliens in *War of the Worlds*, discussed in our next chapter.) Moreover, there are only two possible outcomes to the alien invasion: "Either the aliens fight and are defeated, and leave (only to return at some future point in their hundreds of thousands)" or "they win." Morgan's thinking unconsciously reflects his father's binary approach to the world. We see this binarism illustrated in the following conversation Graham has with his brother Merrill, in a scene in which he divides the world into two groups: believers and unbelievers.

MERRILL: Some people are probably thinking this is the end of the world.

GRAHAM: That's true.

MERRILL: Do you think it could be?

GRAHAM: Yes . . . People break down into two groups. When they experience something lucky, group number one sees it as more than luck, more than coincidence. They see it as a sign, evidence that there is someone up there watching out for them. Group number two sees it as just pure luck, a happy turn of chance. I'm sure that people in group number two are looking at those fourteen lights in a very suspicious way. For them, this situation is a 50-50. Could be bad, could be good, but deep down, they feel that whatever happens they're on their own, and that fills them with fear. Yeah. There are those people. But there's a whole lot of people in the group number one. They see those fourteen lights, they're looking at a miracle, and deep down they feel that whatever's going to happen, there will be someone there to help them, and that fills them with hope. So what you have to ask yourself is, what kind of person are you? Are you the kind that sees signs, sees miracles? Or do you believe that people just get lucky? Or look at the question this way: is it possible that there are no coincidences?

When Merrill asks his brother which type he is, Graham claims to be one of the members of the first group. Graham explains his wife's dying words, "Merrill, swing away," as "the nerve endings in her brain were firing as she died." He suggests to his brother that "some random memory of one of your baseball games popped into her head." However, his tone in describing the people in group two as "them" suggests an unconscious distancing from their position ("Yeah. There are those people."). Hess's binarism suggests that either there is belief or not, either there is hope or there is fear, and either there is the comfort offered by faith or there is profound alienation. The binarism unconsciously suggests a profound anxiety about "chance," "coincidence," or "luck" as arbitrary, random, or meaningless events. As the film will subsequently show with Hess's return to faith, apocalyptic dread replaces the anxiety of the aleatory and meaningless with a preordained narrative authored by God.

Hess's anxiety is an example of narrative dread, or the anxieties prompted by the accidental violence and death of everyday life. In the previous chapter, we saw that the serial killer John Doe responded to random urban crime with an overdetermined theological narrative of the Seven Deadly Sins. He rewrote the future by constructing a master narrative in which he had complete power and control, and in which he was the author and stage director of his crimes, and even of his own demise. In *Signs*, because Hess is traumatized by the arbitrary quality of his wife's death in a tragic accident, he sees his God as cruel and sadistic (he says to God, "I hate you" and "Don't do this to me again" when his son has an asthma attack). As part of this narrative dread, Hess's speech also reflects a profound anxiety about human aloneness in the world; as Kierkegaard had said, "Deep within every human being there still lives the anxiety over the possibility of being alone in the world, forgotten by God, overlooked among the millions and millions in this enormous household" (Kierkegaard, *Journals* 1: 40). The faith that Hess has temporarily disavowed at this point in the narrative will ultimately return, providing him with the hope and comfort ("there will be someone there to help them") the family needs to guide it through its present crisis. For Hess, this will be God, in the form of his wife's words.

In a characteristic move that recurs throughout the film, comic bathos undercuts the elevated gravity of Hess's conversation with his brother. Merrill responds by recounting an inane story:

> I was at this party once. I'm on the couch with Randa McKinney. She was just sitting there, looking beautiful, staring at me. I go to lean in and kiss her, and I realize I have gum in my mouth. So I turn, take out the gum and stuff it in a paper cup next to the sofa. I turn around, and Randa McKinney throws up all over herself. I knew the second it happened it was a miracle. I could have been kissing her when she threw up. That would have scarred me for life. I may never have recovered.

Merrill's silly suggestion that it was fate that Randa McKinney didn't vomit on him deflates the solemnity of the moment, and typifies the shifts in tone between an investment in faith and a parody of superstition;

Hollywood continues to have it both ways, since it is a culturally conservative industry that wants to appeal to as wide an audience as possible.

Apocalyptic Dread

Like other theological and demonic fin-de-siècle cinema and television such as *End of Days*, *Stigmata*, and *Revelations*, in which science and belief are opposing terms, *Signs* brings together an acute apocalyptic dread or anxiety about the future of the world and the increasing political influence of Christian conservatism in the last two decades. Morgan's claim that "everything that people have written about in science books is going to change" suggests that history can only be understood in eschatological terms, and by reframing science in terms of extraterrestrial invasion, Morgan's claim points to a fundamentalist Christian political movement, which as chapter 1 outlined, opposes the scientific premises of liberal humanist education. I suggest that this conservative politics informs the narrative's privileging of faith in times of crisis, and further, that *Signs* is less a science-fiction narrative than it is a philosophical exploration of the relationship between a nostalgic representation of the traditional nuclear family and its dependence on theology. The fact that Morgan is a firm believer in extraterrestrials is a related version of the Hess family's theological beliefs—that there are higher powers, that these forces are beyond human comprehension or intellectual capacity, and that the history of the world is preordained by God.

As part of this theological narrative, the characterization of Graham Hess's youngest child, Bo, who is described as "like an angel," reminds us of the young children Gertie (played by Drew Barrymore) and Elliot (Henry Thomas) in *E.T.: The Extraterrestrial* (Steven Spielberg, 1982) and Carol Anne Freeling (Heather O'Rourke) in *Poltergeist* (Tobe Hooper, 1982). In these films, as in others like *The Sixth Sense* (M. Night Shyamalan, 1999), *Mac and Me* (Stewart Raffill, 1988), *Matilda* (Danny DeVito, 1996), *The Village of the Damned* (Wolf Rilla, 1960), *The Omen* (Richard Donner, 1976), and their respective sequels, children have a special relationship with the supernatural, demonic, or extraterrestrial. The narrative suggests that Bo, like the children in many of these films, has the gift of prophetic second sight. When Morgan has an asthma attack in the basement, she says, "I dreamed this," and earlier on she had said cryptically, "I don't want you to die." However, Hollywood has it both ways again, as Bo is a paradoxical blend of the supernatural and the empirical. She precociously uses scientific language (she is a fan of the animated cartoon *Dexter's Laboratory*) and claims that it is because of the presence of "amoebas" in the water that she leaves glasses of unfinished water all over the house. Morgan describes his sister's neurosis as "like a tic" which she's "always had," but it has clearly been exacerbated by the trauma of the loss of her mother six months before. By voicing a concern that the water is, in her words, "contaminated," Bo's neurosis reminds us of a growing domestic concern about environmental pollution and global warming that became more pronounced in the nineties. Malcolm Bradbury points out that "The ends of millennia are notorious for the rise of apocalyptic fear, and though our Einstein's monsters change from nuclear threat to ozone depletion and global warming, the consciousness of uncertainty is with us again" (qtd. in Melling 168).

Television and Scopic Dread

The crop circle becomes a figure of scopic dread, prompting an intense ambivalence about what one fears to confront. Introducing a report on new crop circles appearing around the world a television reporter says, "What you are about to see may disturb you," and goes on to stress that, "The image has not been adjusted or enhanced in any way. What you are seeing is real. It's unbelievable." Indeed, Merrill rapidly becomes obsessed with watching the television coverage, and stays up all night watching the news in the closet (where he has placed the TV set in order to prevent the children from getting more distressed). The dread of looking is only further heightened when the alien ships suddenly disappear. It soon becomes apparent that the ships have not actually left, but are now invisible beneath a huge optical shield in the sky. Merrill excitedly reports to his brother that the latest news from Mexico City suggests that the ships have disappeared, but "they're not really gone—we just can't see them." The TV then shows footage of a bird flying toward the place where the ships had been, and then abruptly falling out of the sky as if it had struck some invisible physical barrier. This news clip points to the ways in which scopic dread is concerned with what is *unseen*, but which, like the bird's collision with an invisible object, metonymically points to something which is already there.

Wanting to see, yet being terrified of what we might see, becomes closely connected to the narrative function of television as a site of dread. When Merrill watches a breaking news item showing a home video of an alien sighting at a children's birthday party in Passo Fundo, Brazil, he comically foregrounds our own spectatorial frustration, shouting "Move children, vamanos!" as they block the frame (and our point of view). Reaction and point-of-view shots then reveal a shaky and brief image of an alien in the distance; Merrill shrieks and moves back in horror, comically ending up in the closet. The comedy is furthered when Merrill starts wearing a tinfoil hat that the children had created earlier "so the aliens can't read our minds," and like his nephew and niece sits mouth agape in front of the television. In fact, Merrill's increasingly childlike response to the crisis becomes a surrogate for our own insertion into the narrative as spectators. The crop circles are now in India, England, Israel, and Kenya; the television reports they are in over "274 cities, and are expected to spread to 400 worldwide," and Shyamalan repeatedly shows wide-angle shots of the family staring directly into the camera (which stands in for the television set), with the blue-gray light of the screen flickering on their faces. The television reporter then rapidly shifts from the invasion narrative of science fiction to invoking the consolation of religion: "Hundreds of thousands have flocked to temples, synagogues, and churches. God be with us all."

The Hess family's isolation in the country is implicitly counterpointed with the global intimacy and solidarity that television offers as a unifying social practice at times of social crisis. But at the same time that it is a ritualistic site for communal gathering, as it was in the days after 9/11, television is also a source of anxiety and fear, which prompts Graham to hide the television and ban his children from any further obsessional watching. In this way, as a medium for both consoling and provoking anxiety, television figures the paradoxical ambivalence of dread. The close relationship between dread and the scopic is reinforced by the fact that the apocalypse's duration matches its televisual coverage in the narrative; the apocalypse's beginning is signaled when the television abruptly goes off the air ("it's started") and is officially over when television begins transmitting again.

The crisis ends with an eschatological outcome, that is, when people in the Holy Land come up with a method to defeat the aliens. As the television reports, "We know the battle turned around in the Middle East. Three small cities found a primitive method to defeat them." Like the ending of the British science-fiction classic *The Day of the Triffids* (Steve Sekeley and Freddie Francis, 1963), the aliens are defeated by a simple thing—ordinary water. Similarly, according to Revelations, in the battle of Megiddo, faith will defeat the Antichrist. In Graham Hess's mind, his rediscovery of faith allows him to save his family from the aliens. The thematic role that faith and national unity plays in *Signs* was also an important part of the social context of the film's production, as shooting was simultaneous with the events of 9/11 and its immediate aftermath. In fact, the day when Shyamalan shot the narrative's pivotal scene of familial trauma—of Colleen Hess's car accident and death—was September 12, and the cast and crew had a vigil for the New York victims

before commencing shooting. The somberness of the narrative content of
the production schedule for that day also provided an uncanny intersection with the real-life dread occasioned by 9/11. In fact, the fall of the
twin towers was also uncanny; as was widely discussed by both witnesses
and commentators, it was eerily reminiscent of "a scene from a disaster
movie," so frequently had New York City been the setting for apocalyptic
disaster in films from *Deluge* (Felix Feist, 1933) to *The Beast from 20,000
Fathoms* (Eugene Lourie, 1953), *Independence Day* (Roland Emmerich,
1996), *Godzilla* (Roland Emmerich, 1998), and *The Day After Tomorrow*
(Roland Emmerich, 2004). Further, 9/11 occasioned extensive conspiracy
theories, including widespread debate about an image of the collapsing
twin towers that appeared to show the face of the devil (see figure 6.2).
Conspiracy theorists and religious believers were convinced that this
showed the devil gloating at the "evil" committed that day.[3] The interpretation of the image as diabolical points to the wider currency of apocalyptic dread at the turn of the century, and also relies upon the
epistemological authority of the visual image, expressed by the phrase
"seeing is believing."

The prominence of the visual dimension of 9/11 closely aligns itself
with the central theme of *Signs*: that the crop circles signify the end of the
world, and that the alien invasion of the planet is a global test of faith.
The mise-en-scène's dialectical play between what is visible and what
remains unseen connects to the familial trauma that lies buried in Graham Hess's memory. Flashbacks play a key role in the narrative, suggesting the anxiety or memorial dread that overlays repressed events from the
past. Like Selena St. George's repression of her sexual abuse in *Dolores
Claiborne*, it is only when Hess allows himself to fully remember the
traumatic night of his wife's death, and her dying words, that he comes
up with the solution to the film's final crisis, when an alien threatens his
son. Driving home from work one day, Ray Reddy fell asleep at the wheel
and ran over Colleen. With her lower torso crushed by the car, Colleen
was pinned to a tree trunk, remaining alive as long as the car compressed
her. Officer Paski fetched Hess so that he could say good-bye to his wife
before she died; then the police moved the car, and she quickly died.

Memorial Dread

The film shows three flashbacks, which incrementally show the final farewell between Hess and Colleen. The first of these flashbacks occurs
immediately after Graham and Merrill's discussion about those who believe in signs, or who see them as chance. This juxtaposition in editing
suggests the connection between Hess's loss of faith in signs and his wife's

Figure 6.2. The Face of the Devil? 9/11 and Apocalyptic Dread © Mark D. Phillips

death. The flashback simply shows Hess arriving at the scene of the accident, and ends with Paski saying, "She's not in an ambulance, Father." At this point, the restricted narration does not yet reveal that Colleen is dying, nor does it show us the final exchange between husband and wife. The second flashback occurs as the family sits trapped by the aliens in the basement, resigned to their inevitable death.[4] It reveals that Reddy's truck "severed most of [Colleen's] lower half" and that she will not live. Officer Paski tells Hess that "Her body is pinned in such a way that it's alive when it shouldn't be alive." Paradoxically both lifelike and yet (already) dead, Colleen's body is an example of the uncanny's strange mixture of the familiar and unfamiliar, which produces dread. In addition, the severing of Colleen's body becomes a metaphoric figure for the traumatic effect her death will have for both Graham and his family.

The third flashback does not occur until the film's climax, just after the family comes up from the basement. They discover that there is still a wounded alien in the house, which seizes Morgan, who is still unconscious from an asthma attack. When Merrill and Graham surround the alien, it starts spraying Morgan with a poisonous gas. It is only then that Graham Hess finally remembers his wife's dying words to him, as the flashback returns in its lengthiest version.

> COLLEEN: Tell Morgan to play games. It's okay to be silly.
>
> GRAHAM HESS: I will.
>
> COLLEEN: Tell Bo to listen to her brother. He'll always take care of her.
>
> GRAHAM HESS: I will.
>
> COLLEEN: Tell Graham—
>
> GRAHAM HESS: I'm here.
>
> COLLEEN: Tell him . . . to see. Tell him to see. And tell Merrill to swing away.

Colleen's dying words (twice repeated) tell Graham to "see." Hess has not disclosed these words, only telling his brother that she said for him to "swing away." In this way, seeing becomes linked to *revelation*, undoing scopic dread with theology. Hess now believes that his wife's words were prophetic—for they give him the idea to tell Merrill to use his baseball bat and "swing away" at the alien (and thereby rescue Morgan from its grasp). Merrill's bat knocks over a glass of water left by Bo, which sprays over the alien, burning it like acid and killing it.

Up to this point we have had only brief glimpses of the aliens— walking in the corn, on the Hess roof, in a TV clip, and so on. This play between seeing and not seeing, between revealing yet withholding, only enhances the scopic dread of what threatens the family. When Graham

Hess first sees the alien, it is through *its reflection in the television screen*, which underscores the connection between the global crisis of the crop circles and the technological means by which this crisis is mediated and intensified. Further, it is a reflection of the object of familial horror; like Candyman in the mirror in chapter 3, it is another example of *specular dread*, or that dread which attaches to a figure that, in its doubled or mirrored form, embodies the repressions that the family disavows. A close-up shows us that the alien has chameleon defenses: its skin takes on the plaid pattern of Morgan's shirt. The use of the television as visual media-tor for our first prolonged sight of the alien, together with the alien's own camouflaging capacity, suggests that the alien metaphorically acts as a mirror by reflecting the anxieties and ambivalences that beset the family. Appropriately, our final shot of the dying alien appears as a reflection on the television screen. Just as the invasion crisis is bracketed by its televisual meditation, so too is the alien linked to the TV, which here becomes the site of revelation. Moreover, just as the crop circles functioned as naviga-tional devices for the aliens landing on earth, so too do the aliens act as visual markers of dread, as displaced figures for the familial trauma of maternal loss.

The loss of Colleen Hess and the concomitant loss of faith of the familial patriarch have engendered a profound crisis that divides the fam-ily. Under the influence of the alien invasion, even the family dogs turn murderous and attack the children, leading Morgan to kill one in order to protect his sister, Bo. Morgan blames his father, believing that he "let Mom die." Similarly, Merrill blames his brother for succumbing to fear and a lack of faith in the family's capacity to survive: "There's things that I can take. And a couple of things I can't. One of them I can't take is when my older brother, who's everything I want to be, starts losing faith in things." Merrill's confrontation with his brother is a turning point, as Hess's rediscovery of his faith becomes key to the family's survival. When the family was barricaded in the basement and surrounded by aliens, Morgan began to have breathing difficulties because he was without his asthma medication. Graham talked his son through the attack, repeating the phrases "Don't be afraid," and "Believe" in an incantatory way. This was the first moment that he began to use faith to protect his family. Like Abraham, Hess does not have to sacrifice his son in God's test of faith, for which he had earlier said, "I'm not ready."

Ironically, all the traumatic events that happen to the family, from asthma to maternal death, and from childhood neurosis to alien attack, become part of God's master plan, and in the film's celebration of faith they are ultimately more comforting than the dread of "chance" or the even more uncanny "coincidence." In other words, violence is most terrifying when it is meaningless, and the narrative dread that this prompts for the family is displaced onto an apocalyptic framework of alien invasion. Adopting an eschatological narrative allows the Hess family to understand everything that happened to their world in apocalyptic terms, and indeed the very name of their town, "Newtown," subtly connects them to Puritan millennialism. Colleen had reassured Graham that her death "was meant to be." Similarly, Ray Reddy also believes that Colleen's death was preordained: "Most of the ride home, there wasn't a car in sight in either direction. It had to be at that right moment—ten, fifteen seconds when I passed her walking. It was like it was meant to be."

Graham now believes God preordained everything that has happened to the family: "That's why you had asthma. It can't be luck. His lungs were closed. His lungs were closed. No poison got in. No poison got in." When Morgan revives after the alien's death, he says, "Dad, did someone save me?" and Graham responds, "I think someone did." Having survived the crisis, the family's reunification is underscored by the final scene's long take, in which the camera pans back and forth between the four family members (with the family house framed prominently in the background) as they digest the implications of the "miracle" that they have just experienced.

As the introduction noted, dread connects with a presentiment that the future will follow a particular prophesied course, which the decoding of signs can anticipate. Hess now believes that his wife's death was not meaningless, but that her dying words were clues that would save her family long after her death. By finally *remembering* and *seeing*, Hess now understands God's signs, and transforms his scopic and memorial dread into a rediscovery of faith. The existential dread of the aleatory and the meaningless is replaced by signs of the apocalypse, which prophesy and reveal the comforting hand of God. For *Signs*, faith is as simple as the glass of water that destroys the alien, restoring the nuclear family to the imaginary unity that preceded trauma. It offers a way of dealing with the traumas that have beset this family, retrospectively understanding that violence and death have been part of God's plan. In such a way, then, apocalyptic dread, imagined here as the alien invasion that threatens the end of the world, becomes a deeply conservative parable about the integral connection between religion and the survival of the nuclear family.

7

War of the Worlds

Uncanny Dread

ACCORDING TO EXHIBITOR RELATIONS, theatrical receipts were down 7.8% in the summer of 2005, and the only blockbusters that made any money were *Batman Returns, War of the Worlds,* and *The Fantastic Four* (Gross 14). Adapted from the 1898 H. G. Wells novel about invading Martians that strike at the heart of London, *War of the Worlds* (Steven Spielberg, 2005) had seen many previous adaptations, with Paramount originally optioning it for Cecil B. DeMille in the thirties. The most famous adaptations have been Orson Welles's notorious October 30, 1938, CBS Radio broadcast of the Mercury Theater production, which struck terror into the hearts of (some) listeners, and the 1953 Byron Haskin film, but there have been several other TV movies and straight-to-video productions, including two adaptations in 2005 designed to capitalize on interest in Spielberg's release.[1]

War of the Worlds reflects the broader cultural climate of dread and paranoia that the Bush administration continued to stoke, with ever more desperation as the War in Iraq entered its third year, and American service casualties passed eighteen hundred (at the time of the film's release). In fact, the cultural context of this perennial classic of terror points to important sociocultural anxieties in each decade in which it has been adapted for radio, television, or screen. Wells's original story decried the evils of imperial colonialism, comparing the Martians' ruthless extermination of humans with our own and urging us to remember "what ruthless and utter destruction our own species has wrought, not only upon animals such as the vanished bison and the dodo, but upon its inferior races. The Tasmanians, in spite of their human likeness, were entirely swept out of existence in a war of extermination waged by European immigrants, in the space of fifty years" (Wells 11). H. G. Wells's depiction of poison gas, mechanized death, and colossal loss of life anticipated the horrors of World War I, just as Orson Welles's 1938 radio broadcast triggered anxieties in an American public jittery about impending war in Europe. In fact, *War of the Worlds* has been widely understood as prophetic—predicting tanks, aerial bombardment, nuclear war, poison gas, robots, and lasers (Brians 1995).

Spielberg updates Wells's science-fiction invasion drama by shifting its setting from London to contemporary New Jersey and by transforming his unnamed narrator from a married but childless man into a divorced father and Jersey longshoreman named Ray Ferrier (Tom Cruise), whose children—the ever screaming Rachel (Dakota Fanning) and the sullen teenager Robbie (Justin Chatwin)—live with his ex-wife, Mary Ann (Miranda Otto), and her new husband. As with many Spielberg films since *E.T.*, the narrative foregrounds the familial divisions and conflicts that are part of divorce. A deadbeat and inattentive dad (he offers peanut butter sandwiches to a daughter who is allergic to them), Ferrier has just picked up his two kids from Mary Ann for a weekend visit when the invasion begins. Having already promised his ex-wife that he will keep the kids safe, Ferrier finds redemption in rediscovering his paternal role and like Dennis Quaid's character Jack Hall in *The Day After Tomorrow* (Roland Emmerich, 2004), Ferrier also makes an epic journey. He travels from New Jersey to Boston to reunite his children with their mother. Like the disaster movies of the turn of the past century such as *Armageddon, Deep Impact*, and *The Day After Tomorrow*, *War of the Worlds* places the nuclear family at the center of the crisis and links its survival to the national and global crisis.

Indeed, the atmosphere of apocalyptic dread is particularly distinctive in Spielberg's suspenseful remake, which hews closely to the original story, especially in its reuse of the alien ships that march around on tripods using death rays and poison gas to kill. Because the aliens are unused to earth's gravitational field, as Wells explains, they need the tripod legs to "walk" around in their spacecraft. Further, Spielberg's remake repeats the original film's ending in which the invasion suddenly failed, as the aliens succumbed to earthborn microbes against which they had no immunity. Where it differs, besides in its contemporary American setting, is in the film's extensive references to 9/11 and terrorism as the new marker of dread in the twenty-first century, with Spielberg acknowledging that his film was "about Americans fleeing for their lives, being attacked for no reason, having no idea why they are being attacked and who is attacking them" (Rothstein B1). Startling for its vivid portrait of suspenseful urban carnage, the film's imagery includes several set pieces that specifically recall the destruction of the World Trade Center, including the clouds of clothing that float to the ground after the death rays of the aliens vaporize fleeing humans. In response to an electromagnetic pulse sent out by the alien craft, airplanes fall out of the sky. As panic rises in New Jersey and across the globe, missing posters can be seen everywhere as Ferrier tries to keep his family safe, and people ask each other, "Did you lose anyone?" In broader terms, 9/11 is also evoked through the film's iconic images of disaster, which abound: a train that is on fire rockets past stunned survivors waiting at a railroad crossing; a river full of bodies flows past a stunned child's eyes; a downed airplane's wing and tail lie amid the detritus of a suburban street; and a crack in the sidewalk widens and heaves upward as a monumental spacecraft appears from under the earth.

Ironically, a few weeks after *War of the World*'s release in the United States on June 23, 2005, terrorist bombs on the London Underground and a double-decker bus killed fifty-six people, and the United States government nervously anticipated further strikes in the homeland. When the ships first emerge like sleeper cells from their burial sites all over the earth, beginning in Ferrier's hometown of Bayonne, New Jersey, his daughter shrieks, "Is it the terrorists?" As A. O. Scott in the *New York Times* sardonically put it in a recent review of the film, the answer to her question was, "Well, sort of, sweetheart. In a metaphorical sense, that is" (B1). The semantic slippage between intergalactic aliens and the xenophobic anxiety about "immigrant aliens" that has led to acts of profiling and violence against Arabs, both citizens and nonresidents alike, since 9/11 displace American anxieties about the inscrutable and relentless nature of terrorist violence or the "threat from within" onto the representation of a similarly inscrutable, relentless, and violent alien invasion. Indirectly invoking American anxieties of terrorist sleeper cells, one of the film's advertising taglines was "They're already here," alluding to the story's alien spacecraft that have uncannily lain dormant beneath the earth since the dawn of human existence, awaiting the signal to begin the invasion. In the suggestion that the aliens have left "sleeper" tripods buried beneath the earth, Spielberg has altered an important aspect of Wells's story of the invasion, which began when ten rocket cylinders were shot from Mars to Earth over ten days, and which then "unscrewed" to reveal the Martians within. By contrast, Spielberg shows the aliens coming down in mysterious lightning strikes that appear all over the world, and that channel them into their waiting ships. The Spielbergian addition underscores the film's atmosphere of dread. Further, Spielberg shifts the traditional representation of the aliens of classic fifties' science-fiction films like *The Day the Earth Stood Still* (1951), *It Came From Outer Space* (1953), and *Invasion of the Bodysnatchers* (1956), where the aliens appear uncannily *like* human beings, into creatures who appear profoundly different. In other words, whereas the earlier science-fiction films were allegories of similarity as part of their cold war concern with Communist infiltration, here the alien invasion is an allegory about the *anxiety of proximity*, alluding to the invisibility of sleeper-cell Muslim terrorists. Terrorism is a continuing theme in Spielberg's work, and his next film, *Munich* (2005), was an examination of the murders of six Israeli athletes at the 1972 Olympic games by the Palestinian group Black September. Spielberg said this film would be an evenhanded examination of the consequences of terrorism for both victims and attackers, and would look critically at the systematic assassination tactics adopted by Mossad in revenge for the murder of the Israeli athlete. In fact, *War of the Worlds* was originally to be filmed in 2006 after the release of *Munich*, but after gaps opened up in Cruise and Spielberg's schedules, production was hastily approved in August 2004.

In addition to the intertextual role of 9/11 and the war on terror, Spielberg critiques George Bush's invasion of Iraq (2003), with another advertising slogan for the film noting, "This summer, the last war on earth won't be started by humans." Early in the story, and before the invasion begins, another reference to American military policy is made through Robbie's homework project, which his mother warns him not to put off until the last moment. He must write an essay on "the French occupation of Algeria," which recalls Gillo Pontecorvo's classic *Battle of Algiers* (1966, Italy), a film that was notoriously studied by the Pentagon as part of its counterinsurgency research for dealing with the uprisings in Iraq. When the invasion starts, Robbie is angry and pugnacious, and wants to join the army to "get back at them," again echoing some public responses to the 9/11 attacks. Midway through the story, Robbie disappears, so determined is he to join up with the army in its battle against the aliens ("I have to see this"). We assume he is dead, but later he turns up unscathed with his mother in Boston.[2] Occurring offscreen, Robbie's own journey is classic Spielbergian narrative territory in which, as in *A. I.*, a young boy's desire is to reunite with his mother. Here Spielberg changes his traditional preadolescent boy into a teenager, and thus adds oedipal dimensions to this journey of desire. However, the primary focus of the narrative remains with Ferrier's young daughter, Rachel.

On the way to Boston, Ferrier seeks shelter with Harlan Ogilvy (Tim Robbins), who turns out to be a dangerous and paranoid basement dweller, itching to begin an underground war of resistance against the aliens. Spielberg's Ogilvy is a composite of several characters in the original story, including the Curate, Ogilvy, and the Artilleryman. With an intertextual wink to the audience, Spielberg casts Robbins (a public opponent to the 2003 American invasion of Iraq) in the role of Ogilvy, who tells Ferrier that "occupations always fail." Ogilvy is so determined to attack an alien probe that is searching the basement that he imperils Ferrier and his daughter's lives. His paranoia and aggression are such that Ferrier ultimately has to beat him to death, in another important change from the original story, in which the Curate was merely knocked out by the Narrator, and a Martian tentacle dragged him out and killed him. Spielberg also suggests that Ogilvy may be a pedophile, when Ogilvy creepily promises Rachel that he will "look after her" if something happens to her father. Here, then, Spielberg has it both ways: he shows the unforeseen violence that is necessitated by Ferrier's struggle to survive and protect his family, and yet at the same time critiques that violence brought about by militarism and invasion. The dread of what Ferrier has done is intensified by his urging his daughter "not to look" in a number of scenes. He blindfolds his daughter so that she will not see the downed airplane and scene of devastation when he emerges from the basement, warning her that "You're gonna want to look around, but you're not going to." The scene is an embodiment of the ambivalence of scopic dread; on the one hand, the daughter must not see the traumatic crashed plane, so evocative of 9/11, but at the same time, the incongruity of a downed airplane's tails and wings amid suburbia offers a compelling spectacle of disaster for the audience. Like Rachel, we want to look, but the sight threatens to traumatize.

Similarly, Ferrier also kills Ogilvy offscreen, away from both his daughter's and our own eyes, but the editing accentuates this theme of transgressive sight by crosscutting between Rachel (who has been blindfolded by her father so she cannot see) and Ferrier about to kill Ogilvy. Ferrier tells his daughter to sing herself a lullaby, so that she won't hear the sounds of violence in the next room. Then the narration becomes restricted, as the camera frames Ferrier shutting the door, denying the spectator the primal scene of violence. Like Danny in *Cape Fear*, her parent forbids Rachel from looking at traumatic scenes of violence. Elsewhere, when the family stops so that Rachel can go to the bathroom, Ray instructs her to "stay within sight," but she disobeys, and sees a river full of dead bodies (probably from the plane that had crashed earlier, which she was not permitted to see). Finding her, Ray covers her eyes yet again, an action he repeatedly does throughout the film. Ferrier's attempt to control his daughter's vision is both naive and fruitless, if not dangerous, for as Ogilvy says, "*the ones that keep their eyes open*, they're the ones that survive. Running—that's what'll kill ya"(my emphasis). Similarly, Ray's son, Robbie repeatedly expresses his desire to join up with the army in visual terms, as "needing to *see* this" (my emphasis). And as an earlier scene had shown, it is Ferrier who is suffering from shock. Just after Ray has seen the first tripod emerge and kill his neighbors, Ferrier returns to his house covered in ash (again evoking 9/11), and is unable to respond to his children's worried questions. When Rachel touches him, he jumps with fear. Although his traumatic witnessing has induced a powerful dread in Ferrier that he attempts to avoid by later controlling his children's vision, Spielberg suggests that looking and knowing are the only possible responses to trauma.

Vision is also repeatedly emphasized in the design and framing of the tripods. When they first emerge from the earth, close-ups of their headlights appear like giant all-seeing eyes. Atop the long tentacles of the tripods are lights and cameras that they use to probe houses, looking for humans. In one such suspenseful scene, a probe searches the basement where Ray, Rachel, and Ogilvy are hiding, and is temporarily fooled by Ferrier's use of a mirror to confuse it with its reflection. The tripod is a mechanical casing that surrounds the aliens, enabling them to move rapidly around in earth's gravity. The tripod is an apparatus of strength, mobility, and control uncannily similar to the crane we see Ferrier operating on the Jersey docks in the film's opening, but it is also fundamentally an *apparatus of vision*. Ironically, what the aliens cannot see is the microscopic realm of earthborn microbes that ultimately kill them. In the prologue, a series of graphic matches and zooms-out take the spectator from close-ups of these microbes dissolving to close-ups of beads of water, then to shots of a traffic light, and finally all the way out to a long shot of planet earth. This privileged narration enables the spectator to see what is also normally denied to our own vision—the microscopic weapon that will ultimately save us. Rachel had said of the splinter in her finger that she would not let her father touch, "when it's ready, my body will just push it out," and eventually the earth's biological immune system expels the aliens in a similar fashion.

Wells's Curate becomes more prominent in the straight-to-DVD version of *War of the Worlds* (David Latt) that was released simultaneously with Spielberg's film in June 2005. In it the Curate becomes Victor, an Australian priest who mutters about the Rapture and Revelations to the astronomer George (C. Thomas Howell), describing the aliens as "demons" and finally succumbing to despair that those who died were "chosen" and that "we are the Left Behind." This updates Wells's allusions to Revelations, in which his Curate mutters that this is "the great and terrible day of the Lord" (H. G. Wells 83). By alluding to the Rapture, which as the introduction noted has been a popular recent subject for Christian-produced films, Latt's Curate garners an American fundamentalist sheen. In other words, the apocalyptic and specifically Christian eschatological anxieties about the end of the world, so evident in the United States in the last thirty years, become universalized in Latt's version through their articulation by an *Australian* Curate. Similarly, Spielberg's invasion also uses the traditional natural and physical disasters, which in eschatological narratives have been classically interpreted as harbingers of the end, with catastrophic lightning storms in the Ukraine and across the world as the first signs that something is wrong. As one of the New Jersey residents mutters, "God is angry with the neighborhood."

Like Shyamalan in *Signs*, Spielberg intensifies the sonic suspense with ear-piercing foghorn blasts emitted by the tripods as they march around the countryside on the attack. In a paraphrase of the opening lines of H. G. Wells's original story, the film's prologue begins on an ominous note (voiced by Morgan Freeman):

> No one would have believed in the early years of the twenty-first century that our world was being watched by intelligences greater than our own. That as men busied themselves about their various concerns, they observed—and studied. With infinite complacency, men went to and fro about the globe, confident of their empire over this world. Yet, across the gulf of space, intellects vast, and cool, and unsympathetic regarded our planet with envious eyes—and slowly, and surely, drew their plans against us.

As in *Signs* and *The Forgotten*, extreme high-angle shots of human beings absorbed in everyday activities imply the "envious" point of view of alien watchers, and create a sense of scopic dread. Wells's narrator also shows the paradoxical repulsion and fascination of dread's ambivalence. Like the horror spectator, he is dying to take a peek when the Martians first land. Like Poe's narrator in "The Imp of the Perverse," he feels an almost vertiginous compulsion to look down. As Poe's narrator says, "I was a battleground of fear and curiosity. . . . I did not dare to go back towards the pit, but I felt a passionate longing to peer into it" (29).

As we recall, apocalyptic dread is a profound sense of anxiety and ambivalence about the future, and a desire to replace that anxiety with the prophetic signs of the apocalypse. Wells's epilogue notes that the effect of the invasion is that "it has robbed us of that serene confidence in the future which is the most fruitful source of decadence." Nonetheless "the gifts to human science it has brought are enormous, and it has done much to promote the conception of the commonweal of mankind" (H. G. Wells 207). Wells's humanism proffers hope in the same way that the disaster movie of the seventies and nineties like *Poseidon Adventure* and *Independence Day* celebrated the human spirit through a group of survivors learning to work together, overcoming all obstacles, and thereby surviving. Wells's hopeful note is perhaps not so hopeful after all, as he foresees that it could all happen again: "To them and not to us, perhaps, is the future ordained" (H. G. Wells 208). This anxiety about the future is subtly linked to the state of complacency suggested in the prologue. Although Wells was linking this complacency ("our empire over this world") to both the British Empire's military hegemony and to the human mastery of science and technology in 1898, Spielberg explicitly critiques American global hegemony. Spielberg's character Ogilvy says to Ferrier, "The aliens have defeated the greatest power on earth. This is no longer a war. It's an extermination." Later, as people flee over the Hudson River we hear Andy Williams singing, "If I ruled the world." Here Williams's love song is a diegetic melody played by the government authorities over loudspeakers to calm the terrified crowds, but in its dramatic context it also ironically comments on the myth of American military supremacy.

Wells's story repeatedly returns to a profound sense of the uncanny created by this apocalyptic invasion. The Martians' tripod machines which walk around on their long, skinny legs, seem more uncannily alive than the sluglike creatures that pilot them; as Wells's narrator observes, "The contrast between the swift and complex movements of these contrivances and the inert, panting clumsiness of their masters was acute, and for days I had to tell myself repeatedly that these latter were indeed the living of the two things" (H. G. Wells 156). Despite Wells's hopeful belief that the alien invasion has prompted a new collective human spirit of survival and a new direction for scientific research (into Martian biology and technology), a dissonant note remains, which is registered through the uncanny. To Wells's narrator, strangely, the world seems more dead than alive—for he cannot get the images of death and destruction out of his mind: "I go to London and see the busy multitudes in Fleet Street and the Strand, and it comes across my mind that they are but the ghosts of the past, haunting the streets that I have seen silent and wrecked, going to and fro, phantasms in a dead city, the mockery of life in a galvanized body" (H. G. Wells 208). In other words, human beings seem to have become like the Martians; they are "galvanized" or mechanized, in an uncanny simulacrum of body-in-machine, or death-in-life. Similarly, the film's spectacular opening shot of Ray Ferrier operating a crane to lift huge shipping containers would suggest that we are closer than we think to the aliens in our complacent dependence on technology. The final words of Wells's story return us to the Narrator's most intimate space—his marriage with his wife—from whom he has been separated for most of the story. He miraculously discovers her to be alive, after all: "And strangest of all it is to hold my wife's hand again, and to think that I have counted her, and that she has counted me, among the dead" (H. G. Wells 209). There is no such embrace between Ray Ferrier and his wife—only the redemption that he has found in being a good father, by bringing his children safely home. As the film painstakingly suggests in its first half hour, Ray Ferrier has to deal with the ghosts of bad parenting past, and it is only through the global crisis that he is impelled to repair his estranged relationship with his hostile teenaged son (who will not call him "Dad") and his neurotic daughter. Like the families in *Cape Fear*, *Signs*, and *Dolores Claiborne*, the Ferrier family is dysfunctional because it is haunted by unacknowledged failures and personal betrayals that divide parent and child. But unlike the nascent family that flies away in the helicopter at the end of *Jurassic Park* or the newly reunified family in *Signs*, *War of the Worlds* only offers the nuclear family survival, rather than rejuvenation.

War of the Worlds exemplifies the continuity of apocalyptic dread. Like *Signs* it shows anxiety about the future, and links global disaster with the fortunes of a dysfunctional nuclear family. By retroactively imagining the alien invasion in visual and verbal terms that specifically recall the destruction of the twin towers, it links national trauma to a dread of terrorism, with the family becoming the means of negotiating these fears. *War of the Worlds* also underscores the fundamental visual, or scopic, aspect of dread, which fears confronting what is truly terrifying to see, but which ultimately *must* be seen and acknowledged.

Apocalyptic Dread began by examining the ways in which dread infiltrated the cinema at the turn of the millennium. In my case studies, the monster, literal or metaphoric—Cady, Candyman, Joe St. George, John Doe, and the aliens—must be destroyed to preserve the fiction of a reunified family, but in most cases it is at the cost of laying that very fictionality bare. If Kierkegaard were to examine the function of cinematic horror, he might argue that by making concrete and visible our dread in the monster, we only attempt to displace and thereby avoid existential dread. For Kierkegaard it is faith that will prove redemptive, and it must involve the acceptance of dread as the price of absolute freedom. Yet as we have seen in the preceding chapters, the ways in which the demonic, the eschatological, and the supernatural are mapped out across the family and projected across the monstrous body of each horror story only suggest an apocalyptic return to an idealized fantasy of family values, and to a deeply conservative notion of history that can only understand the future in theological and eschatological terms. In Detective Somerset's resigned words, "It's the way it's always been," a dread which can only wait for the Day of Judgment. It is a cryogenics of historical memory that remains frozen.

Notes

1. Apocalyptic Dread, Kierkegaard, and the Cultural Landscape of the Millennium

1. A new acronym entered the Internet lexicon: TEOTWAWKI (tee-OH-tawa-kee) or "The End of the World as We Know It," which reflected a concern that all computers running legacy software (DOS and others) would reset their clocks to an unknown year, possibly 1900, when the millennium arrived at 12:01 a.m. on January 1, 2000, and that business, government, and all infrastructure would collapse because of their reliance on their computer systems. Millions of dollars were spent patching the bug, and the predicted crashes did not eventuate. See Kevin Poulsen, "The Y2K Solution: Run For Your Life!" *Wired* August 1998: 122–67, which noted that survivalist groups were amassing stockpiles of food, water, and other supplies in anticipation of this societal meltdown. Jon Amiel's *Entrapment* (1999) and a number of other TV movies (such as *Y2K*, 1998, 1999) integrated fears about the Millennium bug into their story lines. See Corie Brown, "Searching for a Plot, Hollywood Looks to the Millennium," *Newsweek* June 29, 1998: 14.

2. Frequently prophetic authors recount history up to their own time in symbolic form (Dan. 7.1–8), offering a vision of future salvation brought by God at the end of the present world, as epitomized by the book of Revelation. Passages such as Isaiah 24–27, Zechariah 9–14, and Mark 13 also belong to this type of literature, and other examples include Enoch, Jubilees, and the Apocalypse of Baruch in the Jewish pseudepigrapha, as well as the Apocalypse of Peter in the apocryphal New Testament. Apocalyptic literature is usually pseudonymous and written under the name of a particular prophet, such as Daniel or Enoch.

3. The book of Revelation, also called the Apocalypse, is the last book of the New Testament. Tradition asserts that the apostle John wrote Revelation during his exile on Patmos during the reign of the Roman emperor Domitian, probably about 95 CE. After a prologue, the book comprises two main parts. The first part contains letters to the seven churches of Asia, warning them against false

teachers and offering encouragement, and the second is a series of symbolic visions. See David Herbert Lawrence, *Apocalypse and the Writings on Revelation*, ed. Mara Kalnins (Cambridge: Cambridge UP, 1980); Jacques Ellul, *Apocalypse: The Book of Revelation*, trans. George W. Schreiner (New York: Seabury, 1977); and Leonard Thompson, *The Book of Revelation: Apocalypse and Empire* (New York: Oxford UP, 1988).

4. Evangelicals are born-again Christians, or those who have made a personal decision to follow Christ, such as Billy Graham or groups like the Campus Crusade. Pentecostal Christians include the Assemblies of God and other black, white, and Korean churches, headed by figures like Jimmy Swaggert and Jim Bakker. Pentecostal Christians speak "in tongues" or glossolalia when they believe that they are infused with the Holy Ghost. In *Cape Fear*, Max Cady is a Pentecostal who speaks in tongues as he slowly drowns in the Cape Fear River. Finally, fundamentalists are biblical literalists; usually they are Baptists.

5. The appearance of comets like Hale-Bopp in 1997 and Shoemaker-Levy 9 in 1994 (in its collision with Jupiter), and new diseases like AIDS, SARS, the Ebola virus, and even mad-cow disease have all been suggested as possible signs from God of the approaching end-time, and have often acted as the trigger to cults who commit mass-suicide. "Disturbances in space" in the form of the Hale-Bopp comet was seen as a sign of the end-time by the Heaven's Gate Cult, led by Marshall Applewhite. He and thirty-eight other followers committed mass suicide in 1997.

6. In a 1981 interview Jerry Falwell proclaimed that he saw twenty-two signs of the end-time, citing Mark 13, "For nation will rise against nation, and kingdom against kingdom; there will be earthquakes in various places, there will be famines; this is but the beginning of the birth-pangs." Adopting President George H. W. Bush's phrase "a New World Order" from his state of the union address in 1992, Pat Robertson's eponymous novel suggested that the "one-world Government" foretold in the Book of Revelation was approaching; it invoked classic anti-Semitic conspiracy theories about the influence of the Bilderberger Group, the Trilateral Commission, the World Bank, and the United Nations. In Robertson's *The End of the Age* (Nashville: Thomas Nelson, 1996), he creates a fictional version of apocalyptic prophecy, in which California is devastated in the year 2000 by a heat wave and a meteor, and in which the Antichrist takes over the presidency and rules from Babylon. In the nineties, many prophetic classics of the seventies were re-released, receiving renewed attention and commercial success. Paul Bilheimer's *Destined for the Throne* (1975) had sales of 650,000 by 1988 and continued to sell after 1990; John Walvoord's *Armageddon, Oil, and the Middle East Crisis* (1974) was updated and reissued in 1990 and sold over 600,000 copies from December 1990 to 1991; Hal Lindsay's *The Late, Great Planet Earth* sold 28 million copies; and Salem Kirhan's *Guide to Survival* (1968) has gone through sixteen editions selling five hundred thousand copies. See Melling (77), and Paul Boyer, *When Time Shall Be No More: Prophecy Belief in Modern American Culture* (Cambridge: Harvard UP, 1992).

7. The first eleven novels in this series (1995–2004) have sold over 40 million copies. The seventh book, *Indwelling*, became the first Christian novel to

be number one on the *New York Times* best-seller list. See David Kirkpatrick, "Best-Selling Series Reaches Climax: Jesus' Return," *New York Times* March 29, 2004: A1, A16; and Kevin Sack, "Apocalyptic Theology Revitalized by Attacks," *New York Times* November 23, 2001: A17.

8. Institutionally paranoid films foregrounded themes of conspiracy and corruption in the government, in the police, in the military, in banking, and in the stock market. They ranged from *The Parallax View* (1974) to *All the President's Men* (1976).

9. Terri Schiavo collapsed on February 25, 1990, from causes unknown, and remained in a persistent vegetative state until her death on March 31, 2005. Her parents Bob and Mary Schindler were ultimately unsuccessful in preventing her husband, Michael Schiavo, from having Ms. Schiavo's feeding tube removed, so that she could die. The state legislature of Florida, Congress, Governor Jeb Bush of Florida, and President George W. Bush all became involved in various legal attempts to overturn the court order that permitted Terri Schiavo's feeding tube to be removed, but after the Supreme Court declined to review the matter on March 24, 2005, the tube was removed and Ms. Schiavo subsequently died.

10. In 2005 bills for the teaching of ID or Intelligent Design were under consideration at school boards in Pennsylvania, Alabama, and Georgia. A revival of an earlier argument made by William Paley in *Natural Theology* (1802), ID asserts that biological life is so complex (examples are given of the mammalian blood-clotting mechanism or the bacterial flagellum) that it cannot be explained by Darwin's theory of natural selection. It is argued that consequently, the world must be the product of an "intelligent designer," that is, God. Led by the director of the Discovery Institute of Seattle, Stephen Meyer, a professor at Atlantic University's School of Ministry in Palm Beach and Jonathan Wells, a biologist and author of *Icons of Evolution* (2000), the ID campaign pushes a "teach the controversy" tactic that argues that creationism and ID should be taught in schools alongside evolution. See Evan Ratliff, "The Crusade against Evolution," *Wired* October 2004: 157–61, 202–03; and Raymond A. Eve and Francis B. Harold, *The Creationist Movement in Modern America* (Boston: Twayne, 1990).

11. See Cornelia Dean, "A New Screen Test for IMAX: It's the Bible vs. the Volcano," *New York Times* March 19, 2005: A1.

12. *The Omega Code* had a budget of $8 million. The Trinity Broadcasting Network, the largest independent Christian television station in the United States, was founded by Paul and Jan Crouch in 1973. Adopting the grassroots marketing strategies made famous by *The Blair Witch Project* and also adopted by *The Passion of the Christ*, the film's $600,000 campaign by the producer, Matthew Crouch, directly targeted religious groups and churches With special effects and high-profile actors (Casper Van Dien, Michael York), it earned a gross of $12.6 million (Source Internet Movie Database, November 21, 2005 <http://imdb.com/title/tt0203408/business>) and spawned a sequel, *The Megiddo Code*, which had an even larger budget of $22 million, but which failed to make as much money ($5.9 million gross).

13. See Jerry Adler, "A Matter of Faith," *Newsweek* December 15, 1997: 49–54; "Unbeliever's Quest," *Newsweek* March 31, 1997: 64–65; J. Alter, "The

Age of Conspiricism," *Time* March 24, 1997; S. Begley, "Science Finds God," *Newsweek* July 20, 1998: 46–51; D. V. Biema, "Does Heaven Exist?" *Time* March 24, 1997: 70–78; D. V. Biema, "Mary, So Contrary," *Time* April 10, 1995; D. V. Biema, "Hail Mary," *Time* March 21, 2005; D. Brooks, "Living Room Crusaders," *Newsweek* December 15 1997: 55; H. Chua-Eoan, "Other Faiths, Other Visions," *Time* March 24, 1997: 78; J. Miles, "Religion Makes a Comeback (Belief to Follow)," *New York Times Magazine* December 7, 1997: 56–59; G. Niebuhr, "In Search of Holy Ground," *New York Times Magazine* December 7, 1997; and K. L. Woodward, "Christs and Comets," *Newsweek* April 7, 1997: 40–43.

14. See, for example, *The Rapture* (Michael Tolkin, 1991); *Touched by an Angel* (CBS, 1994); *Powder* (Victor Salva, 1995); *Phenomenon* (Jon Turteltaub, 1996); *Michael* (Nora Ephron, 1996); *Commandments* (Daniel Taplitz, 1997) and *Dogma* (Kevin Smith, 1999).

15. At the same time, so-called body horror films like *Spawn* (Mark A. Z. Dippé, 1997) and *Mimic* (Guillermo del Toro, 1997), like the earlier *Outbreak* (Wolfgang Petersen, 1995), returned to horror's traditional interrogation of the boundaries between the body's inside/outside and self/other, and also reflected heightened anxieties about AIDS.

16. Public television as well as cable networks introduced new series such as *Millennium* (Fox, 1996–99), *Wolf Lake* (CBS, 2001), *Miracles* (ABC, 2003), *Joan of Arcadia* (CBS, 2003), and *Carnivale* (HBO, 2003–05). In the 2005 TV season, the networks continued this trend with a number of new series premiering, including *Lost* (ABC), *Medium* (NBC), and *Point Pleasant* (FOX).

17. The demonic possession cycle of the seventies had its roots in *The Bad Seed* (Mervyn LeRoy, 1956) and the British film *Village of the Damned* (Wolf Rilla, 1960), remade in the United States as *Village of the Damned* (John Carpenter, 1995). It spawned a cycle of films that featured demonic or supernaturally possessed children, including *Patrick* (Richard Franklin, 1978, Australia); *The Godsend* (Gabrielle Beaumont, 1979, UK) ; *The Children* (Max Kalmanowicz, 1980); *Children of the Corn* (Fritz Kiersch, 1984); and *The Good Son* (Joseph Ruben, 1993). *The Omen* begins with Ambassador Thorn's appointment to Rome, where his son dies in childbirth and where he in turn adopts Damien, the "son of a jackal" who was born at the exact time his son died. The president adopts Thorn's son at the end of the film, and in the sequels, will murder his stepbrother, and eventually run for high political office. By placing the demonic threat at the heart of the First Family, this narrative in part reflected anxieties about the political crisis of Watergate and changes to the American family. A recent trend has been the remake of many seventies horror films, including *The Omen* (John Moore, 2006).

18. *Amityville Horror* (Stuart Rosenberg, 1979) rapidly became a franchise. The prequel to the story, *Amityville 2: The Possession* (Damiano Damiani, 1982), was followed by *Amityville 3D* (Richard Fleischer, 1983). Also to follow were the TV movie *Amityville 4: The Evil Escapes* (Sandor Stern, 1989); *Amityville 1992: It's About Time* (Tony Randel, 1992), which linked the house's horrors to the fifteenth-century serial-killer Gilles De Rais; *Amityville Dollhouse* (Steve White, 1996); and another remake, *The Amityville Horror* (Andrew Douglas, 2005). See also the cycle of *Poltergeist* (Tobe Hooper, 1982), *Poltergeist 2: The Other Side* (Brian Gibson,

1986), and *Poltergeist 3* (Gary Sherman, 1988). The return of the devil as a character reminds us of his role in the medieval morality play, which will become narratively explicit in chapter 5 in my discussion of *Se7en*, in which the serial-killer John Doe restages the Seven Deadly Sins as a morality play to preach against sin.

19. Bruce Bartlett, a domestic policy advisor for Ronald Reagan, recently described George W. Bush's foreign policy as informed by a fundamentalist conviction that he is God's messenger. He described Bush's personal faith and policy decisions as guided by "this sort of weird messianic idea of what he thinks God has told him to do." This is a striking example of apocalyptic thinking and one that will be further elaborated in chapter 6. See Bartlett qtd. in Ron Susskind, "Without a Doubt" *New York Times Magazine* October 17, 2004, 44–51, 64, 102: 46.

20. With the exception of the existentialist readings in the film of Ingmar Bergman, Kierkegaard's philosophy has little presence in film theory. Like Kierkegaard, Ingmar Bergman's cultural upbringing was one of Lutheran piety and self-denial. His films are consumed with existential angst and thematize the silence and near-sadistic indifference of God to man's suffering; see *The Seventh Seal* (1957), *The Virgin Spring* (1959), *The Silence* (1963), *Hour of the Wolf* (1968), and *The Shame* (1968); Richard A. Blake, *The Lutheran Milieu of the Films of Ingmar Bergman*, (New York: Arno, 1978); Arthur Gibson, *The Silence of God: Creative Responsibility to the Films of Ingmar Bergman* (New York: Harper, 1969); Charles Ketcham, *The Influence of Existentialism on Ingmar Bergman* (New York: Edwin Mellen, 1986); and Frank Gado, *The Passion of Ingmar Bergman* (Durham, NC: Duke UP, 1986). Carl Dreyer's *Ordet* (1955, Denmark) is also influenced by Kierkegaard's distinction between personal and institutional faith.

21. Kierkegaard divided culture into three spheres: the aesthetic, the ethical, and the religious. In the aesthetic realm, dread appears in the form of fate; in the ethical, dread is guilt; and in the religious sphere, dread is sin.

22. For his discussion of an accident trauma, see Sigmund Freud, "Beyond the Pleasure Principle" trans. James Strachey, ed. Angela Richards, *On Metapsychology: The Theory of Psychoanalysis*, vol. 2 *Penguin Freud Library*, Ser. ed. Angela Richards. London: Penguin, 1984. 269–338, and Sigmund Freud, "Moses and Monotheism" trans. James Strachey, ed. Albert Dickson, *The Origins of Religion*, vol. 13 *Penguin Freud Library*, Ser. ed. Angela Richards. London: Penguin, 1988. 237–386, for his comparison of the trauma of the Jews with that of an accident survivor.

2. *Cape Fear* and Trembling: Familial Dread

1. John McDonald's novel *The Executioners* (1957) was the source material for both films, and it suggests that Cady's criminal behavior was caused by psychosis produced by war trauma. Both the cinematic adaptations of MacDonald's novel (1962, 1991) omit this war context and update the story to a contemporary setting.

2. My focus on the family is also indebted to Robin Wood's classic study of the family and seventies' cinema, *Hollywood from Vietnam to Reagan* (New York: Columbia UP, 1986). Wood argued that from the sixties onward, "the true subject of the horror genre is the struggle for recognition of all that our civilization

represses or oppresses" (28). He argued that audiences had ambivalent relationships with monsters, both identifying with the monster's transgression of social norms and yet remaining discomforted by the very repressed desires that the monster represents.

3. Another link was the production designer, Henry Bumstead, who worked on *To Kill a Mockingbird* and the 1991 *Cape Fear*.

4. In 1960, the campaign to desegregate lunch counters in Greensboro, North Carolina, was followed by SNCC's campaign to desegregate bus stations in Albany, Georgia, in fall 1961, culminating in the March on Washington in 1963. Bull Connor, the police chief in Birmingham, Alabama, used high-pressure fire hoses on black protesters in 1963.

5. Mitchum's own arrest for pot smoking was a further intertextual dimension of the bohemian outsider.

6. Scorsese's dialogical rewriting of the original continues through stylistic and intertextual references to familial horror and melodrama, and cites two films. The first is *Problem Child* (Dennis Dugan, 1990), a comedy about a monstrous child that is a comic remake of *Bad Seed* (Mervyn LeRoy, 1956), which the Bowdens watch in a movie theater. The sadistic comedy of John Ritter's mock paternal violence ("Here's Daddy") in turn cites both *The Tonight Show* ("Here's Johnny") and John Torrance's ironic "Here's Daddy" in *The Shining* (Stanley Kubrick, 1980), in which the father becomes a murderous threat to his wife and child. This intertextual chain of references thus foregrounds the horror that lies not far beneath the surface of familial dysfunction. The second film cited is Douglas Sirk's melodrama *All That Heaven Allows* (1955), which Leigh and Danny are watching on television. Jane Wyman plays a middle-class woman who falls in love with her gardener (Rock Hudson) and subsequently faces social disapproval for her class transgression. The expansion of class as a key component in Scorsese's characterization of Cady intersects with this theme, as we will discuss below. Scorsese's intertextuality also operates on a cinematographic level, as there are a number of matte shots of the family home (and houseboat) at sunset that are citations of Sirk's use of hypersaturated color in his American melodramas of the fifties.

7. Roles like Jeff Bailey in *Out of the Past* (Jacques Tourneur, 1947) typified Mitchum's world-weary star persona. Mitchum's role in *Night of the Hunter* (Charles Laughton, 1955) as an evangelical preacher and killer has obvious parallels with his role as Max Cady. Love and Hate are tattooed on his knuckles, a duality mimicked in Cady's Truth and Justice tattoos.

8. Cady's bumper sticker is "American by birth, Southern by the Grace of God," which aligns the theological, regional, and national in one phrase.

9. See the interview with Wesley Strick in "The Making of Cape Fear," DVD Special Features, *Cape Fear*, Universal Studios, 2001.

10. In fact, this project was not one that originated with Scorsese. The film was originally supposed to be shot by Steven Spielberg, whose company Amblin produced the film. But Scorsese owed Universal Studios a picture after *The Last Temptation of Christ* (1988). Urged by Robert De Niro to direct the film, Scorsese only agreed to take the project if he could transform the Bowden family into a more realistic, conflict-ridden contemporary family. This change led the screen-

writer, Wesley Strick, to develop antagonisms between Sam, Leigh, and Danny Bowden. In one of Scorsese's few ventures into mainstream commercial Hollywood, with its higher budget ($30 million), high production values, and star casting, *Cape Fear* was a relative commercial success, earning $79,100,000 (more in adjusted dollars than the original; see Internet Movie Database, April 15, 2004 <http://imdb.com/title/tt0101540/business>).

11. Some of the images were drawn by the Basses from their archival material, including some unused shots from John Frankenheimer's *Seconds* (1966). These faces are also similar to faces in two music videos ("The Bog," BiGod 20, 1990, and "Creature from the Black Leather Lagoon," The Cramps, 1990), which Danny watches as she tries to drown out the sound of her fighting parents. The repetition of these images suggests that they form part of Danny's unconscious, from which the dread attached to the Cape Fear River is drawn.

12. Thomas Wolfe's (1900–38) coming-of-age story of a young man, Eugene Gant, and his journey from his rural home in Asheville, North Carolina, to Harvard was autobiographical. It is ironic that, from within the film narrative, Danny describes Eugene's journey as "really, um, mystical, almost like a pilgrimage," to which Cady replies, "Like a cop-out. You can't run away from your demons." For Cady, Danny's journey is not to be one of escape to other places, but an eschatological journey "into the light" as his companion. This journey will be both sexual and violent and end in her torture and death on the houseboat.

13. Saturated colors of foreboding skies, angry sunsets, and flickering thunder and lightning (over the prison, over the Cape Fear River) recur as visual leitmotifs, and connect Cady with the natural through weather patterns (lightning, thunder, rain, water). When Cady talks to Bowden in the café, he jokes about moving to California to lecture on "earthquake preparedness." This alignment of natural forces suggests the apocalyptic dimensions of Cady's threat, and also parallels Candyman's similar apocalyptic arrival in Chicago, which we will discuss in chapter 3.

14. In a deleted scene, Danny tells Graciela about her childhood holidays: "We were happy, though, on the Cape Fear River. We'd rent this houseboat and spend the whole summer. All I wanted was for time to just stop and stay perfect right there on the river forever."

15. For more on the Southern idyll's history, see Massood.

16. A reflective and rather revealing conversation occurs in another deleted scene. Leigh sits with Danny, brushing her hair. Reassuring her daughter about how beautiful she is, she says, "Look at all the attention you get." "From who?" asks Danny. "Well, from your Dad, for one. Believe me, he knows a pretty girl when he sees one." Danny: "But Dad loves you, Mom" (to which Leigh does not reply). When asked by her daughter why Leigh cut her hair, she says that she was hoping to "change" something. This scene explicitly reveals the transferal of Sam's affections from his wife to his daughter and suggests that the incestuous displacement of Sam's desire is at the root of the marriage's problems.

17. In Freud's discussion of the uncanny, the fear of losing or damaging one's eyes speaks to castration anxiety. Here Cady's supernatural surveillance has most obviously castrated the weak husband, who is powerless to stop Cady's

rapacious gaze at his wife and daughter. Worse still, he is powerless to counter Leigh's own desire for Cady's gaze.

18. In another deleted scene later in the story, Leigh comes to see Sam in his office to talk about their marriage and asks him if he wants to leave her. Of Cady, she remarks, "Maybe someone who's spent fourteen years alone in jail, maybe they can *see* something better than we can" (my emphasis).

19. It is not insignificant that the first Gulf War occurred in the same year that the film was released. A similar Fourth of July parade occurs at narrative's end in *Mystic River* (Clint Eastwood, 2003). There all the characters watching the parade and each other are fully aware of the communal violence, vigilantism, and murder in which they are complicit. This scene ironically undercuts the ideological function of the parade as a celebration of national survival, demonstrating how illicit violence and the repression of that violence undergird communal and national identity. In this regard, the float with the founding fathers (Washington, Jefferson), who were also slaveholders, also underscores the violence and oppression that was part of the formation of the nation.

20. This femininity also is suggested by Cady's long hair, which is often tied in a bun. When he arrives at the Cape Fear River, he enters the woman's bathroom to clean up, and uses a woman's mascara brush to darken his gray hair.

21. It is also revenge for Lori's earlier patronizing mockery of Cady for not understanding a word: "Debauchery, it's a three-syllable word."

22. My thanks to Judith Halberstam for pointing out these aspects.

23. In another deleted scene, Cady tells Bowden the parable of Lazarus and the Rich Man, in which ultimately Lazarus goes to heaven and the rich man to hell. This underscores the way in which, for Cady, the destruction of class differences can only be understood in theological terms as Christianity's promise of equality and the reversal of material injustices in the afterlife.

24. Edmund rails against his inferior status "Wherefore should I / stand in the plague of custom . . . for that I am some twelve or fifteen moonshines / Lag of a brother? Why Bastard? Wherefore base? / When my dimensions are as well compact, / My mind as generous, and my shape as true, / As honest madam's issue?" *King Lear* (1.2.2–9), *The Arden Shakespeare* ed. K. Muir (New York: Routledge, 1991).

25. This performance is also typical of Lange's star persona built from a multiplicity of melodramatic roles. See her Broadway performances in *A Streetcar Named Desire* (1994, TV movie Glen Jordan 1995), and *Long Day's Journey into Night* (2000), and her cinematic performances in *Frances* (Graeme Clifford, 1982); *Music Box* (Costa-Gavras, 1989); *Men Don't Leave* (Paul Brickman, 1990); *Blue Sky* (Tony Richardson, 1991, release delayed until 1994); *A Thousand Acres* (Jocelyn Moorhouse, 1997); and *Cousin Bette* (Des McAnuff, 1998).

26. Though it is only briefly alluded to in several cryptic conversations, Sam Bowden is working on a legal case involving Broadbent's daughter and son-in-law, a Savings and Loan, and stolen money that the son-in-law has hidden. It could be a divorce case, or a corruption investigation into the S & L. Broadbent later offers to get his daughter to perjure herself in this case, but Bowden refuses any more legal improprieties. The case connects illicit actions (theft, deception)

to marriage and thereby reiterates the film's connection of personal and criminal actions. Fred Dalton Thompson was a senator for Tennessee from 1994–2002, and was chair of the Senate's 1997 subcommittee to investigate campaign fund-raising abuses. He was a lawyer on the Watergate committee and appeared in the archival footage of the hearings in Oliver Stone's *JFK* (1991)—ironically, a film that is itself an artful blend of fictionalized reality. Prior to *Cape Fear*, Thompson played a succession of roles as Government officials and military leaders: *In the Line of Fire* (Wolfgang Petersen, 1993); *Barbarians at the Gate* (Glenn Jordan, 1993); *Thunderheart* (Michael Apted, 1992); *Class Action* (Michael Apted, 1991); *Days of Thunder* (Tony Scott, 1990); *Die Hard 2* (Renny Harlin, 1990); *The Hunt for Red October* (John McTiernan, 1990); *No Way Out* (Roger Donaldson, 1987), and *Flight of the Intruder* (John Milius, 1991), as well as a recurring role on the television series *Law and Order* (NBC, 2004–present).

27. Although Cady wins, he is also subtly othered in the judge's mispro-nunciation of his name as "Maximilian Caddy" suggesting an unconscious asso-ciation of Cady with a Jew.

28. As Bowden (Peck) teeters between unruffled man of law and methodi-cal vigilante, he is admonished by his wife, Peggy (Polly Bergen), "I can't believe we're standing here talking about, about *killing* a man," and when her husband runs out of the house with a gun, Peggy calls the police. Yet, in an earlier dream sequence of Sam's, their positions reverse: we hear Peggy say to Sam, "A man like that doesn't deserve civil rights." The dream (which may recall an actual conver-sation) continues with Samuel Bowden's rejection of the law as repressive tool; he says, "But darling you can't put a man in jail for what he *might* do, and thank heaven for that." Bowden's comments are an ironic contrast to a later scene in which Chief Dutton (Martin Balsam) scolds Bowden for advocating just that: "I couldn't arrest a man for something that *might* be in his mind. That's dictatorship. Now Sam, you're a citizen, would you want it any other way?" The structural duality of Bowden's dream sequence, where Peggy plays id to Bowden's superego, suggests that Bowden's legal rationalism is in conflict with his subconscious vigi-lantism and that he has already internalized the myth of the white colonial family under siege.

29. Yellow fever is an acute respiratory disease transmitted in warm cli-mates by mosquitoes breeding in stagnant water. Cady's association with water is established with the Cape Fear River in the opening credit sequence.

30. In the 1962 *Cape Fear*, Bowden, in a frustrated plea to Dutton, says, "What am I supposed to do? Pull up the drawbridge, sit home with a loaded gun . . . . That's kind of an artificial way to live, wouldn't you say?" Here, conceiv-ing the defense of the home as a man's castle is acknowledged as an archaic response. Instead, in keeping with his rigorously legal approach, Bowden enlists the police in his plan of defense.

3. Strange Fruit: *Candyman* and Supernatural Dread

1. Notable exceptions of horror films which foreground race include *Night of the Living Dead* (George A. Romero, 1968) and *The People under the Stairs* (Wes

Craven, 1991). In *Night of the Living Dead*, Ben, the African American protagonist, is an important antecedent to *Candyman*. Ben leads a group of survivors to
take refuge in a home, where zombies besiege them. Again, the family is a site of
threat, with the horror surfacing from the basement, in the guise of a daughter
who has become a zombie and attacks her family. Although Ben survives the
zombies, he is later murdered—in effect, lynched—by a mob of rednecks, who
assume Ben is a zombie because he is black. They use *meat hooks* to hoist Ben's
body onto a bonfire, where his body is burnt to ashes—a parallel corporeal annihilation to Candyman's fate.

2. Candyman borrows certain conventions from another urban legend, the
"Bloody Mary" story (the avenging spirit's name has dozens of variants, ranging
from Mary Whales to Mary Worth to Svarte Madame). One version of the legend
recounts that Mary was horribly disfigured or killed as the result of an accident.
Although there are many variants, common elements include the mirror, the ritualized repetition of her name in front of a mirror, and an ominous outcome to the
invocation. For more details, see *Urban Legends*, October 11, 2002 <http:::://
www.snopes.com/horrors/ghosts/bloody.htm>; and Janet Langlois, " 'Mary Whales,
I Believe in You': Myth and Ritual Subdued," *Indiana Folklore* 11.1 (1978): 5–33.

3. The ten deadly plagues cited in *Exodus* did not include bees but were:
water turned into blood, frogs, gnats, beetles, murrain or cattle disease, boils, hail,
locusts, darkness, and the slaying of the firstborn (Exodus 7–11 RSV). The locust
swarm most often represents the scourge of God, and the locusts in *The Exorcist*
(William Friedkin, 1973) and *Exorcist 2* (John Boorman, 1977) continue this tradition in horror.

4. Because he was blessed by God the prophet Daniel survived the famous
den of lions, yet cursed by white men, Daniel Robitaille does not survive, and he
is torn apart as if by wild beasts. See Daniel 6: 1–28.

5. See, for example, the photographic exhibition Without Sanctuary:
Lynching Photography in America, which continues to tour nationally. See also
Philip Dray, *At the Hands of Persons Unknown: The Lynching of Black America* (New
York: Random, 2002); and Jonathan Markovitz, *Legacies of Lynching: Racial Violence
and Memory* (Minneapolis: U of Minnesota P, 2004).

6. *Candyman: Farewell to the Flesh* (Bill Condon, 1995). A further sequel
was *Candyman 3: Day of the Dead* (Turi Meyer, 1999).

7. Gunning convincingly argues for the white supremacist conflation of
black male citizenship and sexual threat to white womanhood in the Reconstruction period, which is figured in the work of Thomas Dixon's *The Leopard's Spot*
and *The Clansman* (the latter would be the source material for D. W. Griffith's *The
Birth of a Nation*). In these texts' imaginary triangulation of a white woman under
threat from a black man (with a white man as self-appointed avenger), neither the
historical rape of black women by white men, nor the sexual desires of white
women for black men, could be empirical or ideological possibilities. The latter
issue is key to the film's depiction of both Helen and Caroline Sullivan's desire for
Daniel Robitaille. The pretexts for historical lynchings ranged from allegations of
black assault to voodoism. A number of specific forbidden categories for African
American men involved social contact with white women, including insulting,

eloping, courting, cohabitation, or sexual congress. Lynching had four principal and continuous effects: first, the maintenance of social control over the black population through unpredictable terrorism; second, the suppression of black economic, political, and social competition; third, the stabilization of the white class structure and the preservation of the white aristocracy; and fourth, the systematic targeting of black political leadership. With the demise of slavery after the Civil War, miscegenation became an even greater taboo, as sexual and political agency became joint targets in the violence then directed against African American males with newly gained suffrage. See Martha Hodes, "The Sexualization of Reconstruction Politics: White Women and Black Men in the South after the Civil War," *Journal of the History of Sexuality* 3.3 (1993): 402. *Candyman: Farewell to the Flesh* continues to explore the issue of miscegenation. In the sequel, we learn that Caroline and Daniel's child Isabel is the grandmother of Annie Tarrant (Kelly Rowan), the main protagonist. The repressed secret of this family is that they are of black descent, but Annie's mother, Octavia Tarrant, as the holder of this family's secret, keeps the photo of her "mulatto" mother locked in a drawer. The Tarrant family's decayed mansion on Esplanade Avenue in New Orleans turns out to be the original plantation house in which Daniel Robitaille was born, and which Caroline Sullivan purchased after Robitaille's death, in order to live there with their daughter. There Annie Tarrant discovers Caroline's mirror in the ruined slave quarters, and with its shattering, Candyman is destroyed.

8. The more recent lynchings and mutilation of Garnett Johnson in Independence, Virginia (1997), James Byrd in Jasper, Texas (1998), and torture and sodomization of Abner Louima in New York City (1997) reinforce the contemporary currency of *Candyman*'s investigation of the pathological brutalities of racist violence on black male bodies.

9. In Clive Barker's short story "The Forbidden," which was the source for *Candyman*, human waste pervades the projects: "[T]he smell, even in the cold weather, was unpleasant. In high summer, it must have been overpowering" (Barker 71). The film and sequels also emphasize the malodorous presence of urine and shit in Cabrini-Green. Bernadette exclaims, "Jesus, it stinks in here" when she and Helen first explore the abandoned apartment of one of Candyman's first murder victims, Ruthie-Jean.

10. Sugar was a colonialist staple, particularly in Cuba, in the Antilles, in Brazil, and throughout the Caribbean. Sugar was traded for slaves in the West Indies as one of the legs in the Triangle trade between England, Africa, and the West Indies. Like cotton, sugar harvesting was a labor-intensive industry dependant on slavery. See Richard S. Dunn and Gary B. Nash, *Sugar and Slaves: The Rise of the Planter Class in the English West Indies, 1624–1713* (Durham, NC: U of North Carolina P, 2000).

11. Location scouts for the production consulted with community leaders, including the Cabrini-Green resident Henrietta Thompson, who served as a consultant to the production (and model for character Anne-Marie). The production also hired members of the Vicelords and Disciples gangs as extras, closed certain floors of Cabrini-Green as a precaution against the random sniper fire responsible for many of the murders there, and restricted shooting to daylight hours with

limited crews (Gramercy Pictures, *Candyman* 3). Cabrini-Green has been the site for gang warfare for over fifty years, and one site known as "Death Corner," near Jenner Elementary School, is particularly notorious. In 1981 in a nine-week span, ten Cabrini-Green residents were murdered and thirty-five were wounded by gunshots, which in turn prompted then Chicago mayor Jane Byrne to take up symbolic residence there for several weeks in a political stunt (ironically to call it her "home"). In 1992, the year of the film's release, Dantrell Davis, a young Cabrini-Green resident, was shot on his way to school. The film alludes to this when Bernadette says to Helen, "I heard that a kid got shot there the other day." In the mid-1990s, plans to demolish Cabrini-Green and replace it with mixed income low-rise housing were announced, and on September 27 1995, demolition began. See also Cornelia Grumann, "CHA Watch: Redrawing Cabrini's Future," *Chicago Tribune* Internet Edition. March 30, 1996 <http://pqasb.pqarchiver.com/chicagotribune/index.html?ts=1079636767>; and "Cabrini-Green Homes," Chicago Housing Authority, July 28, 2004 <http://thecha.org/housingdev/cabrini_green_homes.html >.

12. Actually, the sequel shows one inconsistency in this regard. As Annie Tarrant visits a New Orleans cemetery, she sees the tomb of Daniel Robitaille, next to that of Caroline Sullivan and their child, Isabel. This contradicts the first film, which tells us that Robitaille's ashes were scattered over the site of the future Cabrini-Green (although Caroline may have subsequently placed his ashes in the tomb).

13. The 1969 Brooke Amendment, which specified that tenants should pay no more than 20% of their income for rent (later altered under Ronald Reagan to 25%, then 30%) with the rest to be subsidized by the federal government, had one unforeseen consequence, which was to drive out working-class families and concentrate the poor within public housing. Over two-thirds of Cabrini-Green residents were below the poverty line. African Americans comprise 85% of the public housing population in Chicago. By 1992, there were 5.5 violent crimes per month per 100 residents. See David C. Ranney and Patricia A Wright, "Race, Class and the Abuse of State Power: The Case of Public Housing in Chicago," V172, The Natalie P. Voorhees Center for Neighborhood and Community Improvement, February 6, 2000. October 7, 2000 <http://www.uic.edu/cuppa/upp/faculty/ranny/Race%20Relations%20Abstracts%20Paper%20draft%205.htm>.

14. Freud's etymological examples of heimlich included "bees who make the lock of 'Heimlichkeiten' (i.e. sealing-wax)" ("Uncanny" 344).

15. See Arnold Hirsch, *Making the Second Ghetto: Race and Housing in Chicago, 1940–1960* (New York: Cambridge UP, 1993); Nicolas Lemann, *The Promised Land* (New York: Knopf, 1991); Thomas Lee Philpott, *The Slum and the Ghetto: Neighborhood Deterioration and Middle-Class Reform: Chicago, 1880–1930* (New York: Oxford UP, 1978).

16. Cabrini-Green is bounded on its north side by Ranch Triangle, Lincoln Park, and Old Town triangle, on its east by Old Town and the Gold Coast, on its south by the Near North Side, and on its west by Goose Island. See David Peterson, "A Great Chicago Land Grab: Burying Public Housing in Chicago," *Z Magazine* (April 1997): 34–37.

17. See also Aviva Breifel and Sianne Ngai, "How Much Did You Pay for This Place? Fear, Entitlement and Urban Space in Bernard Rose's *Candyman*," *Camera Obscura* 37 (January 1996): 71–92. Although Cabrini-Green and Lincoln Village share a secret history as mirror images of each other, art design makes them markedly different. The production designer Jane Stewart's description of her design of Helen's apartment and Cabrini-Green underscores the problematic racial binaries implicit in the film's mise-en-scène: "The environments in which Helen lives and works are all essentially sterile, modernist and utilitarian. Cabrini-Green, on the other hand, is dark, mysterious and totally irrational" (Gramercy Pictures pack, *Candyman* 5).

18. The theme of white paranoia about black criminality continues in the film's sequel. Reappearing in *Candyman: Farewell to the Flesh*, Professor Purcell looks uneasily at a black man behind him in a public bathroom. A few minutes later, Candyman appears in his place and murders Purcell. The scene also evokes the dread of sodomy, in that Purcell is both racially and sexually uncomfortable in a scene that could also be read as sexual cruising.

19. There is an urban legend that has widely circulated over the last thirty years that claims that Halloween sweets are poisoned or contain needles or razor blades. There are confirmed examples of this form of tampering, but not of poisoning. This led to the present-day practice of making sure all sweets distributed to children are in unopened packages; see *Urban Legends Reference Pages*, May 17, 2004 <http://www.snopes.com/horrors/poison/hallowee.htm > and <http://www.snopes.com/horrors/mayhem/needles.htm>.

20. In the sequel, Professor Purcell believes that his former student succumbed to a form of psychotic overidentification with Candyman and has written a book about Helen. On a promotional book tour, he shows a slide of a news article with the headline "Helen Lyle: Murderer or Victim?" adding: "Cabrini-Green, Chicago, 1992. Helen Lyle became so obsessed by the myth that she took on the persona of the Candyman, killing her victims with a hook. Residents believed it was the Candyman. And in a way it was."

21. In "The Forbidden," the original motivation for the bonfire was the occasion of Guy Fawkes Day. This traditional British festival on November 5 commemorates Fawkes's failure to blow up James 1 and Parliament in 1605.

4. *Dolores Claiborne:* Memorial Dread

1. A big-budget Hollywood production, *Dolores Claiborne* was marketed as a thriller largely to cash in on Kathy Bates's Academy Award–winning performance as a disturbed and homicidal fan in *Misery* (Rob Reiner, 1990), another adaptation of a Stephen King novel. The film's gross was disappointingly low ($24.3 million), because it was not marketed toward melodrama's traditional target audience of younger and older women (Source Internet Movie Database, November 21, 2005 <http://imdb.com/title/tt0109642/business>. Bates's idiosyncratic career has included playing the detective in *Diabolique* (1996), the working-class character Molly Brown in *Titanic* (1997), and the fierce idealist in *Primary Colors* (1998). Her nontraditional looks and size (by the normative standards of

the Hollywood star system) are a partial explanation for her varied roles. Although highly acclaimed for her performance in the theatrical production of *Frankie and Johnny at the Clair de Lune*, she was replaced by Michelle Pfeiffer in the film *Frankie and Johnny* (1991), because she did not fit the conventional Hollywood version of the glamorous and sexual female star. Jennifer Jason Leigh has also chosen idiosyncratic roles, which often include those of psychologically or emotionally disturbed young women: see *Single White Female* (1992), *Mrs. Parker and the Vicious Circle* (1994), *Bastard out of Carolina* (1996), *Washington Square* (1997), *A Thousand Acres* (1997) and *The Love Letter* (1998).

2. One reviewer described the film as "a slightly overcooked mystery that manages to cram a host of fashionable hot-button topics—including euthanasia, drug and alcohol dependency and repressed memory syndrome—into a little more than two hours." See Mick LaSalle, "A Powerhouse Acting Duet: Leigh, Bates Are Electric in *Dolores Claiborne*," *San Francisco Chronicle*, Online Edition, March 24, 1995 <http://www.sfgate.com/cgi-bin/article.cgi?f=/c/a/1995/03/24/DD44813. DTL>. Critics also remarked on its generic antecedents as a "women's picture" that foregrounded female relationships and the sacrifices women make for family. Richard Schickel's review observed, "At no point in *Dolores Claiborne* is its eponymous protagonist tied to a railroad track or strapped down in the path of a rapidly impending train or buzz saw. And a good thing too, for this adaptation of Stephen King's best seller . . . also lacks a hero, or indeed any remotely admirable masculine figure, eager to race to her rescue." He calls Dolores a protagonist "who resembles the heroine of a gaslit theatrical enterprise of the nineteenth century." See Richard Schickel, "Woman Under the Influence," *Time* March 27, 1995, Online Edition September 1, 1999 <http://www.time.com/time/archive/preview/ 0,10987,1101950327-133948,00.html>. Hollywood melodramas that have thematized sexual, physical, and domestic violence include *Looking for Mr. Goodbar* (Richard Brooks, 1977), *Nuts* (Martin Ritt, 1987), *Prince of Tides* (Barbra Streisand, 1991), *Bastard Out of Carolina* (Anjelica Huston, 1996), and *A Thousand Acres* (Jocelyn Moorhouse, 1997).

3. However, this is not to deny the profound interconnections between private space and political concerns, which feminism's slogan "the personal is political" foregrounded. In particular, feminist theory has helped us understand the connections between domestic space and patriarchal oppression. See Sandra M. Gilbert and Susan Gubar, *The Madwoman in the Attic: The Woman Writer and the Nineteenth-Century Literary Imagination* (New Haven: Yale UP, 1979).

4. Video Image, Cinesite, and the Computer Film Company created the film's special effects.

5. For an overview of melodrama theory, see Elsaesser.

6. Here the linguistic association of moon is with Joe's rectum, the dark side metaphorically becoming unpredictable male violence.

7. This thinly veiled reference to Dolores's class status as "servant," also invokes the architectonics of Gothic Victorian space. Its separate entrances and staircases for servants spatialized an upper-class desire to make servants invisible at the same time as their ubiquity was required for work. The one threat to this newly established bourgeois zone of Victorian familial privacy was the presence of servants, who because of their privileged access to the family were often key

witnesses in murder trials in the nineteenth century. As Vera's servant, Dolores's intimate spatial access to the wealthy Donovan household leads to the emotional intimacy between her employer and herself, through which she eventually learns that Vera killed her husband.

8. Like Selena St. George, Detective John Mackey is also a professional investigator. He tries to draw Selena to his side, believing her to be the only witness to Dolores's crimes. Both Selena and Mackey are single (Mackey's wife has died of cancer). Remarking that they both live alone, have no children, and are workaholics, he observes, "We're probably more alike than you'd care to believe." Obsessed with revenge, the retired detective is particularly determined to convict Dolores Claiborne for Vera Donovan's murder, because he is convinced that Dolores already "got away" with killing her husband earlier. The detective's obsessive drive to find evidence to convict Dolores is motivated by his frustrated desire for a perfect work record of closed cases (the death of Joe is the only case out of eighty-six in his entire career that he never solved to his satisfaction). For Mackey, Dolores's crime is ideologically transgressive, for to kill a husband is to kill the embodiment of patriarchal law, and Dolores's character is everywhere transgressive, in speech and body. Sententiously quoting the Bible in a warning to Selena, Detective Mackey attempts to justify his obsessive behavior, by linking it to a theological dread of crime and punishment: "For God shall bring every work into judgment, with every secret thing, whether it be good or whether it be evil." He believes that Dolores has killed her husband for pleasure and Vera Donovan for profit (a multimillion dollar inheritance she unexpectedly receives).

9. A match on action also acts as a link between father and daughter in flashback 10. This begins with a shot from Selena's point of view of a glass of Scotch placed before her by her mother (in the present), followed by a match-on-action of Joe St. George's hand tremulously lifting the drink (in the past).

10. Unlike Annie Johnson, the black servant whose labor and maternal love are appropriated by the white family in Douglas Sirk's film (1959), Dolores controls the narrative's point of view. *Imitation of Life* (starring Lana Turner, Sandra Dee, Juanita Moore, and John Gavin) was a remake of John Stahl's 1934 *Imitation of Life* (starring Claudette Colbert, Louise Beaver, and Warren William); both were adaptations of the Fannie Hurst novel. Its principal theme explored the personal and psychological impact of racism, emphasizing its psychological effect on the young, light-skinned daughter, Sarah Jane (Susan Kohner). Her resentment and self-hatred of her racial and class identities are evident as she tries to pass for white, and functions in a different way from the selfish and spoiled white daughters who are ashamed of their mothers in *Mildred Pierce* and *Stella Dallas*.

11. The Gothic also shares a strong thematic component of masochism; see Michelle A. Masse, *In the Name of Love: Women, Masochism, and the Gothic* (Ithaca: Cornell UP, 1992). The tradition of "procrastinated rape" figured in tales of male seduction and female virtue besieged in the eighteenth century novel. See Samuel Richardson's *Pamela* (1740–41) and *Clarissa* (1747–48), and Henry Fielding's parody *Shamela* (1741). I thank Bob Stam for reminding me of this connection.

12. Public anxiety about female murderers often points to underlying essentialist ideas of women as maternal, emotional, and life-enhancing. The notoriety of certain female murderers is because they transgress these very codes, as

with Lizzie Borden who killed her parents, or Susan Smith and Andrea Yates, who killed their children. See Helen Birch, ed., *Moving Targets: Women, Murder and Representation* (Berkeley and Los Angeles: U of California P, 1994); Lynda Hart, *Fatal Women: Lesbian Sexuality and the Mark of Aggression* (Princeton: Princeton UP, 1994); and Neil Noddings, *Women and Evil* (Berkeley and Los Angeles: U of California P, 1989).

13. The slippage between bitch and witch also reminds us that the Christian persecution of witches targeted political, sexual, or gender nonconformists, labeling their transgressive behavior demonic.

14. Stanley Kubrick's *The Shining* (1976) is another important film in the horror genre in which the axe is a homicidal weapon within a familial context. Jack Torrance axes down the bathroom door, and shrieks: "Hi honey, I'm home," destabilizing the familial "safety" that these words suggest.

15. The foreground action between the two characters was shot in a controlled environment on a 360-degree "blue-screen" set inside Acadia University Hockey Arena in Wolfville overlooking the Bay of Fundy in Nova Scotia. The assistant director Josh McLaglen shot the background activity of the boats in the bay on location at Blue Rocks Cove. The dramatically changing sky leading up to and out of the total eclipse was laid by the Computer Film Company (CFC) using plates of cloud formations photographed in Nova Scotia, and animated by Yannick Sirrs and Rob Hodgson. Finally, all four elements were composited together by means of CFC's digital animation to create a total eclipse (information courtesy of Castle Rock Entertainment, Columbia Pictures Corporation and Internet Movie Database Online, December 1, 2004).

5. *Se7en* in the Morgue: Dystopian Dread

1. Khondji used Panavision Primo lenses for sharp contrasts and Kodak stock 93 for interiors, 45 for daytime, and 87 for nighttime exteriors, offering up rich blacks. A few hundred of the twenty-five hundred first-run theatrical prints were created using a silver-retention process called CCE. With silver retention, the silver leached out during conventional film processing is rebonded to the print, thus greatly increasing luminosity in the light portions of the image with rich blacks and desaturated colors. See Chris Darke, "Inside the Light," *Sight and Sound* 6.4 (1996): 18–20.

2. Francis Fukuyama conceives of history as having reached its *ne plus ultra* in democratic consumer capitalism, which with the fall of the Berlin Wall and the Soviet Union in 1991 marked the end of the cold war and the terminus to history. See Francis Fukuyama, *The End of History and the Last Man* (New York: Free Press, 1992). Jameson's understanding of the postmodern suggests that originality is no longer possible and that repetition and recycling have become the new aesthetic norm. See Fredric Jameson, *Postmodernism, or the Cultural Logic of Late Capitalism* (London: Verso, 1991).

3. In the film's deleted prologue, we see Somerset inspecting his new home with a realtor. He carries around a piece of wallpaper from this house in his wallet

and refers to it as "my future." This hopeful anticipation of retirement will vanish by the film's end, with Somerset's decision to remain on the police force.

4. *The Silence of the Lambs* spawned two sequels: *Hannibal* (Ridley Scott, 2001) and *Red Dragon* (Brett Ratner, 2002). In the last fifteen years there have been dozens of serial killer films, including *Apartment Zero* (Martin Donovan, 1988), *Henry: Portrait of a Serial Killer* (John McNaughton, 1990), *Jennifer 8* (Bruce Robinson, 1992), *Basic Instinct* (Paul Verhoeven, 1992), *Sliver* (Phillip Noyce, 1993), *Citizen X* (Chris Gerolmo, TV 1995), *Switchback* (Jeb Stuart, 1997), *The Minus Man* (Hampton Fancher, 1999), *The Bone Collector* (Phillip Noyce, 1999), *Mindhunters* (Renny Harlin, 2004), *Suspect Zero* (E. Elias Merhige, 2004), *Saw* (James Wan, 2004), and *Saw II* (Darren Lynn Bousman, 2005).

5. House of Representatives Hearings before a Subcommittee of the Committee on Government Operations, *The Federal Role in Investigation of Serial Violence*, 99th Congress, Second Session, April 9–May 21, 1986. For the statistical debate over the incidence of serial killing in the United States, see Steven A. Egger, *Serial Killers: An Elusive Phenomenon* (New York: Praeger, 1990).

6. In the Mithraic narrative, the soul travels through the seven heavenly spheres, progressively purifying itself from each sin: (in astrological order) the Moon-Envy, Mercury-Greed, Venus-Lust, Mars-Anger, Jupiter-Ambition, Saturn-Sloth, and the Sun-Pride. There are also seven terraces of Dante's Purgatory and seven cardinal virtues. In the book of Revelation symbolic groups of seven include candlesticks, angels, trumpets, churches and the seven last days of revelation. (Dyer, 8)

7. Of *Taxi Driver*, Christopher Sharrett remarks that the film "suggests the millennialism dominant in American art to have a collective psychopathological foundation" (228). Bickle's "last stand" prefers death to reform and presents massive violence as redemptive ritual. Bickle shares Doe's misogyny (" the women I killed were filth, bastard prostitutes just standing around littering the streets. I was just cleaning up a bit."). Cinematic vigilantes include the characters played by Charles Bronson, Clint Eastwood, Chuck Norris, Sylvester Stallone, Steven Seagal, and Mel Gibson in American cinema of the late seventies and eighties.

8. In *The Silence of the Lambs* Hannibal Lecter demonstrates his power to inhabit the body of his victims. Escaping from prison, he hides beneath facial skin he has just removed from one of his victims. Buffalo Bill constructs his own female transvestitism from the skin of his female victims. Max Cady also becomes a transvestite (as Graciela the maid) in order to fool Detective Kersek.

9. The cluttered contents of Doe's apartment include journals and crime scene photographs; they were all created by teams of art designers, photographers, and artists. A company named PHD created three entire journals from Doe's 2000 journals, sections of which are shown in the opening credit sequence as well as read aloud from by Detective Somerset. Doe's fifty-two photographs of Sloth's starvation were created by Melanie McDaniel with Annette Haellmigk and Fernando Favila, and evidence photos of Doe's other crime scenes were by Peter Sorel.

10. The name John Doe had its origins in English legal history. Used as early as 1659, John Doe was the name for a fictitious plaintiff, and John Roe was the name for a fictitious defendant in a legal process called ejectment, in which

a dispossessed owner tried to recover his land. A technical requirement up until an Act of Parliament in 1852, landowners who wanted to establish their rightful titles would first have to use fictitious tenants in the ejectment action. Thus, the first legal use of the term John Doe (and its variants John Stiles and Richard Miles and later variants Jane Doe/Jane Roe) was always fictitious. Later it could be used to conceal a person's identity (as in *Roe v. Wade*) or because a person's real name was not known (such as in the case of an unknown body). In *Se7en*, it is not known whether John or "Jonathan Doe" is an assumed or actual identity.

11. Cultural representations of serial killers have engaged with three principal discursive systems as explanatory models. These three competing, often mutually contradictory, discourses—forensic criminology, psychology, and Gothic monstrosity—are all self-reflexively foregrounded and debated in *Se7en*. The first, forensic criminology with its behavioral profile, as developed by the FBI National Center for the Analysis of Violent Crime (NCAVC) and Behavioral Science Unit, and prominently featured in *The Silence of the Lambs*, has according to both Philip Jenkins and Richard Tithecott become the dominant model for representation in both journalism and cinema (Jenkins 212 ff; Tithecott 17–33). The serial killer presents a particular problem in what Foucault has called the "dividing practices" between the law and psychiatry. As the psychologist Karl Menninger has stated, "In attempting to assess the criminal responsibility of murderers, the law tries to divide them (as it does all offenders) into two groups, the 'sane' and the 'insane.' The 'sane' murderer is thought of as acting upon rational motives that can be understood, though condemned, and the 'insane' one as being driven by irrational senseless motives. But murderers who seem rational, coherent and controlled and yet whose homicidal acts have a bizarre, apparently senseless, quality pose a difficult problem" (qtd. in Seltzer 298). For McNaughton's rule for the legal definition of "insanity" see Lee Willemen and David B. Cohen, *Psychopathology* (New York: McGraw, 1990) 57. Cinematic representations of the serial killer have reflected the shift of nomenclature from psychopath to sociopath to antisocial personality disorder in naming and explaining his or her behavior. See Georges Canguilhem, *The Normal and the Pathological*, trans. Carolyn Fawcett and Robert S. Cohen (New York: Zone, 1989), and the American Psychiatric Association, *DSM-IV* (147ff.) for definitions of psychosis. Detective Mills dismissively describes John Doe as "insane," "a nutbag," and "a lunatic . . . who [probably is] dancing around his room in his grandma's panties, rubbing himself in peanut butter," while Somerset strongly disagrees, drawing attention to Doe's rational and systematic behavior.

12. Somerset's UFO image nicely encapsulates the ways in which the dread of the end of the world that is most explicit in alien invasion science-fiction and disaster movies of the nineties also pervades a crime film like *Se7en*.

13. The cabinet of curiosities or *Kunstkabinett* is an aesthetic form used by the avant-garde—for example, in the work of the group FLUXUS. It may contain photos, ordinary household objects, or mechanical devices whose arrangement within a cabinet provides a different aesthetic context for the viewer. When the detectives finally discover Doe's apartment, we see five cabinets completed and a sixth (Lust) with a photo of the planned victim and a receipt to a leather shop. These cabinets include GLUTTONY, a Warholian stack of soup cans and shopping

receipts for their purchase; GREED, some bloodied law textbooks from Eli Gould's office along with press clippings of Gould's famous clients; SLOTH, photos of Victor's physical decay over one year, with specimen jars of his right hand, urine, and feces; and LUST (incomplete).

14. The lyrics of the song "Closer to God" are in keeping with Doe's messianic mission as agent of catastrophe. The harsh, synthesized beats of this piece, together with Howard Shore's score (who also did the foreboding score for *The Silence of the Lambs*), are another key component in creating an atmosphere of ominous dread.

15. For the "minus man" see Lew McCrary's novel *The Minus Man* (New York: Penguin, 1991), which foregrounds the serial killer characteristics of anonymity, ubiquity, and transparency. Paradoxically, it is only through their acts of murder that they construct a sense of identity.

16. This was Lucifer's sin, and the reason for his expulsion from paradise by God, which is explored in Milton's *Paradise Lost*.

6. *Signs* of the End of the World: Apocalyptic Dread

1. Shyamalan claims the influence of three key films in the writing of *Signs*: *The Birds* (Alfred Hitchcock, 1963), *Night of the Living Dead* (George A. Romero, 1968), and *Invasion of the Body Snatchers* (Don Siegel, 1956). In each of these films, supernatural forces besiege individuals or the family.

2. Crop circles first appeared widely in the mid-1970s and 1980s. With over a hundred annual circles sightings, Wiltshire, England to this day, remains the center of crop circles (in fact, crop circle tourism has also sprung up in southern England). Early circles featured simple designs and usually appeared in fields of wheat, rape, oat, or barley, in which the stalks were flattened but not broken. In 1991, in Hampshire, two residents, Doug Bower and Dave Chorley, came forward to say they had begun making crop circles in 1978 using a simple device involving a board and rope (which Officer Paski alludes to in the film). Bower's and Chorley's work became increasingly influential and spread around the world, with crop circles appearing on all six continents and increasing in design complexity. This form of "agrarian art" includes the mythology that has grown up around the astounding shapes, for as John Lundberg, leader of the Circlemakers, says, "The art form isn't just about the pattern making. The myths and folklore and energy [that] people give them are part of the art." Other "croppies" or cereologists, as they are known, insist that the complexity of the designs must mean they have been created by extraterrestrials. See Hillary Mayell, "Crop Circles: Artworks or Alien Signs?" *National Geographic*, August 2, 2002 <http://news.nationalgeographic.com/news/2002/08/0801_020801_cropcircles.html>.

3. See case file # ULRR0085 on the Web site of the Urban Legends Research Center, October 14, 2004 <http://www.ulrc.com.au/html/report.asp?CaseFile=ULRR0085&Page=1&View=Request>. A host of conspiracy theories were triggered by 9/11, and many urban legends claimed that the fall of the Twin Towers was predicted in the following lines, purportedly from Nostradamus: "In the City of God there will be a great thunder / Two brothers torn apart by Chaos, while the

fortress endures, the great leader will succumb / The third big war will begin when the big city is burning—Nostradamus 1654." It bears noting that Nostradamus died in 1566, and that the last line was never written by him. See case file ULRR0083 <http://www.ulrc.com.au/html/report.asp?CaseFile=ULRR0083&Page=1& View=Request>.

4. The connection between the aliens and Colleen's death is also reiterated in another scene, when Graham receives a cryptic phone call from Ray Reddy that is abruptly disconnected (the only word we hear is "Father"). A long shot of Hess tracks slowly backward to show a dressmaker's mannequin wearing a blue dress that clearly belonged to Colleen, which serves as an uncanny reminder of her continuing presence in his life. Prompted by the strange phone call, Hess goes over to Reddy's house, where he discovers that Reddy has trapped an alien in his kitchen. In this way, the camera's slow disclosure of the mannequin, together with the word "Father," subtly draws a connection between the alien crisis, Colleen's death, and Graham's loss of faith. Reddy and Graham have a brief conversation, akin to a confession, which is the first time they have communicated since the accident that killed Colleen. Reddy apologizes to Graham for making him "question [his] faith," and he muses that if this is the end of the world, he is not going to be in the front of the line for heaven for "killing a reverend's wife."

7. *War of the Worlds:* Uncanny Dread

1. Previous *War of the Worlds* adaptations include a TV series aka *Second Invasion* (George Bloomfield, Timothy Bond, et al., Paramount, 1988–90). In 2005 there were two other adaptations: the straight-to-DVD release H. G. Wells's *War of the Worlds*/aka *Invasion* (David Michael Latt, Asylum Productions, 2005), and *The War of the Worlds* (Timothy Hines, Pendragon, 2005).

2. In a shot of Ferrier at the end of the film, Spielberg points to the symbolic significance of Ferrier's odyssey to Boston as a key historical site in the American Revolution. After successfully making it to Boston, Ferrier examines a statue of a minuteman covered in red creeper vines, and notices that the vines are dying. This is the first signal that the aliens are succumbing to infection and that the invasion has failed. Like *Independence Day*, the allusion to the Revolutionary War aligns the global crisis with an American story of national survival.

Works Cited

American Psychiatric Association. *Diagnostic and Statistical Manual IV.* Washington: American Psychiatric Association, 1994.

Ammerman, Nancy T. "North American Protestant Fundamentalism." *Media, Culture, and the Religious Right.* Ed. Linda Kintz and Julia Lesage. Minneapolis: U of Minnesota P, 1998. 55–114.

Anz, Wilhelm. "Kierkegaard on Death and Dying." *Kierkegaard: A Critical Reader.* Ed. Jonathan Rée and Jane Chamberlain. New York: Blackwell, 1998. 39–52.

Barker, Clive. "The Forbidden." *In The Flesh.* New York: Poseidon, 1986. 65–108.

Bennett, Stephen. "The Day the Earth Stood Still." May 17, 2004. American Family Association. October 4, 2004 <http://www.afa.net/homosexual_agenda/GetArticle.asp?id=144>.

Berger, James. "Twentieth-Century Apocalypse: Forecasts and Aftermaths." *Twentieth Century Literature* 46.4 (2000): 387–95.

Bignell, Jonathan. *Postmodern Media Culture.* Edinburgh: Edinburgh UP, 2000.

Brians, Paul. "Study Guide for H. G. Wells' *The War of the Worlds* (1898)." July 10, 2005 <http://ww.wsu.edu:8080/~brians/science_fiction/warofworlds.html.>.

Broderick, Mick. "Heroic Apocalypse: Mad Max, Mythology and the Millennium." *Crisis Cinema: The Apocalyptic Idea in Postmodern Narrative Film.* Ed. Christopher Sharrett. Washington: Maisonneuve, 1993. 251–72.

Byars, Jackie. *All That Heaven Allows; Rereading Gender in 1950s Melodrama.* Chapel Hill: U of North Carolina P, 1991.

Caruth, Cathy, ed. *Trauma: Explorations in Memory.* Baltimore: Johns Hopkins UP, 1995.

———. *Unclaimed Experience: Trauma, Narrative and History.* Baltimore: Johns Hopkins UP, 1996.

Castle Rock Entertainment. *Dolores Claiborne.* Dir. Taylor Hackford. "Production Information" Castle Rock Entertainment Presspack 1995. 4–5.

Clover, Carol. *Men, Women and Chainsaws: Gender in the Modern Horror Film.* Princeton: Princeton UP, 1992.

Cubitt, Sean. *Aliens R Us: The Other in Science Fiction Cinema*. London: Pluto, 2002.

Derrida, Jacques. *The Gift of Death*. Trans. David Willis. Chicago: U of Chicago P, 1995.

———. "On a Newly Arisen Apocalyptic Tone in Philosophy." *Raising the Tone of Philosophy: Late Essays by Immanuel Kant*. Ed. Peter Fenves. Baltimore: Johns Hopkins UP, 1993.

———. "Whom to Give to (Knowing Not to Know)." *Kierkegaard: A Critical Reader*. Ed. Jonathan Rée and Jane Chamberlain. Malden, MA: Blackwell, 1998. 151–74.

Dixon, Wheeler Winston. *Visions of the Apocalypse: Spectacles of Destruction in American Cinema*. London: Wallflower, 2003.

Doane, Mary Ann. *The Emergence of Cinematic Time: Modernity, Contingency, the Archive*. Chicago: U of Chicago P, 2002.

Dyer, Richard. *Seven*. London: BFI, 1999.

Edmundson, Mark. *Nightmare on Main Street; Angels, Sadomasochism and the Culture of the Gothic*. Cambridge: Harvard UP, 1997.

Elsaesser, Thomas. "Tales of Sound and Fury: Observations on the Family Melodrama." *Home Is Where the Heart Is: Studies in Melodrama and the Woman's Film*. Ed. Christine Gledhill. London: BFI, 1987. 43–69.

Fiedler, Leslie. *Love and Death in the American Novel*. New York: Anchor, 1992.

Foucault, Michel, ed. *I Pierre Rivière, Having Slaughtered My Mother, My Sister and My Brother . . . A Case of Parricide in the Nineteenth Century*. Lincoln: U of Nebraska P, 1975.

———. *Madness and Civilization*. New York: Random, 1965.

Fowkes, Katherine, A. *Giving Up the Ghost: Spirits, Ghosts, and Angels in Mainstream Comedy Films*. Detroit: Wayne State UP, 1998.

Freud, Sigmund. "The Uncanny." *Art and Literature* trans. James Strachey, Ed. Albert Dickson. vol. 14. *The Penguin Freud Library*, Ser. Ed. Angela Richards. London: Penguin, 1990. 335–76.

Gramercy Pictures. *Candyman*. Dir. Bernard Rose. "Production Notes." Tristar & Polygram Filmed Entertainment Presspack, 1992.

———. *Candyman: Farewell to the Flesh*. Dir. Bill Condon. "Production Notes." Tristar & Polygram Filmed Entertainment Press Pack, 1995.

Gross, Daniel. "Detroit Is So Hollywood and Vice Versa." *New York Times* July 10, 2005: Natl. edn. sec. 4: 14.

Gross, Louis S. *Redefining the American Gothic*. Ann Arbor: UMI, 1981.

Gunning, Sandra. *Race, Rape and Lynching: The Red Record of American Literature*. New York: Oxford UP, 1996.

Hagedorn, John M. "Violence, Gangs and the Redivision of Space in Chicago." Guggenheim Proposal. September 4, 2002. 1–18. October 10, 2002 <http://gangresearch.net/Globalization/guggenheim/GugProposal2.htm>.

Heidegger, Martin. "The Quest For Being." *Existentialism from Dostoevsky to Sartre*. Ed. Walter Kaufmann. New York: Meridian. Rev. ed. 1975. 233–79.

Hendershot, Heather. *Shaking the World for Jesus: Media and Conservative Evangelical Culture*. Chicago: U Chicago P, 2004.

Hinson, Hal. "Dolores Claiborne." *Washington Post,* Online Edition Mar. 24, 1995. <http://www.washingtonpost.com/wpsrv/style/longterm/movies/videos/doloresclaibornerhinson_c00eba.htm>.

Hoberman, J. "Sacred and Profane." *Sight and Sound* 1.10.1992: 8–11.

Jameson, Fredric. "Progress versus Utopia; or Can We Imagine the Future?" *Science Fiction Studies* 9.2 (1982), reprinted in *Art Aftr Modernism: Rethinking Representation,* ed. Brian Wallis. New York: New Museum of Contemporary Art, 1984. 238–52.

Jenkins, Harold, ed, *William Shakespeare's Hamlet.* London: Routledge, 1990.

Jenkins, Philip. *Using Murder; The Social Construction of Serial Homicide.* New York: Aldyne de Gruyter, 1994.

Keane, Stephen. *Disaster Movies: The Cinema of Catastrophe.* London: Wallflower, 2001.

Kierkegaard, Søren. *The Concept of Dread.* 1844. Trans. Walter Lowrie. Princeton: Princeton UP, 1944.

———. *Fear and Trembling.* 1843. Trans. Alistair Hannay. London: Penguin, 1985.

———. *Journals and Papers.* Ed. and trans. Howard V. Hong and Edna H. Hong. 7 vols. Bloomington: Indiana UP, 1967–78.

King, Geoff, and Tanya Krzywinska. *Science Fiction Cinema: From Outerspace to Cyberspace.* London: Wallflower, 2000.

Kirban, S. *666 and 1000.* n.p.: AMG, 1970.

Kirkpatrick, David. "Best-Selling-Series Reaches Climax: Jesus' Return." *New York Times,* March 29, 2004: A1. Natl. edn.

———. "The Return of the Warrior Jesus." *New York Times* Apr. 5, 2004: A1, A6. Natl. edn.

Lindsay, Hal. *The Late, Great Planet Earth.* New York: Bantam, 1971.

Lowder, Jeffrey Jay. "The God of Terrorism." June 21, 1998. Secular Web. June 2, 2004 <http://www.infidels.org/secular_web/feature/1998/robertson.html>.

Lyden, John C. *Film as Religion: Myths, Morals and Rituals.* New York: New York UP, 2004.

Malone, Peter. *Movie Christs and Antichrists.* New York: Crossroad, 1990.

Martin, Joel W., and Conrad E. Ostwalt Jr., eds. *Screening the Sacred: Religion, Myth, and Ideology in Popular American Film.* Boulder: Westview, 1996.

Massood, Paula. "The Antebellum Idyll and Hollywood's Black Cast Musicals." *Black City Cinema; African American Experiences in Film.* Philadelphia: Temple UP, 2003. 11–43.

Melling, Philip. *Fundamentalism in America: Millennialism, Identity, and Militant Religion.* Edinburgh: Edinburgh UP, 1999.

Mintz, Steven. "The Family." *The Columbia Companion to American History on Film.* Ed. Peter C. Rollins. New York: Columbia UP, 2004. 352–62.

Moylan, Tom. *Scraps of the Untainted Sky: Science Fiction, Utopia, Dystopia.* Boulder: Westview, 2000.

Natoli, Joseph. *Memory's Orbit: Film and Culture, 1999–2000.* Albany: State U of New York P, 2003.

———. *Postmodern Journeys: Film and Culture, 1996–1998.* Albany: State U of New York P, 2001.

———. *Speeding to the Millennium: Film and Culture, 1993–1995*. Albany: State U of New York P, 1998.

Newman, Kim, *Apocalypse Movies: End of the World Cinema*. New York: St. Martin's, 1999.

Nietzsche, Friedrich. *Thus Spake Zarathustra*. Trans. A. Tille. Rev. ed. Ed. M. M. Bozman. London: J. M. Dent, 1957.

Page, Susan. "Churchgoing Closely Tied to Voting Patterns." *USA Today* June 2, 2004 <http://aolsvc.news.aol.com/elections/article.adp?id=200406030709099 90023>.

Penley, Constance. "Time Travel, Primal Scene, and the Critical Dystopia." *Close Encounteres: Film, Feminism and Science Fiction*. Ed. Constance Penley, Elisabeth Lyon, et al. Minneapolis: U of Minnesota P, 1991. 63–81.

Pinedo, I. C. *Recreational Terror: Women and the Pleasures of Horror Film Viewing*. Albany: State U of New York P, 1997.

Poe, Edgar Allan. "The Imp of the Perverse." *The Norton Anthology of American Literature*. Ed. Nina Baym, et al. 3rd ed. Vol. 1. New York: Norton, 1989. 1438–1441.

Poniewozik, James. "Spirits of the Age." *Time* Feb. 15, 2005: 55–56.

Prawer, S. S. *Caligari's Children: The Film as Tale of Terror*. New York: Oxford UP, 1980.

Reardon, Patrick. "Cabrini's Hellish History." Aka "We're Crying for Help, Cabrini, the Day After: Anguish, an Arrest, a Call for Troops; City's Public Housing Is Promise Unfulfilled." *Chicago Tribune* Oct. 15, 1992. March 30, 1996 <http://pqasb.pqarchiver.com/chicagotribune/index.html?ts=1079636767>.

Ressler, Robert, and Tom Shachtman. *Whoever Fights Monsters: My Twenty Years Tracking Serial Killers for the FBI*. New York: St. Martin's, 1992.

Robertson, Pat. *The New World Order*. New York: W., 1992.

———. *700 Club*. September 18, 2004 <http://www.infidels.org/secular_web/feature/1998/robertson.html>.

Rothstein, Edward. "Martians Attack, with Extra Baggage." *New York Times*, July 11, 2005: B1, B3. Natl. edn.

Savoy, E. "The Face of the Tenant: A Theory of American Gothic." *American Gothic: New Interventions in a National Narrative*. Ed. Robert K. Martin and Eric Savoy. Iowa City: U of Iowa P, 1998.

Scott, A. O. "Another Terror Attack, but Not by Humans." *New York Times* June 29, 2005: B1, B3. Natl. edn.

Seltzer, Mark. *Serial Killers: Death and Life in America's Wound Culture*. New York: Routledge, 1998.

Sharrett, Christopher. "The American Apocalypse: Scorsese's *Taxi Driver*." *Crisis Cinema: The Apocalyptic Idea in Postmodern Narrative Film*. Ed. Christopher Sharrett. Washington: Maisonneuve, 1993. 221–36.

Shorto, Russell. "Belief by the Numbers." *New York Times Magazine* Dec. 7, 1997: 60–61.

Simpson, Philip L. *Psycho Paths: Tracking the Serial Killer Through Contemporary American Film and Fiction*. Carbondale: Southern Illinois UP, 2000.

Spencer, Lloyd. "Allegory in the World of the Commodity: The Importance of Central Park." *New German Critique* 34 (Winter 1985): 59–77.

Strozier, Charles. *Apocalypse: On the Psychology of Fundamentalism.* Boston: Beacon, 1994.

Summers, Montague, ed. and trans. *The* Malleus Maleficarum *of Heinrich Kramer and James Sprenger.* New York: Dover, 1928.

Tithecott, Richard. *Of Men and Monsters: Jeffrey Dahmer and the Construction of the Serial Killer.* Madison: U of Wisconsin P, 1997.

Todorov, Tzvetan. *The Fantastic: A Structural Approach to a Literary Genre.* Trans. Richard Howard. Cleveland: Case Western Reserve UP, 1939.

Tolnay, Stewart, and E. M. Beck. *A Festival of Violence: Southern Lynchings, 1882–1930* Chicago: U of Illinois P, 1995.

Turner, Alice K. *The History of Hell.* New York: Harcourt, 1993.

Vidler, Anthony. *The Architectural Uncanny: Essays in the Modern Unhomely.* Cambridge: MITP, 1992.

Waxman, Sharon. "Hollywood Rethinking Films of Faith After 'Passion.' " *New York Times,* Mar. 15, 2004: B5. Natl. edn.

———. "The Passion of the Marketers: Studios Give Christians Their Movie Moment." *New York Times* July 18, 2005: C1, C3. Natl. edn.

Wells, H. G. *War of the Worlds.* 1898. Introduction and notes by Alfred MacAdam. New York: Barnes, 2004.

Wells, Paul. *The Horror Genre: From Beezlebub to Blair Witch.* London: Wallflower, 2000.

Wiegman, Robyn. "The Anatomy of Lynching." *Journal of the History of Sexuality* 3.3 (1993): 445–68.

Wood, Robin. *Hitchcock's Films.* New York: Castle, 1969.

———, *Hollywood; From Vietnam to Reagan.* (New York: Columbia UP, 1969.

Zamora, Lois Parkinson. *The Apocalyptic Vision in America: Interdisciplinary Essays in Art and Culture.* Bowling Green: Popular, 1982.

Index